BY ROBERT D. KAPLAN

The Return of Marco Polo's World: War, Strategy, and
   American Interests in the Twenty-first Century

Earning the Rockies: How Geography Shapes America's Role
   in the World

In Europe's Shadow: Two Cold Wars and a Thirty-Year
   Journey Through Romania and Beyond

Asia's Cauldron: The South China Sea and the End of
   a Stable Pacific

The Revenge of Geography: What the Map Tells Us About
   Coming Conflicts and the Battle Against Fate

Monsoon: The Indian Ocean and the Future of American Power

Hog Pilots, Blue Water Grunts: The American Military
   in the Air, at Sea, and on the Ground

Imperial Grunts: The American Military on the Ground

Mediterranean Winter: The Pleasures of History and Landscape
   in Tunisia, Sicily, Dalmatia, and the Peloponnese

Warrior Politics: Why Leadership Demands a Pagan Ethos

Eastward to Tartary: Travels in the Balkans, the Middle East,
   and the Caucasus

The Coming Anarchy: Shattering the Dreams of the Post
   Cold War

An Empire Wilderness: Travels into America's Future

The Ends of the Earth: From Togo to Turkmenistan, from
   Iran to Cambodia

The Arabists: The Romance of an American Elite

Balkan Ghosts: A Journey Through History

Soldiers of God: With Islamic Warriors in Afghanistan
   and Pakistan

Surrender or Starve: Travels in Ethiopia, Sudan, Somalia,
   and Eritrea

THE RETURN
OF MARCO POLO'S
WORLD

RANDOM HOUSE

NEW YORK

THE RETURN
OF MARCO
POLO'S WORLD

War, Strategy, and
American Interests in
the Twenty-first Century

Robert D. Kaplan

Published in the United States by Random House, an imprint and division
of Penguin Random House LLC, New York.

RANDOM HOUSE and the HOUSE colophon are registered trademarks of Penguin
Random House LLC.

Essays in this work were originally published in the following publications: *The American
Interest:* "The Wounded Home Front" and "The Great Danger of a New Utopianism";
The Atlantic: "The Art of Avoiding War," "Elegant Decline: The Navy's Rising Importance,"
"When North Korea Falls," "Rereading Vietnam," "Iraq: The Counterfactual Game,"
"No Greater Honor," "In Defense of Henry Kissinger," "Samuel Huntington: Looking
the World in the Eye," and "Why John Mearsheimer Is Right (About Some Things)";
The National Interest: "The Tragedy of U.S. Foreign Policy," "The Post-Imperial Moment,"
"Fated to Lead," and "Traveling China's New Silk Road"; *The Washington Post:* "On Foreign
Policy, Donald Trump Is No Realist."

Hardback ISBN 978-0-8129-9679-1

Ebook ISBN 978-0-8129-9680-7

Printed in the United States of America on acid-free paper

randomhousebooks.com

9 8 7 6 5 4 3 2 1

First Edition

Title-page and part-title page images: Courtesy of the U.S. military. Photograph by
Sgt. Ken Scar, 7th MPAD

Book design by Victoria Wong

To Elizabeth M. Lockyer

The origins of hot wars lie in cold wars, and the origins of cold wars are found in the anarchic ordering of the international arena. . . . Theorists explain what historians know: War is normal.

—Kenneth N. Waltz, 1988

Preface and Acknowledgments

The lead, anchoring essay in this collection was written for the Pentagon's Office of Net Assessment in the late summer of 2016 and was subsequently released for public view. Here and there, very sparingly, I have updated it. The other essays, going back as far as seventeen years, remain exactly as they were upon original publication. Thus, the reader will find occasional repetitions in terms of ideas and of phrases even, as well as assumptions that, from hindsight, I obviously got wrong.

At the Office of Net Assessment, I thank Air Force Colonel (Ret.) James H. Baker and Dr. Andrew D. May for their help and interest. Net Assessment commissioned the essay through the Center for a New American Security (CNAS) in Washington, for which I thank CEO Michele Flournoy, President Richard Fontaine, Director of Studies Shawn Brimley, Creative Director Melody Cook, and other members of the CNAS staff. In particular, I am especially grateful for the guidance of CNAS's director of the Defense Strategies and Assessments Program, Navy Captain (Ret.) Jerry Hendrix. Others who provided guidance and insights as I wrote this essay, for which I am grateful, include Dr. Shamila Chaudhary, Senior Advisor to the

Dean, Johns Hopkins School of Advanced International Studies; Svante Cornell, Director of the Central Asia–Caucasus Institute at the Johns Hopkins School of Advanced International Studies; Reva Goujon, Vice President of Global Analysis at Stratfor; Army Colonel Valery Keaveny, Jr.; Air Force Lieutenant Colonel Robert Lyons; Marine Lieutenant Colonel Peter McAleer; Army Lieutenant General H. R. McMaster; Marine Lieutenant Colonel David Mueller; Evan Osnos, staff writer for *The New Yorker*; Karim Sadjadpour, Senior Associate at the Carnegie Endowment for International Peace; Navy Admiral (Ret.) James Stavridis, Dean of the Fletcher School of Law and Diplomacy at Tufts University; and Jim Thomas, Distinguished Senior Fellow at the Center for Strategic and Budgetary Assessments. Any mistake or incorrect analysis herein is entirely my own, however.

Regarding the other essays, I am deeply grateful for the support over the years of all the editors at *The Atlantic, The American Interest, The National Interest,* and *The Washington Post,* especially James Bennet, James Gibney, Cullen Murphy, Scott Stossel, Adam Garfinkle, and Jacob Heilbrunn.

Anna Pitoniak at Random House energetically oversaw the production and presentation of this book, with good advice throughout. My literary agents, Gail Hochman, Marianne Merola, and Henry Thayer, provided their usual, exceptional support. The late Carl D. Brandt advised me well in the early phases of this book project, as did Henry Thayer in the latter stages. Elizabeth M. Lockyer, with help from Diane and Marc Rathbun, meticulously organizes my professional life. And my wife, Maria Cabral, remains there with decades' worth of love and support.

Contents

REFLECTIONS

MARCO POLO REDUX

STRATEGY

1.

The Return of Marco Polo's World and the U.S. Military Response

AS EUROPE DISAPPEARS, EURASIA COHERES. The supercontinent is becoming one fluid, comprehensible unit of trade and conflict, as the Westphalian system of states weakens and older, imperial legacies—Russian, Chinese, Iranian, Turkish—become paramount. Every crisis from Central Europe to the ethnic-Han Chinese heartland is now interlinked. There is one singular battle space.

What follows is a historical and geographical guide to it.

The Dispersion of the West

Never before in history did Western civilization reach such a point of geopolitical concision and raw power as during the Cold War and its immediate aftermath. For well over half a century, the North Atlantic Treaty Organization (NATO) condensed a millennia-long tradition of political and moral values—*the West,* in shorthand— into a robust military alliance. NATO was a cultural phenomenon before it was anything. Its spiritual roots reach back to the philosophical and administrative legacies of Greece and Rome, to the emergence of Christendom in the early Middle Ages, and to the Enlightenment in the seventeenth and eighteenth centuries—from which the ideas of the American Revolution emerged. Of course, key nations of the West fought as an alliance in the First and Second World Wars, and those emergency contingencies constituted forerunners to NATO's more secure and elaborate structures. Such structures, in turn, were buttressed by a continent-wide economic system, culminating in the European Union (EU). The EU gave both political support and quotidian substance to the values inherent in NATO—those values being, generally, the rule of law over arbitrary fiat, legal states over ethnic nations, and the protection of the individual no matter his race or religion. Democracy, after all, is less about elections than about impartial institutions. The end of the Long European War, 1914–89, saw those values reign triumphant, as communism was finally defeated and NATO and the EU extended their systems throughout Central and Eastern Europe, from the Baltic Sea in the north to the Black Sea in the south. And it categorically was a *long European war,* as wartime deprivations, political and economic, existed in Soviet satellite states until 1989, when the West triumphed over Europe's second totalitarian system, just as it did over the first in 1945.

Civilizations often prosper in opposition to others. Just as Christendom achieved form and substance in opposition to Islam after the latter's conquest of North Africa and the Levant in the seventh and eighth centuries, the West forged a definitive geopolitical paradigm in opposition to Nazi Germany and Soviet Russia. And because the aftershocks of the Long European War extended to the very end of the twentieth century, with the dissolution of Yugoslavia and chaos inside Russia, NATO and the EU remained as relevant as ever, with NATO demonstrating its expeditionary capability in the case of Yugoslavia, and the EU building inroads into the former Warsaw Pact to take advantage of Russia's infirmity. This era was called the Post Cold War—that is, it was defined in terms of what came before it and what still continued to influence it.

The Long European War, which lasted three-quarters of a century, influences events still, and constitutes my entry point for describing a new world far beyond Europe that the U.S. military now must grapple with. And because Europe's current predicament constitutes an introduction to that new world, I begin with it.

It was the monumental devastation of two world wars that led European elites, beginning in the late 1940s, to reject the past altogether, with all of its inherent cultural and ethnic divisions. Only the abstract ideals of the Enlightenment were preserved, which in turn led to political engineering and economic experimentation, so that the specific moral response to the human suffering of 1914–18 and 1939–45 was the establishment of generous social-welfare states, which meant highly regulated economies. As for the national-political conflicts that gave birth to the two world wars, they would not be repeated because, in addition to other aspects of supranational cooperation, European elites imposed a single monetary unit on much of the continent. Except in the most disciplined northern European societies, however, those social-welfare states have proven unaffordable, just as the single currency has caused the weaker economies of southern Europe to pile up massive debt. Alas, the post–World War II attempt at moral redemption has led over time to an intractable form of economic and political hell.

The irony deepens. Europe's dull and happy decades in the second half of the twentieth century were partially born of its demographic separation from the Muslim Middle East. This, too, was a product of the Cold War phase of the Long European War, when totalitarian prison-states in such places as Libya, Syria, and Iraq were propped up for decades by Soviet advice and support, and afterward took on a life of their own. For a long time Europe was lucky in this regard: It could reject power politics and preach human rights precisely because tens of millions of Muslims nearby were being denied human rights, and with them the freedom of movement. But those Muslim prison-states have all but collapsed (either on their own or by outside interference), unleashing a tide of refugees into debt-ridden and economically stagnant European societies. Europe now fractures from within as reactionary populism takes hold, and new borders go up throughout the continent to prevent the movement of Muslim refugees from one country to another. Meanwhile, Europe dissolves from without, as it is reunited with the destiny of Afro-Eurasia as a whole.

All this follows naturally from geography and history. For centuries in early and middle antiquity, Europe meant the entire Mediterranean Basin, or *Mare Nostrum* ("Our Sea") as the Romans famously called it, which included North Africa until the Arab invasion of Late Antiquity. This underlying reality never actually went away: In the mid-twentieth century, the French geographer Fernand Braudel intimated that Europe's real southern border was not Italy or Greece, but the Sahara Desert, where caravans of migrants now assemble for the journey north.*

* Fernand Braudel, *The Mediterranean and the Mediterranean World in the Age of Philip II*, trans. Sian Reynolds (1949; reprint, New York: Harper & Row, 1972), vol. 1, 171.

Europe, at least in the way that we have known it, has begun to vanish. And with it the West itself—at least as a sharply defined geopolitical force—also loses substantial definition. Of course, the West as a civilizational concept has been in crisis for quite some time. The very obvious fact that courses in Western civilization are increasingly rare and controversial on most college campuses in the United States indicates the effect of multiculturalism in a world of intensified cosmopolitan interactions. Noting how Rome only partially inherited the ideals of Greece, and how the Middle Ages virtually lost the ideals of Rome, the nineteenth-century liberal Russian intellectual Alexander Herzen observed that "[m]odern Western thought will pass into history and be incorporated in it, will have its influence and its place, just as our body will pass into the composition of grass, of sheep, of cutlets, and of men. We do not like that kind of immortality, but what is to be done about it?"[*]

Indeed, Western civilization is not being destroyed; rather, it is being diluted and dispersed. After all, how exactly does one define globalization? Beyond the breakdown of economic borders, it is the worldwide adoption of the American form of capitalism and management practices that, merging with the advance of human rights (another Western concept), has allowed for the most eclectic forms of cultural combinations, wearing down in turn the historical division between East and West. Having won the Long European War, the West, rather than go on to conquer the rest of the world, is now beginning to lose itself in what Reinhold Niebuhr called "a vast web of history."[†] The decomposition that Herzen spoke of has begun.

---

[*] Alexander Herzen, *My Past and Thoughts,* trans. Constance Garnett (1968; reprint, Berkeley: University of California Press, 1973), 390.

[†] Reinhold Niebuhr, *The Irony of American History* (1952; reprint, Chicago: University of Chicago Press, 2008), 74.

A New Strategic Geography

As Europe disappears, Eurasia coheres. I do not mean to say that Eurasia is becoming unified, or even stable in the manner that Europe was during the Cold War and the Post Cold War—only that the interactions of globalization, technology, and geopolitics, with each reinforcing the other, are leading the Eurasian supercontinent to become, analytically speaking, one fluid and comprehensible unit. *Eurasia* simply has meaning in the way that it didn't use to. Moreover, because of the reunification of the Mediterranean Basin, evinced by refugees from North Africa and the Levant flooding Europe, and because of dramatically increased interactions across the Indian Ocean from Indochina to East Africa, we may now speak of *Afro-Eurasia* in one breath. The term "World-Island," early-twentieth-century British geographer Halford Mackinder's phrase for Eurasia joined with Africa, is no longer premature.*

The slowly vanishing West abets this development by depositing its seeds of unity into an emerging global culture that spans continents. Further encouraging this process is the erosion of distance by way of technology: new roads, bridges, ports, airplanes, massive container ships, and fiber-optic cables. It is important, though, to realize that all this constitutes only one layer of what is happening, for there are more troubling changes, too. Precisely because religion and culture are being weakened by globalization, they have to be reinvented in more severe, monochromatic, and ideological form by way of the communications revolution. Witness Boko Haram and the Islamic State, which do not represent Islam per se, but Islam igniting with the tyrannical conformity and mass hysteria inspired by the Internet and social media. As I have written previously, it isn't the so-called *clash of civilizations* that is taking place, but the

---

* Halford J. Mackinder, *Democratic Ideals and Reality,* Defense Classic Edition (Washington, DC: National Defense University Press, 1942), 45–49.

clash of artificially reconstructed civilizations. And this only hardens geopolitical divides, which, as the collapse of Middle East prison states indicates, are in evidence not only between states but within states themselves.

The combination of violent upheavals and the communications revolution in all its aspects—from cyber interactions to new transportation infrastructure—has wrought a more claustrophobic and ferociously contested world: a world in which territory still matters, and where every crisis interacts with every other as never before. This is all intensified by the expansion of megacities and absolute rises in population. No matter how overcrowded, no matter how much the underground water table and nutrients in the soil have been depleted, people will fight for every patch of ground. On this violent and interactive earth, the neat divisions of Cold War area studies and of continents and subcontinents are starting to be erased as the Long European War passes from living memory. Europe, North Africa, the Near East, Central Asia, South Asia, Southeast Asia, East Asia, and the Indian subcontinent are destined to have less and less meaning as geopolitical concepts. Instead, because of the erosion of both hard boundaries and cultural differences, the map will manifest a continuity of subtle gradations, which begin in Central Europe and the Adriatic, and end beyond the Gobi Desert where the agricultural cradle of Chinese civilization begins. Geography counts, but legal borders will matter less so.*

This world will be increasingly bound by formal obligations that exist both above and below the level of government, a situation that recalls the functionality of feudalism. Just as the medieval Al-Andalus region in Spain and Portugal saw a rich confection of Muslim, Jewish, and Christian civilizations, where the Arabs ruled but forced conversions to Islam did not occur, this emerging world—outside of conflict zones, of course—will be one of tolerance and

---

* Parag Khanna, *Connectography: Mapping the Future of Global Civilization* (New York: Random House, 2016), 14.

pungent cultural mixes, into which the liberal spirit of the West will dissolve and only in that way have its place. As for the regional conflicts, they almost always will have global implications, owing to how every part of the earth is now increasingly interwoven with every other part. To wit, local conflicts involving Iran, Russia, and China over the decades have led to terrorist and cyber attacks on Europe and the Americas.

Geographical divisions will be both greater and lesser than in the twentieth century. They will be greater because sovereignties will multiply; that is, a plethora of city-states and region-states will emerge from within existing states themselves to achieve more consequence, even as a supranational organization like the EU wanes and one like ASEAN is destined to have little meaning in a world of intimidation and power.* Geographical divisions also will be lesser because the differences—and particularly the degree of separation—between regions like Europe and the Middle East, the Middle East and South Asia, and South Asia and East Asia will decline. The map will become more fluid and baroque, in other words, but with the same pattern repeating itself. And this same pattern will be encouraged by both the profusion and hardening of roads, railways, pipelines, and fiber-optic cables. Obviously, transportation infrastructure will not defeat geography. Indeed, the very expense of building such infrastructure in many places demonstrates the undeniable fact of geography. Anyone in the energy exploration business, or who has participated in a war game involving the Baltic states or the South China Sea, knows just how much old-fashioned geography still matters. At the same time, critical transportation infrastructure constitutes yet another factor making geography—and, by inference, geopolitics in our era—more oppressive and claustrophobic. To be sure, connectivity, rather than simply leading to more peace, prosperity, and cultural uniformity as techno-optimists like to claim, will

* ASEAN is the Association of Southeast Asian Nations.

have a much more ambiguous legacy. With more connectivity, the stakes for war will be greater, and the ease in which wars can proliferate from one geographic area to another will also be greater. Corporations will be the beneficiaries of this new world, but being (for the most part) unable to provide security, they will ultimately not be in control.

Nothing is more illustrative of this process than the Chinese government's attempts to build a land bridge across Central and West Asia to Europe, and a maritime network across the Indian Ocean from East Asia to the Middle East. These land and sea conduits may themselves be interlinked, as China and Pakistan, as well as Iran and India, hope to join the oil and natural gas fields of distant, landlocked Central Asia with the Indian Ocean to the south.* China is branding these infrastructure projects "One Belt, One Road"—in effect, a new Silk Road. The medieval Silk Road was not a single route but a vast and casual trading network, tenuously linking Europe with China both overland and across the Indian Ocean. (The Silk Road was only named as such—the *Seidenstrasse*—in the late nineteenth century by a German geographer, Baron Ferdinand von Richthofen.) The relative eclectic and multicultural nature of the Silk Road during the Middle Ages meant, according to historian Laurence Bergreen, that it was "no place for orthodoxy or single-mindedness." Medieval travelers on the Silk Road encountered a world that was, furthermore, "complex, tumultuous, and menacing, but nonetheless porous." Consequently, with each new traveler's account, Europeans saw the world not as "smaller and more manageable," but as "bigger and more chaotic."† This is a perfect description of our own time, in which the smaller the world actually

---

* Robert D. Kaplan, *Monsoon: The Indian Ocean and the Future of American Power* (New York: Random House, 2010), chap. 1.
† Laurence Bergreen, *Marco Polo: From Venice to Xanadu* (New York: Knopf, 2007), 44, 68.

becomes because of the advance of technology, the more permeable, complicated, and overwhelming it seems, with its numberless, seemingly intractable crises that are all entwined. The late-thirteenth-century Venetian merchant Marco Polo, who traveled the length and breadth of the Silk Road, is most famously associated with this world. And the route he traveled provides as good an outline as any for defining the geopolitics of Eurasia in the coming era.

Faded Empires in Marco Polo's Path

Marco Polo, who began his twenty-four-year-long trek to Asia by sailing down the eastern shore of the Adriatic in A.D. 1271, would spend considerable periods of time in Palestine, Turkey, northern Iraq, Iran in its entirety (from the Azeri and Kurdish north to the Persian Gulf), northern and eastern Afghanistan, and China's ethnic-Turkic Xinjiang Province, before arriving at the court of the Mongol emperor, Kublai Khan, in Cambulac (modern-day Beijing). From Cambulac he would make forays across the whole of China and into Vietnam and Myanmar. His return route to Venice would take him across the Indian Ocean: through the Strait of Malacca to Sri Lanka, up India's western coast to Gujarat, and on side trips to Oman, Yemen, and East Africa. If the early-twenty-first-century world has a geopolitical focus, this would be it: the Greater Indian Ocean from the Persian Gulf to the South China Sea, and including the Middle East, Central Asia, and China. The current Chinese regime's proposed land-and-maritime Silk Road duplicates exactly the one Marco Polo traveled. This is no coincidence. The Mongols, whose Yuan Dynasty ruled China in the thirteenth and fourteenth centuries, were, in fact, "early practitioners of globalization," seeking to connect the whole of habitable Eurasia in a truly multicultural empire. And Yuan China's most compelling weapon was— despite the Mongols' bloody reputation—not the sword but trade:

gems, fabrics, spices, metals, and so on. It was trade routes, not the projection of military power, that emblemized the "Pax Mongolica."* Mongol grand strategy was built on commerce much more than on war. If you want to understand China's grand strategy today, look no further than Kublai Khan's empire.

Yet, for Kublai Khan it didn't altogether work. Persia and Russia were beyond Chinese control, and the Indian subcontinent, separated from China by the high wall of the Himalayas, with seas on both sides, remained its own geopolitical island. All the while, though, the Great Khan strengthened his base in what always has been Chinese civilization's arable cradle, in central and eastern China, away from the Muslim-minority areas of the western desert. In all of this, the geopolitical characteristics of Marco Polo's world roughly approximate our own.

To be sure, Marco Polo equated the future itself with China. Coal, paper money, eyeglasses, and gunpowder were Chinese marvels unknown in Europe at the time, while the city of Hangzhou, with a giant moat and hundreds of bridges over its canals, was in Marco Polo's eyes as beautiful as Venice. But traveling in Tibet he also saw the dark side of Yuan Chinese rule, with its wanton destruction and forced incorporation of a distant province.

Aside from the geopolitical island of India, two especially consequential territories that Marco Polo describes in his *Travels* are Russia and Persia (or Iran, as it is now called). Russia he describes, just barely and from afar, as a profitable wasteland rich in furs, whereas Persia dictates much of his route. Persia, that is, Iran, is second only to China in Marco Polo's eyes—in a similar way that the Persian Empire dominated the paths of both Alexander the Great and Herodotus. For Persia was history's first superpower in antiquity, uniting the Nile, Indus, and Mesopotamia with trade links to China. As was so often the case in history, it was all about Persia, whose

* Ibid., 27, 94, 152.

language by the High Middle Ages was the main vehicle for the spread of Islam throughout the East.* Thus, a map of thirteenth-century Eurasia during Marco Polo's lifetime—overlaid by the "Empire of the Great Khan" and the "Khans of Persia"—is now the backdrop to something far more complex and technological.†

In all this complexity, keep in mind that empire remains the organizing principle of world affairs, given that the imperial experiences of Turkey, Iran, Russia, and China explain the geopolitical strategy of each country to this day. That same legacy also explains how each country could weaken or partially disintegrate. For it is the constancy of history that continues to define Eurasia—not only the stability wrought by empire, but also the chaos that emerged in the interregnum between imperial dynasties, as crises in the capital led to ungovernability in the far-flung provinces. And because of the way communications technology empowers individuals and small groups—in addition to the instability that erupts from the increasing interconnectedness of crises worldwide—threats to imperial-oriented power centers are now greater than ever. And this is to say nothing of the acute economic challenges all these states face, particularly Russia and China, whose own internal stability can never be taken for granted.

So think of the first cartographic stratum of the new Eurasian map as composed of Faded Empires: undeclared empires albeit, though still operating from an imperial mindset, whose official territorial control, in the cases of Turkey and Iran, is far less than that of their former imperiums—and greater in the cases of Russia and China. For what makes Russia and China especially vulnerable is the fact that these states still encompass territory of truly imperial dimensions, stretching beyond the homelands of their ruling ethnic

---

* Peter Frankopan, *The Silk Roads: A New History of the World* (New York: Knopf, 2015), 1–6; Touraj Daryaee, *The Oxford Handbook of Iranian History* (New York: Oxford University Press, 2012), 3–4, 6.
† *The Travels of Marco Polo: The Complete Yule-Cordier Edition* (1903; reprint, New York: Dover, 1993), vol. 1, inset after 144.

and religious groups. George Kennan said that the strongest argument for imperialism was "contingent necessity," meaning "unless we took those territories, somebody else would and that this would be still worse."* For this reason, imperialism in one form or another will never die.

Turkish, Iranian, and Central Asian Power

Turkey and Iran, thanks largely to their long and venerable imperial legacies, are the most coherent states in the Near East, further buttressed by their natural geographies neatly encompassing the Anatolian land bridge and the Iranian plateau. By "coherent" I do not mean that their current regimes are altogether stable, only that their institutions have a degree of depth far greater than in the Arab world, so that they will likely recover from bouts of instability, such as the failed coup and consequent crackdown in Turkey in the summer of 2016. Turkey and Iran are messes, but don't think for a moment that much of the Arab world isn't an even greater mess. Take Saudi Arabia: a comparatively young and artificially drawn kingdom with no imperial legacy to draw upon, and with great regional differences between Najd and the Hejaz, whose water-starved population may double in a few decades, making it, in political terms, less and less coherent. Moreover, mainly because of the natural gas revolution in the United States, Saudi Arabia is no longer the global swing producer of hydrocarbons. Energy expert Daniel Yergin writes, "The new Saudi strategy is to use oil revenues to diversify the economy and build the world's largest sovereign wealth fund as the investment engine for development." The target, he writes, "is to increase non-oil government revenues at least sixfold by 2030."† Neverthe-

---

* George F. Kennan, *American Diplomacy* (1951; reprint, Chicago: University of Chicago Press, 2012), 17.
† Daniel Yergin, "Where Oil Prices Go from Here," *Wall Street Journal*, May 16, 2016.

less, even if the Kingdom achieves all or part of this goal—and that is very doubtful—it is safe to say that Saudi Arabia's geopolitical power has, at best, peaked.

Turkey's dynamic regional policies under President Recep Tayyip Erdoğan mark a return to a more historically rooted Ottoman imperial strategy—something, in turn, that was first introduced by the late prime minister Turgut Özal in the 1980s and early 1990s. Özal, a deeply religious Muslim like Erdoğan (but without the latter's authoritarian tendencies), saw so-called neo-Ottomanism as pluralistic and multi-ethnic, thus providing a basis for peace between Turks and their fellow-Muslim Kurds, and also allowing for Turks to reach out to Turkic peoples in Central Asia, as well as to fellow Muslims in the Arab and Persian worlds. It was not an aggressive and antidemocratic strategy, in other words. To be sure, the "narrow . . . western orientation" of Turkish foreign policy that we in the West both admired and considered normal during the middle decades of the Cold War, when the military ruled Turkey, was actually an aberration—the singular invention of that fierce secularist, Mustafa Kemal "Atatürk," who abjured Ottoman imperialism, and by the way, was no democrat.* The dictatorial Kemalist state so geopolitically convenient to the West will never come back. Turkish society has become too sophisticated for that. And yet it must also be said that Erdoğan, in his own very compulsive authoritarianism, and in his attempt to subdue the Kurds within Anatolia itself, is to some degree a Kemalist, striving in vain for a mono-ethnic Turkish state, even as his vision of Turkey as a power broker in the Levant is very Ottoman. This is not a contradiction, though. Because of the way that ethnic Kurdish areas overlap Turkey, Syria, Iraq, and Iran, protecting Turkey's modern, Kemalist borders at a time of war in Syria and Iraq requires a forward policy of Ottoman-like expan-

* Nora Onar, "Neo-Ottomanism, Historical Legacies and Turkish Foreign Policy," Centre for Economics and Foreign Policy Studies, Istanbul, October 2009.

sion. Turkey's worst nightmare is losing control of ethnic Kurdish areas in eastern Anatolia. Thus, it must always be on the offensive in some oblique form.

That is why we see Turkey building an oil pipeline in northern Iraq and having in the recent past supported the Kurdish Democratic Party there against the pro-Iranian Patriotic Union of Kurdistan, while also working against Kurdish defense units in Syria. Clearly, Kurdistan itself is weak and fragmented, despite its media image as being the only success story to emerge from the Iraq War. Kurdistan will ultimately provide the long-term geopolitical battleground for Turkey versus Iran: something that is a revival of the Ottoman-Safavid imperial conflicts of early modern history.

Whereas Turkey's imperial tradition (Seljuk and Ottoman) lay wholly within the Islamic ages, making the values of Erdoğan's rule actually very natural, Iran's imperial tradition (Median, Achaemenid, Parthian, and Sassanid) predates Islam. The exception was the Safavid Dynasty, whose adoption of Shi'ite Islam in 1500 led to a disastrous war with the Sunni Ottoman Empire that cut off Iran from Europe.* It is this history that creates a certain tension between Iran's Islamic ideology and Iran's idea of itself as a successful great power in the Near East. To wit, Hassan Rouhani, the Iranian president whose ministers negotiated the nuclear agreement with the West, would like Iran to evolve into a regional economic power, with a revitalized capitalist-style system, open to the world, much like China has become. But the Supreme Leader, Ayatollah Ali Khamenei, sees Iran as more like the old Soviet Union, whereby if it compromises its Islamic ideology it is likely to disintegrate, given how ethnic Persians dominate Iran's mini-empire of minorities. Karim Sadjadpour of the Carnegie Endowment for International Peace calls this division "the Pragmatists versus the Principlists [those who believe in first Principles]." Ali Vaez of the International

---

* Graham E. Fuller, *The Center of the Universe: The Geopolitics of Iran* (Boulder, CO: Westview Press, 1991), 192–93.

Crisis Group divides each of these two groups, in turn, into those who are more and less radical, so that there are at least four distinct factions competing for influence within Iran's multiple power centers. This extremely decentralized arrangement "inherently favors continuity," according to Vaez.* Both Vaez and Sadjadpour suggest that Iran will not move over the coming years—despite the nuclear agreement—toward the Chinese model. The model of the old, pre-Gorbachev Soviet Union is more likely to hold. That is, rather than become a truly dynamic postmodern empire-of-sorts and attractor force in both the Middle East and Central Asia, with a normalized relationship with the West, Iran may continue for a number of more years as a corrupt, resource-rich, grievance-driven state.

Though smaller in numbers than those who want to see a more revitalized Iran, the clerical and Revolutionary Guard elites will fight and die to stay in power because they have literally nowhere else to go—while many of Rouhani's supporters in the government could always flee to the West (where they were educated at the same time that the hard-liners were fighting in the trenches of the Iran-Iraq War). As one analyst advises, considering the mass violence that the Iranian hard-liners are perpetrating in Syria to keep Bashir al-Assad in power, just imagine what they are prepared to do to keep themselves in power inside Iran. Remember that dictatorships collapse often when the dictator himself—because of age and infirmity—loses the sheer will to remain in power. Examples of this include the Iranian shah in 1979, Nicolae Ceauşescu in Romania in 1989, and Hosni Mubarak in Egypt in 2011. That certainly won't happen soon to the murderous elites now ruling Iran.

Iran will likely continue onward as a semi-dysfunctional power with an aggressive foreign policy in the Levant. There may be small uprisings in future years in places like Baluchistan in the southeast of the country and in Khuzestan in the southwest, but they will be

* Ali Vaez, "Iran After the Nuclear Deal," International Crisis Group, Brussels, December 15, 2015.

containable. Iran, with a civilizational sense of itself to no less a degree than China or India (or Turkey even), will not dissolve like the artificial states of the Levant and other parts of the Arab world; nor will Iran progress, however. In terms of atmosphere, if not in the specifics, both Iran and Turkey in the coming years might come to resemble the Turkey of the long decade of the 1970s, when Turkey was nominally democratic, but a political and institutional mess, dominated by the cult of the military, with a weak, center-left prime minister, Bulent Ecevit, who ended up invading Cyprus.

Turkey and Iran, both slowly calcifying under very different types of authoritarian regimes, elected or not, will, nevertheless, remain safe from outright collapse, despite political upheavals to come, especially after Iran's Supreme Leader dies. Their old-new rivalry over Kurdistan eventually will come to overshadow the greater disintegration of Syria and Iraq, whose formal power centers in Damascus and Baghdad will never again govern effectively because of all the regional players—with their vastly different geopolitical agendas—implicated in the fighting everywhere between the Mediterranean and the Iranian Plateau. The map of former Syria and Iraq will continue to resemble a child's messy finger-painting with Sunni and Shi'ite war bands expanding and contracting their areas of control—the result being flimsy and radical micro-states, with cities like Mosul and Aleppo oriented as much toward each other as toward their former respective capitals, in the way of old caravan routes. Given a somewhat diminished Saudi Arabia to the south, the continued cratering in the desert reaches of the Levant will further leverage the strength of the politically troubled Turkish and Iranian plateaus. Remember that right now there are millions of Arab refugees from these wars stuck in the region whose children are not being educated, making the next generation even more prone to radical Islamist propaganda. Concomitantly, it is in both the Turkish and Iranian national interest—whatever Ankara and Tehran may say publicly—to keep the Arabs weak, divided, and warring against each other. In sum, even the collapse of ISIS and the survival—or removal—of the Bashar al-Assad regime will not lead to any real form of stability.

Turkish and Iranian influence, because of the deep religiosity of the regimes in Ankara and Tehran, is strikingly limited in the post-Soviet Caucasus and Central Asia. The energy powerhouse of Azerbaijan helps illustrate what I mean. Azerbaijan's ethnic and linguistic affinity with Turkey resulted in extremely close relations between Baku and Ankara in the 1990s, when Turkey, like Azerbaijan, was secular. But the more Islamic that Turkey becomes, the more it becomes estranged from Azerbaijan, which still unabashedly reveres Atatürk's devotion to secularism, even if Turkey itself no longer does. Then there is Turkey's decision to work with Russia to develop a gas pipeline from Siberia to Europe under the Black Sea, which competes with Azerbaijan's own gas export plans.* As for Iran, theoretically it should wield considerable influence in the Caucasus and Central Asia—owing to its demographic, cultural, and linguistic weight—for Persia remains, in historical terms, the organizing principle of this entire region. Moreover, Iran is traditionally a Central Asian power as much as a Middle Eastern one. But Tehran's sterile Islamic ideology repulses these countries, whose traditions are still influenced by Soviet atheism, as well as by Turkic syncretism and shamanism (which, along with the brutal repression of regime opponents, are the real reasons why Islamic rebellions have not taken hold, at least yet, in the region). This is where Iran's Islamic ideology interferes with its largely pre-Islamic imperial tradition. Thus, as we move eastward along Marco Polo's path and leave behind the faded imperial influence of Turkey and Iran, we very quickly run up against that of China, whose prestige here is greater than that of either Turkey, Iran, Russia, or America for that matter.

---

* Selena Williams, "Improved Ties Bode Ill for Rival Gas Lines," *Wall Street Journal*, August 10, 2016.

The Russian invasion of Greater Georgia in 2008 was a pivot point in this process. Until then, Armenia was aligned with Russia, and Georgia was aligned with the United States and Europe. Also aligned with the West was energy-rich Azerbaijan, owing to its oil and natural gas pipelines that bypass Russia and run from Baku through Georgia and Turkey to the Mediterranean. But the Muslim Azeris saw the American desertion in 2008 of Georgia—a Christian nation, no less, during its hour of need—and realized that Washington no longer could be trusted in a crisis, even if the Azeris themselves continued to detest the Russians. And yet the Russians now sell arms to the Azeris, even while they take the Armenians for granted. In the late 1970s, Moscow deserted its ally Somalia for Somalia's archenemy Ethiopia, because the latter was a wealthier and more populous country. Moscow would like to similarly trade up in the Caucasus, from Armenia to Azerbaijan. But it cannot as yet since the regional situation is actually far more complicated still.

Here is the context: The Azeri leadership, as well as the leaderships of Uzbekistan, Kazakhstan, and other former Soviet republics in inner Asia—secular and authoritarian all—have been terrified by the Arab Spring and the Islamic uprisings that subsequently have taken advantage of it. They also have been terrified by Russia's aggression in Ukraine, as well as by tensions between Russia and Turkey, and by the drop in energy prices. They have no friends in this unraveling world, it seems, and the United States appears to matter increasingly less to them, especially as its eventual withdrawal—perhaps in defeat—from nearby Afghanistan could leave a vacuum there. So gradually, with the help of Chinese economic and political support, these former Soviet republics have been strengthening their institutions, quietly removing pro-Russian elements from their bureaucracies and delinking their economies measurably from Russia's. In general, they have been standing up to the Russians—so that Russia's leverage only remains pivotal in Kazakhstan and Kyrgyzstan (because of the former's very long border with Russia and the latter's institutional weakness). The larger picture here is that state legitimacy in Central Asia, despite the artificial creation of many of these republics by Stalin, in the short run at least has proven somewhat stronger than expected. (The small states of Kyrgyzstan and Tajikistan, with their divisive mountainous geographies, are obvious exceptions. Uzbekistan, following the death of leader Islam Karimov, will be the real test case, though.)* In sum, Russia, with its own declining economy, is stymied in the region, and the Chinese, with the roads, railways, bridges, tunnels, and pipelines they are building, are recalling the days of the Tang Dynasty in the eighth and ninth centuries, when Chinese imperial influence extended across Central Asia into northeastern Iran. In 2013, China moved demonstrably ahead of Russia in terms of regional trade, doing $50 billion in commerce with the five former Soviet Central Asian republics, compared to Russia's $30 billion. Chinese companies now own almost a quarter of Kazakhstan's oil production and more than half of Turkmenistan's gas exports.†

"Central Asia is unique in that it is the only place where all the great powers converge," writes Zhao Huasheng, a professor at Fudan University in Shanghai. After all, historic Central Asia consists not only of the former Soviet republics, but also of Mongolia, Chinese Xinjiang (East Turkestan), and Afghanistan. And in addition to the impact of China and Russia in the former Soviet republics (shaped, in turn, by their own imperial legacies), the United States remains militarily engaged in Afghanistan, while Iran through much of its imperial history has been dominant in western Afghanistan, as has India in eastern Afghanistan.‡ Indeed, while we have been ac-

---

* Interview with Svante Cornell of Johns Hopkins University's School of Advanced International Studies, April 21, 2016.

† William T. Wilson, "China's Huge 'One Belt, One Road' Initiative Is Sweeping Central Asia," *National Interest*, July 27, 2016.

‡ Zhao Huasheng, "Central Asia in Chinese Strategic Thinking," in *The New Great Game: China and South and Central Asia in the Era of Reform*, ed. Thomas Fingar (Stanford, CA: Stanford University Press, 2016), 182.

customed to conceptually seeing the former Soviet republics as a separate unit, their destiny increasingly will be interwoven with what happens next door in restive Xinjiang and war-torn Afghanistan.* This does not mean that Central Asia is where world power will be predominantly decided, but it does mean that Central Asia will be a register of those power relationships. That is, Central Asia will show us who has the upper hand, and who does not.

Russia and the Intermarium

To the north of all this complexity and turmoil lies Russia, whose Eastern Orthodox imperium did not take part in the historical ages (the Renaissance and the Enlightenment) that made Europe what it is today, even as the medieval czars long before Napoleon and Hitler faced invasion from Swedes, Poles, and Teutonic Knights—and thus chose to ally with the Mongols. Vladimir Putin's Eurasianism is deeply rooted in this past, and so "empire is the Russian state's default option."† Putin knows that the mid-seventeenth-century czarist imperial expansion south into the medieval heartland of Kievan Rus (Ukraine, that is) toward the Black Sea paid great dividends, for it marked the early disintegration of Russia's ultimate enemy, the Polish-Lithuanian Commonwealth.‡ Stalin knew this history in his bones, too, and was therefore guided by a so-called *revolutionary-imperial* paradigm to defend Russia against real and perceived threats, especially those coming from Central and Eastern Europe. And because the Middle East adjoins Central-Eastern Europe, its anarchy is something that Putin also cannot now ignore,

---

* Igor Torbakov, "Managing Imperial Peripheries: Russia and China in Central Asia," in Fingar, ed., *The New Great Game*, 245.

† Stephen Blank, "The Intellectual Origins of the Eurasian Union Project," in *Putin's Grand Strategy: The Eurasian Union and Its Discontents*, ed. S. Frederick Starr and Svante E. Cornell (Washington, DC: Central Asia–Caucasus Institute & Silk Road Studies Program of the Johns Hopkins University–SAIS, 2014), 15.

‡ Nikolas K. Gvosdev and Christopher Marsh, *Russian Foreign Policy: Interests, Vectors, and Sectors* (Washington, DC, and London: Sage/CQPress, 2012), 13–24.

especially given Russia's equities in the adjacent Caucasus. Therefore, Putin looks at the Greater Middle East and Central-Eastern
Europe and sees a single region. Russia's own Eurasian geography
lends itself to this realization.

What all this adds up to is that the geographical heart of the
challenge posed by Russia becomes the Black Sea Basin: here is
where Russia intersects with Ukraine, Turkey, Eastern Europe, and
the Caucasus. Or explained another way, where Europe meets the
Near East and where the former Russian, Ottoman, and Habsburg
imperial conflict systems all merge. To be sure, the Greater Black
Sea region constitutes a geopolitical concept that unites the wars in
Syria and Ukraine, and puts Turkey front and center alongside the
Caucasian and Balkan pivot states of Azerbaijan and Romania to
counter Russia.* The Black Sea is no less a conflict system than the
Caribbean was in the nineteenth century and the South and East
China seas are today. Yet the Black Sea does not register within the
logic of Cold War area studies around which the U.S. defense and
security bureaucracy remains organized. This is because the Black
Sea falls within and among other regions, and thus emblemizes the
fluid and organic geography that now gives definition to Eurasia in
the first place. Putin intellectually grasps this better than we do. His
tactical skill is rooted in an accurate geographical conception.

Thus, both Ukraine and Syria are inseparable from Putin's challenge to the Baltic states and the Balkans. This reality rejuvenates
the 1920s concept of the *Intermarium,* Latin for "between the
seas"—the Baltic and Black seas, that is. The Intermarium constitutes the contested rimland from Estonia in the north to Romania
and Bulgaria in the south, and to the Caucasus in the east that once
framed the conflict zone between Germany and Russia and now
frames the conflict zone between the United States and Russia.[†]

* George Friedman, "Ukraine, Iraq and a Black Sea Strategy," Stratfor, September 2, 2014.
† Robert D. Kaplan, *In Europe's Shadow: Two Cold Wars and a Thirty-Year Journey Through Romania and Beyond* (New York: Random House, 2016), 195–97.

American power worldwide will therefore be heavily determined by its ability to keep Russia from "Finlandizing" this contested rimland.

Meanwhile, Europe is no longer geopolitically protected from Russia the way it was during the Post Cold War: nor, as I've said, is Europe protected from the Levant and North Africa, as the Mediterranean Basin by way of Muslim migration becomes truly unified for the first time in hundreds of years. Thus, we are back to a much older cartography that recalls the High Middle Ages, in which "the East" did not begin in any one particular place because regions overlapped and were more vaguely defined, even as the sense of a homeland was strictly local, limited to a city or town and its surrounding countryside. To wit, the Near East, however much it may be denied, begins inside Europe itself now, given the comparatively weak institutions, the comparatively high levels of corruption, and the demonstrable presence of Russian organized crime groups that burden the states of the Balkans with a higher level of political instability than the states of Central and Western Europe. This is itself a legacy of communism and the Long European War. Yes, the dichotomy of the Orient and the Occident is breaking down the world over, even as subtle gradations continue to persist.

Tang China and the Lesson of Afghanistan

In Eurasia, Russia will be contained by China much more than by the United States. In fact, the whole underlying logic of Russia's Eurasian Customs Union is to limit, to the extent that it can, Chinese influence.* China constitutes a very distinct imperial mindset. Because it was a vast empire for thousands of years under many dynasties, China simply takes for granted its superiority, and conse-

---

* Blank, *Putin's Grand Strategy*, 21–22.

quently has never sought to influence others in the proper way of governance. (This puts it at odds with the democratic universalism of the United States, which has sought religious-like conversion to its principles worldwide.)* China's particular imperial tradition allows it to deal with all sorts of regimes, good and evil, without any notion of guilt. For untold centuries, Beijing's only problem was the so-called barbarians on the steppelands partially encircling Han China's arable lowland cradle: the Tibetans, the Turkic Muslim Uighurs, the Inner Mongolians, and others, who either had to be violently subdued, bribed, or demographically overwhelmed, exactly as they must be today.

China's twenty-two urban clusters, each containing at least one megacity, all happen to be located within Han China's arable cradle, which constitutes the territory of Chinese imperial dynasties throughout history and excludes this semicircle of steppelands. It was only in the mid-eighteenth century that the last of those dynasties, that of the Qing or Manchus (who were themselves outsiders), expanded into the barbarian desert and steppe regions, thus preparing the geographical context of the current Chinese state—a state that overlaps with Muslim Central Asia. And yet this dangerous periphery that has threatened the Han cradle still exists—not only inside China, but beyond its current borders.† China hopes its Silk Road development strategy can make a political end run around these volatile minority regions, economically pacifying these minorities as it were, though it also might bring Muslim Uighur separatists in western China into greater contact with radical Islamists in South Asia, Central Asia, and the Middle East. Uighur separatists already have received training in the Pakistan-Afghanistan border

---

* Henry Kissinger, *On China* (New York: Penguin, 2011), 17.
† Michael D. Swaine and Ashley J. Tellis, *Interpreting China's Grand Strategy: Past, Present, and Future* (Santa Monica, CA: RAND, 2000), 26, 41–44; Khanna, *Connectography*, Map 20.

area.* In other words, connectivity does not necessarily lead to a more peaceful world, especially because changes in the status quo, even for the better, can lead to more ethnic unrest.

For example, in Xinjiang (East Turkestan), the very process of economic modernization, in which the Muslim Uighurs actually can benefit, plays a part in shaping a more radical identity for them, immersed as the Uighurs are in economic competition with the Han Chinese.† Whereas the Han have viewed the Tibetans somewhat like the Americans have viewed the Navajo—as exotic reminders of how they successfully conquered a continent—the Han view the Uighurs with absolute dread. For Islam represents an alternative identity for the Uighurs, one unconnected to the Chinese state. Unlike the Tibetans with their Dalai Lama, the Uighurs don't have an elite leader and educated bureaucracy with which to communicate with Beijing; rather, they represent an inchoate, undirected force of upheaval that could be triggered by an environmental or other emergency. The Uighurs, as one astute China observer told me, are the bomb under the carpet of the Chinese state. Remember that the core argument of the late Harvard professor Samuel Huntington's theory of a *clash of civilizations*—which those who criticized Huntington either overlooked or completely failed to grasp—was that ethnic and cultural tension is central to the process of modernization and development itself.‡ China's rapid-fire modernization is now mightily testing Huntington's thesis.

China's infrastructure expansion across Central Asia is directly related to its maritime expansion in the South and East China seas. After all, China is only able to act aggressively in its adjacent seas

* Michael Clarke, "Beijing's March West: Opportunities and Challenges for China's Eurasian Pivot," *Orbis,* Spring, 2016; John W. Garver, *China and Iran: Ancient Partners in a Post-Imperial World* (Seattle: University of Washington Press, 2006), 132; Fingar, *The New Great Game,* 44.

† Ben Hillman and Gray Tuttle, *Ethnic Conflict and Protest in Tibet and Xinjiang: Unrest in China's West* (New York: Columbia University Press, 2016), 8, 122, 142, 241–42.

‡ Samuel P. Huntington, *The Clash of Civilizations and the Remaking of World Order* (New York: Simon & Schuster, 1996), 20.

because it is now, for the time being, secure on land to a degree it has never been in its history. Threatened constantly by the peoples of the steppe in the west, southwest, and north, with the exception of the voyages of Admiral Zheng He during the Ming Dynasty in the early fifteenth century, China never actually did have a maritime tradition in the east. But globalization, with its exaggerated emphasis on sea lines of communication, has necessitated Chinese power projection into the blue-water extensions of its own continental landmass. Because that requires China to remain secure on land, it also means the permanent subjugation of the Muslim Uighurs, Tibetans, and Inner Mongolians. And thus we have the One Belt, One Road strategy. In short, China's ethnic demons within its borders lead it to push out militarily and economically well beyond its borders.

China's new Silk Road is very much in keeping with its medieval precedent, when Tang armies threaded their way through the space between Mongolia and Tibet to establish protectorates as far as Iranian Khorasan. Indeed, almost touching China's dangerous steppeland periphery through much of Late Antiquity, the Middle Ages, and the early modern era was Persia, whose linguistic and imperial domain stretched from the Mediterranean to Central Asia. Both China and Persia were rich, settled agricultural civilizations besieged by warlike desert peoples, even as they were in contact with each other because of the Silk Road. And both were great empires humiliated by Western powers during the modern era. Such is the emotional and historical bedrock for sustaining Sino-Iranian relations today.* Iran's deputy head of railways, Hossein Ashoori, says, "Our goal in the Silk Road plan is first to connect Iran's market to China's [rather than to Central Asia per se]."† Thus, even as the theme of the Eurasian interior is weaker and weaker states, with the great former

---

* Garver, *China and Iran,* 4, 22, 24.
† Najmeh Bozorgmehr, "First Freight Trains from China Arrive in Tehran," *Financial Times,* May 9, 2016.

empires weakening at a somewhat slower pace than the rest, there also will be more intensified linkages and interactions between all of them.

So forget the dichotomy between the pessimists who predict anarchy and the optimists who predict greater connectivity: Both trends will happen simultaneously. And there is no contradiction in this, as long as one thinks outside the paradigm of linear progress with which the liberal mind is obsessed. Think again of Marco Polo's world: one of great, overwhelming danger for the traveler in which a Silk Road nexus—with all its sinews of wealth creation— nevertheless existed.

Of all these countries, Pakistan will be the chief register of China's ability to join its Silk Road across Eurasia with its maritime Silk Road across the Indian Ocean. This branch of the Silk Road will require the full force of China's proposed $46 billion investment, in order to build an 1,800-mile superhighway and high-speed railway from Pakistan's Arabian Sea port of Gwadar (a port that China already has built) north across the Baluchistan desert and the Karakoram mountains into China's western Xinjiang Province. Nothing since independence in 1947 has the potential to help stabilize Pakistan—calming its frontier insurgencies—than the completion of this project, and nothing would do more to firm up China's domination of its own steppeland periphery. In fact, Chinese pressure, much more than American pressure, may have caused the Pakistanis to crack down on terrorist networks in North Waziristan some years back, since the proposed Silk Road gives Beijing leverage in Islamabad that Washington can only dream of having.

It is doubtful, however, that China can save Pakistan. While it is true that Pakistan's government is increasingly being held accountable by a burgeoning media and nongovernmental organizations— thereby expanding civil society at the top end of the spectrum in Islamabad and Lahore—and it is also true that interparty warfare in Islamabad has lessened somewhat, the country in fundamental ways continues to deteriorate. Electricity blackouts ("load shedding," as they are called) are more persistent now than ever, and water shortages are worsening. The situation is fluid. Nuclear power and coal imports may soon alleviate the power blackouts, even as the army has reportedly moved away somewhat from encouraging Islamic radicalism. But Pakistan's population growth is still above 2 percent annually, meaning its population doubles every thirty-five years. (The median age is 22.7 years old.) Corruption is rife, even as there are no significant anticorruption drives. Karachi, a sprawling city of slums and fortified villas with a population of 24 million, is defined by criminal networks and refugees from the violent tribal areas abutting Afghanistan. Because of security concerns, more and more Pakistani political conclaves have been held not in Pakistan at all, but in Dubai. Still, the Pakistani state will not collapse, as it basically consists of around one hundred wealthy families. (It is such families who will benefit the most financially from the Silk Road project.) This oligarchy is actually similar to the one in the Philippines, another vast, institutionally weak, overcrowded state with a difficult geography. Of course, Pakistan, unlike the Philippines, has a reported two hundred nuclear weapons, even as it is reportedly building smaller, tactical ones and dispersing them around the country, so that they may be harder for the Americans to locate.

The pattern continues, in other words: In the vast area between a cratering Levant and an internally troubled China, no state is improving its capacity to govern effectively. They are all either weakening or headed nowhere good.

Pakistan's chronic instability could well limit China's ability to complete its Silk Road project from the Indian Ocean northward into western China, with a band of separatist violence from Baluchistan in the south to Xinjiang in the north perpetually simmering along the whole route. In this way, China, as a secure domestic entity, might only exist within, say, its greater arable cradle, from which tentacles of lucrative trade protrude outward. Thus, the true map of China and its shadow zones, again, would resemble the medieval one that Marco Polo knew. In terms of the dry-land portion of the earth, no region will do more by itself to tell us who wields more power and how stable things really are in the early twenty-first century than Greater Central Asia, encompassing the Caucasus, Iran, Afghanistan, and Pakistan.

Consider Afghanistan for a moment. The U.S. military can arguably save face in Afghanistan, but it cannot stabilize it. If anyone holds the key to economically and perhaps even politically stabilizing Afghanistan, it is mainly China through resource extraction, and also the Caspian Sea countries through the building of a natural gas transport network south through Afghanistan to the Indian Ocean. Meanwhile, India and Iran work together to counter the influence of Pakistan and Saudi Arabia in Afghanistan. If the Indians and the Iranians can build the Char Bahar port and transport project, linking that Iranian port on the Indian Ocean with Central Asia, with a spur line into Afghanistan, it can then compete with the China–Pakistan Silk Road project extending northward from Gwadar. As for the Russians, who have an interest in fighting Islamic extremism in Afghanistan because of Afghanistan's contiguity with the former Soviet Union, they continue to develop their intelligence contacts with both Pakistan and Iran. Afghanistan provides a signal lesson about the limits of American power, coupled with the continued relevance of geography, which Washington elites fail to respect at their peril.

Afghanistan, which has been at war in one form or another for almost four decades, and Pakistan, which has never really been safe from tribal insurgencies and political turmoil for almost seven decades, demonstrate that the configuration of the Indian subcontinent into two larger states and several smaller ones may not be the last word in human political organization there. To wit, the political map may evolve over time: Pakistan can partially crumble into a rump Greater Punjab with Baluchistan and Sind gaining more de facto independence, with vast implications for India. And it is the Indian subcontinent that I am talking about: Since parts of Afghanistan were incorporated into various Indian imperial dynasties, governments in New Delhi always have considered Afghanistan in conceptual terms as part of a Greater India, stretching from the Iranian Plateau in the west to the Burmese jungles in the east. Whereas China seeks to expand vertically south to the Indian Ocean, India seeks to expand horizontally along or close to the Indian Ocean, with a special growing influence in the Persian Gulf.* Therein lies the contest between these two faded empires.

The Flattening Himalayas and the Nationalist Undercurrent

Indeed, the defeat of distance effected by military technology has created a new strategic geography of rivalry between India and China. Indian ballistic missiles can reach cities in China's arable cradle while Chinese fighter jets can reach the Indian subcontinent. Indian warships are in the South China Sea while Chinese warships sail throughout the Indian Ocean, with China deeply involved in port development projects in the Bay of Bengal and Arabian Sea that virtually surround India on three sides. The high wall of the Himalayas no longer separates these two great civilizations, and hasn't for some time. Trade routes linking China and India, by way of Tibet, Nepal, West Bengal, and Myanmar—joining Lhasa, Kathmandu, and Kolkata—will only further mature, with peaceful commerce cushioning the impact of this new strategic geography.† But these widened tentacles of vehicular transport also might be used for Chinese tanks to enter India. Again, connectivity does not neces-

---

* British policy in the Middle East and the Gulf "emanated more from the British Raj in India than it did from Whitehall." In fact, geography dictates that India's geopolitical concerns are the same whether under British colonial or independent Indian administrations in New Delhi. Fuller, *The Center of the Universe*, 235.
† Bibek Paudel, "The Pan Himalayan Reality That Awaits South Asia," *The Wire*, March 4, 2016; Khanna, *Connectography*, 86.

sarily presage a more peaceful world. Eurasia is cohering into both a single trade and conflict system.

Oxford historian and archaeologist Barry Cunliffe writes that the maritime network of the Portuguese in the late fifteenth and early sixteenth centuries—whose ports and trading posts punctuated the entire Indian Ocean seaboard—helped bring the vast Eurasian landmass into a new global system.* The Chinese, with their investments in Indian Ocean ports (in Myanmar, Bangladesh, Sri Lanka, Pakistan, Djibouti, and Tanzania), are doing for the postmodern era what the Portuguese did for the late medieval and early modern ones, even while the map lines connecting these new and expanded ports approximate Marco Polo's return route. The "nexus" of China, the Middle East, and Africa now accounts for more than half of world trade, writes Parag Khanna.†

This is truly a Chinese maritime empire we are talking about. Like that of the Portuguese, it is mainly limited to the coast, and does not guarantee China pivotal influence inland. Myanmar's political liberalization offers the example of a country reaching out to India and the United States to avoid domination by China: Geography still rules, but globalization and the communications revolution amplify the opportunities for out-of-area powers. Furthermore, while the ships of the Portuguese and the Spanish may have invented the global system, that system's very complexity now has reached a point where it embraces a multidimensional and interlocking tendency for violent conflict.

And keep another thing in mind: Both China and Russia have influence of increasing imperial dimensions, even as they weaken internally from economic stresses of a profound and structural kind. The very fragility of these highly centralized, Politburo-style regimes inside their own countries makes them increasingly aggressive be-

---

* Barry Cunliffe, *By Steppe, Desert, and Ocean: The Birth of Eurasia* (Oxford: Oxford University Press, 2015), 472.
† Khanna, *Connectography*, 242.

yond their borders, since nationalism can serve as a unifying element in times of societal stress. China and Russia are the hinge states on which the organization of this entire Eurasian conflict system depends, and given the constricted and copious interactions from one end of the supercontinent to the other, future palace coups and intrigues in Beijing and Moscow can trigger fires throughout the Eastern Hemisphere.

The surface of this world will be cosmopolitan, but with nationalism—as China and Russia demonstrate—still composing the bedrock. To be sure, city-states such as Qatar, Dubai, and Singapore illustrate that cosmopolitan surface. One can't help but think of the eclectic cities of the Levant at the turn of the twentieth century: Alexandria, Smyrna, and Beirut, where, writes historian Philip Mansel, "people switched identities as easily as they switched languages."* And regarding Odessa of the same period, there was "nothing national" about this cosmopolitan city.† Salonica, too, fell within this exciting category; but here, more darkly, as ethnic nationalism began to take hold, "Muslims turned into Turks, Christians into Greeks," explains Columbia professor Mark Mazower.‡ For the easygoing Ottoman imperial tolerance, which allowed for such a high degree of cosmopolitanism in the first place, was giving way to the hardened national and ethnic divides that have been a feature of the industrial and postindustrial ages. Imperialism and cosmopolitanism go together, in other words, since empires are by definition multi-ethnic and multi-religious, whatever their bad reputation. But the end of formal imperialism and the continued internal weakening of faded empires that we see now are not friendly to postmodern forms of those multicultural Levantine cities. The city-

* Philip Mansel, *Levant: Splendour and Catastrophe on the Mediterranean* (New Haven, CT: Yale University Press, 2010), 2.
† Charles King, *Odessa: Genius and Death in a City of Dreams* (New York: Norton, 2011), 108.
‡ Mark Mazower, *Salonica, City of Ghosts: Christians, Muslims and Jews, 1430–1950* (New York: Knopf, 2005), 13.

states of the Persian Gulf and Singapore, with their international workforces, may somewhat resemble old Alexandria and Smyrna—but certainly not Aleppo, Mosul, or Karachi, where the collapse of European imperial rule spawned authoritarian and sectarian states that either have disintegrated or (in the case of Pakistan) are extremely dysfunctional. In such places, communal violence is the norm, and there is no sense of a *patria*.

Because the Gulf states and Singapore depend upon a vibrant world trading order, which in turn depends on a stable balance of power, they provide little fundamental security of their own and, therefore, in geopolitical terms constitute an illusion. Violent Shi'ite separatism in eastern Saudi Arabia, a war between Saudi Arabia and Iran, and warfare in the South China Sea could wreck these city-state economies. The continued accumulation of corporate wealth, which these city-states represent, is more fragile and contingent than we think.

Consider the port of al-Duqm, which I visited recently, built midway along a largely bleak and uninhabited Omani coastline. A multibillion-dollar rail and shipping complex taking advantage of Indian Ocean traffic between Asia, the Middle East, and Africa, al-Duqm did not even exist a few years ago. It is a testament to the continued power of location—of geography. Because al-Duqm lies just outside the Persian Gulf, but is proximate to it, conflict within the Gulf actually increases the importance of al-Duqm, whose rail and pipeline terminuses (in the future originating as far north as Kuwait) will fill waiting ships that dock in safety outside the Strait of Hormuz. Moreover, al-Duqm was built in the expectation that the U.S. Fifth Fleet soon will want a more secure harbor than those available inside the Gulf. Al-Duqm, which shrinks the Eurasian trading system down to one port complex, is a monument to pessimism: It assumes future conflict and the instability that comes with connectivity.

The Contracting Rimland and the Meaning of Bulgaria

This increasingly crowded and interconnected world will have so many layers of horizontal linkages between one part of Afro-Eurasia and another that it will be increasingly difficult for the United States to exert pressure on it. China, Russia, and Iran will be part of the same supply chain of trade and transportation that works to thwart U.S. influence. In the past, Eurasia was simply too vast to work to the advantage of any one power. The Mongol Empire from Genghis Khan to Tamerlane (and including Kublai Khan) was the singular, stunning exception to this. But as technology has collapsed distance, advancing the possibilities of trade and supply chains, there is now the possibility of some semblance of Eurasian unity among China, Russia, and Iran, with China as the first among equals, just as in Marco Polo's day. But whereas in the High Middle Ages the Yuan Empire posed no challenge to Europe, in a more shrunken, tightly wound world of high technology, the challenge to the United States of such a Eurasian trading network is obvious.

Of course, opportunities will arise for the United States, ironically due to this very connectivity—as when Myanmar uses the United States to balance against China. And as the principal geographical satellite of the Afro-Eurasian landmass,* North America will remain pivotal to world history even while it is protected from many of the disruptions that will overtake Afro-Eurasia itself. For this is a world that will be more volatile precisely because of the growth of middle and working classes that are less stoical than the rural poor, of which there will be less. Indeed, it is the shantytown, the incubator of misery and utopian ideology, that will help define the megacities of Afro-Eurasia. The more urbanized, the more educated, and even the more enlightened the world becomes, counter-

---

* Mackinder, *Democratic Ideals and Reality,* 46–48.

intuitively, the more politically unstable it becomes, too.* This is what techno-optimists and those who inhabit the world of fancy corporate gatherings are prone to miss: They wrongly equate wealth creation—and unevenly distributed wealth creation at that—with political order and stability.

Nevertheless, the United States has a problem. For a century it has sought to prevent any one power from gaining the same degree of dominance in the Eastern Hemisphere that it itself possesses in the Western Hemisphere. And that is still certainly possible. While one power per se may not gain such dominance, however, a grouping of powers might, with a de-Westernized Europe, Russia, Turkey, and Iran leveraging the power of China through trade and Silk Road connectivity. Eurasia is getting smaller, and that may make it harder for the United States to play one power on the supercontinent off against the other. Think of a world with more conflict and disruption, amplified by technology and the growth of megacities, while at the same time evincing a degree of economic unity, encouraged by new infrastructure on land and maritime platforms at sea in the Greater Indian Ocean, that will thwart American influence in the Old World. The United States will remain the most potent individual power, but that will mean less and less as powers on the same supercontinent find themselves more closely linked by trade.

Yet, given the political weakening and stagnation I have described throughout the Greater Middle East and Central Asia, this is a very contradictory picture I have laid out. And that is the point. For the world is going in different directions, and the sheer scale of activity will make dominance from any one geographical point like ours harder.

Perhaps no place provides an insight into the challenge faced by the United States more than Bulgaria, just one of the many countries that are invisible to the Washington policy elite and consequently

---

* Samuel P. Huntington, *Political Order in Changing Societies* (New Haven, CT: Yale University Press, 1968), 47.

are never part of its conversation. Bulgaria is a member of NATO and the European Union, but it is located at the far southeastern end of Europe—historically part of the Near East, or "Turkey in Europe," as much of the Balkans were labeled in the late nineteenth century. Bulgaria was the most loyal Warsaw Pact satellite of the Soviet Union during the Cold War. In the 1990s and first decade of the 2000s, following America's victory in the Cold War, and a time when NATO and the EU appeared invincible, Bulgaria saw its future wholly inside the West. American and Western power back then was such that, even as few in Washington focused on the country, it was safe within our embrace. Bulgaria's border with Turkey, its proximity to Russia, and its closely related Slavic language did not seem to matter as much as they used to. American power, it appeared, had defeated geography. Fast-forward to today: Bulgaria is still in NATO and the EU, but the Russians and the Turks are aggressively competing for the destiny of the country, with Turkey being among Bulgaria's biggest trading partners and the Russians, especially, involved in various forms of subversion, from organized crime to encouraging nationalist parties. Bulgaria, because of its weak institutions, and the increasing inability of Brussels to project power into its own far-flung hinterlands, is a compromised country whose political integrity nobody trusts. The unipolarity that defined the Post Cold War is over, the West itself is dissipating, and we are back to classical geography—particularly in Europe.

Indeed, what was supposed to have been a monochrome superstate from Iberia to the Black Sea, integral to the very conception of the West, is now decaying into various color tones on a neo-medieval map, with various layers of political and even civilizational identity: There is still the EU, but also individual states, regions, and city-states, with liberalism barely holding off the forces of populist nationalism. To say that this does not undermine the strength of NATO is to be in denial, especially as regional military groupings (Baltic-Scandinavia, Visegrad) strengthen within Europe. NATO will continue to exist in full, but, even more so in the future than in the past, emergencies will require the United States to force the alliance into action. Without powerful arm-twisting by the United States, even an Article 5 violation by Russia may not rouse NATO on its own, beyond the holding of meetings and more meetings.

Yet, as the example of Bulgaria indicates, Russia does not require an invasion, only a zone of influence in the Intermarium that it can achieve by gradually compromising the democratic vitality of rimland states. (Hungary, in particular, is well on its way in this regard.) Again, Eurasia and the Near East increasingly begin inside Europe.

A stark realization emerges: America can defend its interests modestly defined, but it cannot change the world into a version of itself. In a word, we cannot ultimately defend Bulgaria—let alone Iraq or Afghanistan—from within.

The Geopolitics of a Naval Power

Our response to this entire dilemma begins with defining accurately who we are. In geopolitical terms, the United States is a maritime power, operating from the greatest of the island satellites of the Eurasian supercontinent, whose mission is to defend a free trading order from which we ourselves benefit. In the tradition of the British imperial navy, we protect the global commons. Free trade works in tandem with liberal democracies but does not necessarily require them. Countries such as Morocco, Egypt, Jordan, Oman, Taiwan, and Singapore have over the span of the decades fallen under the category of enlightened dictatorships that nevertheless have been conducive to liberal values worldwide. Our allies are mainly democracies but not always so, as these examples suggest. The world is intractable enough (and becoming more so) without our needing to impose our values on other countries' internal systems. Thus, we should start with asking how we can act with caution and restraint, without drifting into neo-isolationism. Air and naval power are actually suited to a restrained foreign policy, since it is about projecting power over broad reaches of the earth without getting bogged down with land forces in any one place, and without incurring significant casualties. We must keep our limitations in mind, especially as the two signal advantages of U.S. power projection since the end of World War II have been steadily eroding: the advantage of being the only major country whose infrastructure was not either decimated or severely damaged between 1941 and 1945, and the advantage of having had a big internal market that for a long time protected its workers from the rigors of global competition. Our middle class was built on this internal market, and thus was willing and able for decades to support vast military expenditures.

But while our position has been eroding, the internal positions of Eurasia's two principal hinge states, Russia and China, have been eroding further. They have ethnic, political, and economic challenges of a fundamental, structural kind compared to which ours pale in significance. Their very future stability and existence as unitary states can be questioned, whereas ours cannot. And the world I have been describing in Eurasia, defined by nonstop crises and political stagnation and weakness—a world where chaos and wealth creation go hand in hand—is one that will help keep our competitors preoccupied. State capacity in Eurasia is declining. Meanwhile, energy rich and self-sufficient, bordered by oceans and the Canadian Arctic, we have breathing room that the Eurasian powers do not, even if we will not be able to influence the power balance on the supercontinent in the way that we used to. The age of comparative anarchy is upon us.

Here it is wise to review why we have had so much influence in the Asia-Pacific region, even as we are located half a world away, and even in the face of a rising China, which constitutes East Asia's geographic and economic core. It isn't only our naval presence that buys us so much influence there. It is our naval presence merged with the realization among all Pacific nations that—precisely because we are only a distant geographical satellite of Eurasia—we have no territorial ambitions in their region. To repeat, North America's very distance from East Asia means our influence there cannot be overbearing, and thus we are trusted. We are the reputational power and honest broker, defending a system of free trade upon which every regional economy depends.

Therefore, it is time now to extend the concept of the Asia pivot to encompass the entire navigable rimland of Eurasia, including not only the Western Pacific but the Indian Ocean as well, with our influence following exactly the path of Marco Polo's return by sea, from China to Venice. Sea power is the compensatory answer for shaping geopolitics—to the extent that it can be shaped—in the face of an infernally complex and intractable situation on land. Here is where the ideas of Alfred Thayer Mahan meet those of Halford Mackinder.

Sea power does not mean domination at sea. It does not necessarily mean a significant expansion of our navy. It means conceptually merging our presence in the Persian Gulf region with that in the South and East China seas. It means leveraging the growing naval presence of India, a de facto American ally, in the Arabian Sea and the Bay of Bengal. More specifically, we will require the twenty-first-century equivalent of coaling stations in rimland locations whose stability is defensible, where we can pre-position locations and conduct long-range strikes off ships: Oman, Diego Garcia, India, and Singapore come to mind.

Our land strategy should be secondary, and should follow from our air and naval strategy, not the other way around. A land strategy that is paramount defines an imperial military more than does an air and sea strategy, since land forces are synonymous with occupation. We must move away from domain control to domain denial, since our only motive to be on the ground in the Greater Middle East and

Central Asia is for smackdown or disruption purposes. (In retrospect, that is how we should have handled Afghanistan after 9/11.) As we learned to our horror at the turn of the twentieth century in the Philippines, as well as in the 1960s in Vietnam, and again in the last decade in Iraq, *to invade is to govern.* Once you decide to send in ground forces in significant numbers, it becomes your job to administer the territory you've just conquered—or to identify someone immediately who can. That's why, particularly since the end of the military occupation of Japan in 1952, we have been both more comfortable and better off as a status quo power, accepting regimes as they are, democratic or not.

The geopolitical situation I have outlined in the vast space between Europe and China is such that America should use every opportunity to stay militarily disengaged, unless an overwhelming national interest forces our hand. (And that may happen from time to time in a world of cyberattacks and nuclear proliferation.) Still, the instability and complexity that we see now will only intensify in inner Asia. Thus, there will not be more but actually fewer opportunities to intervene successfully on a grand scale, even as the temptation to do so may grow.

Our interests in terms of the bar for military intervention are mainly negative: to prevent a nonstate actor—or a state actor working in sync with a nonstate one—from planning or launching an attack on ourselves or our allies; and to prevent a Silk Road trading network from creating a demonstrably hostile Eurasian superpower or alliance-of-sorts, with the same level of influence in the Eastern Hemisphere that the United States enjoys in the Western Hemisphere. Britain's historic effort to prevent any one power from gaining dominance over the European mainland is similar to ours now in Eurasia. But our Western Pacific and Indian Ocean sea power can work to restrain that, without the need for large-scale ground force intervention. To be sure, China's island reclamations in the South

China Sea and its port development projects in the Indian Ocean all work to push our navy away from the Eurasian mainland. This is where the Iranian-Indian alliance to develop the Char Bahar port in Iranian Baluchistan, to undermine the Chinese-Pakistani port project in Pakistani Baluchistan, actually works in our favor.

At least along Marco Polo's route we always should seek to occupy the territory between neo-isolationism and imperial-style interventionism. That means more drones, more precision-guided missiles, more cyber capabilities, and more special operations forces for various missions, not fewer. We must be comfortable operating at levels smaller than that of a brigade, in other words. This is how we guard our negative interests and shape the battlespace to the degree that we can, while lessening the risk of outright occupation anywhere. Foreign Internal Defense—the low-key training of local forces that compete with forces hostile to U.S. interests—is the way we will forge outcomes, where such a possibility even exists. To this end, we will need to strengthen our Foreign Area Officer program with first-tier recruits, not second- and third-tier ones as we often do now. The decline of states in general in inner Asia means a future of more refugees. We will have to become expert at using refugee camps for intelligence gathering, at a time in history when our adversaries try to weaponize refugees. Obviously, diplomacy will be altogether crucial in many of these efforts, in which there will be no victory parades, even as the Westphalian system of modern states weakens and calcifies.

Of course, we must maintain robust land forces for the sake of unpredictable contingencies, as well as to demonstrate clearly that we always reserve the right to intervene—even if we don't, or shouldn't. The fact is, a robust land force in and of itself affects the power calculations of our adversaries to our advantage. This may seem like a prohibitively expensive insurance policy, but the cost of not maintaining deployable land forces would be far greater in terms of the temptations offered to expansionist, autocratic states such as Russia, China, and Iran, especially as they internally weaken and consequently employ nationalism as a solidifying force.

Yet, despite the threats of Russian and Chinese expansionism, particularly in the Baltic, Black, and South China seas, the more important underlying dynamic will be the crises of central control inside Russia and China themselves as their authoritarian systems degenerate. This will happen alongside decaying Turkish and Iranian imperial structures, even while Europe itself becomes more fractured and less trustworthy—and besieged as the years go on with refugees from sub-Saharan Africa, to say nothing of the Middle East. Alas, as I've indicated, modernism with its neatly defined bureaucratic states and borders is receding in the rearview mirror across Eurasia. The current bout of populist nationalism that we see is merely its swan song.

To recap: At a more profound and yet less obvious level, there is, as the French philosopher Pierre Manent intimates, a growing emphasis on city-states and the half-hidden traditions of empire, even while the problems of modern states increase.* We may be back to what Manent calls the age-old political formulations of city, empire, and tribe, or *ethnos*. Meanwhile, across Eurasia, the state itself—that more recent invention—suffers. Thus, the map increasingly will be defined by a new medievalism, as the Westphalian model, with which the United States has traditionally been comfortable intervening and interacting, becomes increasingly less relevant. Europe will form the crucible of this age of comparative anarchy—the place that millions from these weakening states desperately want to get into. But an America that consciously seeks to keep its powder dry and maintains a degree of sea control in the Eastern Hemisphere will be, at least in geopolitical terms, relatively safe.

* Pierre Manent, *Metamorphoses of the City: On the Western Dynamic*, trans. Marc LePain (Cambridge, MA: Harvard University Press, 2013), 5, 18.

The Peloponnesian War?

But can America keep its powder dry? As I write, Washington elites are busy demonizing the rulers of Russia and China, and are obsessed with going toe-to-toe with those two autocratic powers in the Baltic, Black, and South China and East China seas. There may be grounds for arguing, as I and others have, for a more robust response to Russian and Chinese probing operations in these areas. After all, an altogether weak response to probing tempts the other side to miscalculate its strength—a common cause of wars. But given just how many scenarios exist for an outbreak of hostilities in these increasingly fraught conflict zones, the question nobody asks, and that is utterly absent from the policy debate, is: Once violent hostilities begin, how do you *end* a war with Russia or China?

Like the nations involved in World War I, the United States, Russia, and China in the twenty-first century will have the capacity to keep on fighting even if one or the other loses a major clash or missile exchange. This has far-reaching implications. For the problem is, both Russia and China are dictatorships, not democracies. Therefore, losing face for them would be much more catastrophic than it would be for an American president. Politically speaking, they may be unable to give up the fight. And so we, too, might have to fight on, until there is some form of a regime change, or a substantial reduction in Moscow's or Beijing's military capacity. The world would not be the same after. We imagine a war in the Baltic Sea basin or the South China Sea as short, intense, and contained. But who knows what it might unleash? Washington has done almost no thinking about that. After World War I, after Iraq even, we never should imagine war as easy, or surgically confined to one place.

We assume, without too much thinking, that any regime change in these places will be for the better. But it easily could be for the worse. Both Putin and Xi Jinping are rational actors, holding back more extreme elements. They are bold, but not crazy. The idea that more liberal regimes might replace them is an illusion. Given their decaying authoritarian systems and the buildup both of ethnic tensions and economic problems inside Russia and China, the alternative danger is that rather than another strong ruler or a move toward stable democracy, we will see a partial breakdown of order itself in Moscow and perhaps even in Beijing, upon which, as I have written, the very coherence of Eurasia hinges. Remember the overarching theme of this essay: the tightly wound interconnectedness of weakening states and faded empires across Eurasia. The world of the digital age is like a taut web. Tweak one string and the whole network vibrates. This means a flareup in the Baltic or South China Sea is not only about the Baltic or South China Sea. Nothing is local anymore. Connectivity itself magnifies the effect of military miscalculation. The Peloponnesian War that engulfed all of Greece had its origins in relatively minor conflicts involving Corcyra and Potidaea, which helped drive tensions between Athens and Sparta to the breaking point. Because of the way technology has collapsed distance, Eurasia is now no less a coherent conflict system than were the city-states of ancient Greece. And the basic unit of our world, the state, is itself in decline in too many places. In the interest of thinking tragically in order to avoid tragedy, policy makers need to worry about how not to provoke more anarchy than the world has already seen.

Beginning in the late nineteenth century and leading up to World War I, the "Eastern Question"—what to do about the weakening Ottoman Empire in the Balkans and the Middle East—dominated European geopolitics. The Eastern Question has now been replaced by the Eurasian Question: what to do about the weakening of states on the supercontinent, as older imperial legacies move to the forefront.

2.

The Art of Avoiding War

THE ATLANTIC, JUNE 2015

The Scythians were nomadic horsemen who dominated a vast realm of the Pontic steppe north of the Black Sea, in present-day Ukraine and southern Russia, from the seventh century to the third century B.C. Unlike other ancient peoples who left not a trace, the Scythians continued to haunt and terrify long after they were gone. Herodotus recorded that they "ravaged the whole of Asia. They not only took tribute from each people, but also made raids and pillaged everything these peoples had." Napoleon, on witnessing the Russians' willingness to burn down their own capital rather than hand it over to his army, reputedly said: "They are Scythians!"

The more chilling moral for modern audiences involves not the Scythians' cruelty, but rather their tactics against the invading Persian army of Darius, early in the sixth century B.C. As Darius's infantry marched east near the Sea of Azov, hoping to meet the Scythian war bands in a decisive battle, the Scythians kept withdrawing into the immense reaches of their territory. Darius was perplexed, and sent the Scythian king, Idanthyrsus, a challenge: *If you think yourself stronger, stand and fight; if not, submit.*

Idanthyrsus replied that since his people had neither cities nor cultivated land for an enemy to destroy, they had nothing to defend, and thus no reason to give battle. Instead, his men harassed and skirmished with Persian foraging parties, then quickly withdrew, over and over again. Each time, small groups of Persian cavalry fled in disorder, while the main body of Darius's army weakened as it marched farther and farther away from its base and supply lines. Darius ultimately retreated from Scythia, essentially defeated, without ever having had the chance to fight.

Killing the enemy is easy, in other words; it is finding him that is difficult. This is as true today as ever; the landscape of war is now vaster and emptier of combatants than it was during the set-piece battles of the Industrial Age. Related lessons: Don't go hunting ghosts, and don't get too deep into a situation where your civilizational advantage is of little help. Or, as the Chinese sage of early antiquity Sun Tzu famously said, "The side that knows when to fight and when not will take the victory. There are roadways not to be traveled, armies not to be attacked, walled cities not to be assaulted." A case in point comes from the ill-fated Sicilian Expedition of the late fifth century B.C., chronicled by Thucydides, in which Athens sent a small force to far-off Sicily in support of allies there, only to be drawn deeper and deeper into the conflict, until the prestige of its whole maritime empire became dependent upon victory. Thucydides's story is especially poignant in the wake of Vietnam and Iraq. With the Athenians, as with Darius, one is astonished by how the obsession with honor and reputation can lead a great power toward a bad fate. The image of Darius's army marching into nowhere on an inhospitable steppe, in search of an enemy that never quite appears, is so powerful that it goes beyond mere symbolism.

Your enemy will not meet you on your own terms, only on his. That is why asymmetric warfare is as old as history. When fleeting insurgents planted car bombs and harassed Marines and soldiers in the warrens of Iraqi towns, they were Scythians. When the Chinese harass the Filipino navy and make territorial claims with fishing boats, coast guard vessels, and oil rigs, all while avoiding any confrontation with U.S. warships, they are Scythians. And when the warriors of the Islamic State arm themselves with knives and video cameras, they, too, are Scythians. Largely because of these Scythians, the United States has only limited ability to determine the outcome of many conflicts, despite being a superpower. America is learning an ironic truth of empire: You endure by *not* fighting every battle. In the first century A.D., Tiberius preserved Rome by not interfering in bloody internecine conflicts beyond its northern frontier. Instead, he practiced strategic patience as he watched the carnage. He understood the limits of Roman power.

The United States does not chase after war bands in Yemen as Darius did in Scythia, but occasionally it kills individuals from the air. The fact that it uses drones is proof not of American strength, but of American limitations. The Obama administration must recognize these limitations, and not allow, for example, the country to be drawn deeper into the conflict in Syria. If the United States helps topple the dictator Bashar al-Assad on Wednesday, then what will it do on Thursday, when it finds that it has helped midwife to power a Sunni jihadist regime, or on Friday, when ethnic cleansing of the Shia-trending Alawites commences? Perhaps this is a battle that, as Sun Tzu might conclude, should not be fought. *But Assad has killed many tens of thousands, maybe more, and he is being supported by the Iranians!* True, but remember that emotion, however righteous, can be the enemy of analysis.

So how can the U.S. avoid Darius's fate? How can it avoid being undone by pride, while still fulfilling its moral responsibility as a great power? It should use proxies wherever it can find them, even among adversaries. If the Iranian-backed Houthis are willing to fight al-Qaeda in Yemen, why should Americans be opposed? And if the Iranians ignite a new phase of sectarian war in Iraq, let that be their own undoing, as they themselves fail to understand the lesson of the Scythians. While the Middle East implodes through years of low-intensity conflict among groups of Scythians, let Turkey, Egypt, Israel, Saudi Arabia, and Iran jostle toward an uneasy balance of power, and the United States remain a half step removed—caution, after all, is not the same as capitulation. Finally, let the United States return to its roots as a maritime power in Asia and a defender on land in Europe, where there are fewer Scythians, and more ordinary villains. Scythians are the nemesis of missionary nations, nations that obey no limits. Certainly America should reach, but not—like Darius—overreach.

3.

The Tragedy of U.S. Foreign Policy

THE NATIONAL INTEREST, AUGUST 1, 2013

For over two years, the civil war in Syria has been synonymous with cries of moral urgency. *Do something!* shout those who demand the United States intervene militarily to set the situation there to rights, even as the battle lines now comprise hundreds of regime and rebel groupings and the rebels have started fighting each other. *Well, then,* shout the moral interventionists, *if only we had intervened earlier!*

Syria is not unique. Before Syria, humanitarians in 2011 demanded military intervention in Libya, even though the regime of Muammar Qaddafi had given up its nuclear program and had been cooperating for years with Western intelligence agencies. In fact, the United States and France did lead an intervention, and Libya today is barely a state, with Tripoli less a capital than the weak point of imperial-like arbitration for far-flung militias, tribes, and clans, while nearby Saharan entities are in greater disarray because of weapons flooding out of Libya.

The 1990s were full of calls for humanitarian intervention: in Rwanda, which tragically went unheeded; and in Bosnia and Kosovo, where interventions, while belated, were by and large successful. Free from the realpolitik necessities of the Cold War, humanitarians have in the past two decades tried to reduce foreign policy to an aspect of genocide prevention. Indeed, the Nazi Holocaust is only one lifetime removed from our own—a nanosecond in human history—and so Post Cold War foreign policy now rightly exists in the shadow of it. The codified upshot has been R2P: the "Responsibility to Protect," the mantra of humanitarians.

But American foreign policy cannot merely be defined by R2P and *Never Again!* Statesmen can only rarely be concerned with humanitarian interventions and protecting human rights to the exclusion of other considerations. The United States, like any nation—but especially because it is a great power—simply has interests that do not always cohere with its values. That is tragic, but it is a tragedy that has to be embraced and accepted.

What are those overriding interests? The United States, as the dominant power in the Western Hemisphere, must always prevent any other power from becoming equally dominant in the Eastern Hemisphere. Moreover, as a liberal maritime power, the United States must seek to protect the sea lines of communication that enable world trade. It must also seek to protect both treaty and de facto allies, and especially their access to hydrocarbons. These are all interests that, while not necessarily contradictory to human rights, simply do not operate in the same category.

Because the United States is a liberal power, its interests—even when they are not directly concerned with human rights—are generally moral. But they are only secondarily moral. For seeking to adjust the balance of power in one's favor has been throughout history an amoral enterprise pursued by both liberal and illiberal powers. Nevertheless, when a liberal power like the United States pursues such a goal in the service of preventing war among major states, it is acting morally in the highest sense.

A telling example of this tension—one that gets to the heart of why *Never Again!* and R2P cannot always be the operative words in statesmanship—was recently provided by the foreign affairs expert Leslie H. Gelb. Gelb noted that after Saddam Hussein had gassed close to seven thousand Kurds to death in northern Iraq in 1988, even a "truly ethical" secretary of state, George Shultz, committed a "moral outrage." For Shultz basically ignored the incident and continued supporting Saddam in his war against Iran, because weakening Iran—not protecting the citizens of Iraq—was the primary American *interest* at the time.

So was Shultz acting immorally? Not completely, I believe. Shultz was operating under a different morality than the one normally applied by humanitarians. His was a public morality; not a private one. He and the rest of the Reagan administration had a responsibility to the hundreds of millions of Americans under their charge. And while these millions were fellow countrymen, they were more crucially voters and citizens, essentially strangers who did not know Shultz or Reagan personally, but who had entrusted the two men with their interests. And the American public's interest clearly dictated that of the two states, Iran and Iraq, Iran at the time constituted the greater threat. In protecting the public interest of even a liberal power, a statesman cannot always be nice, or humane.

I am talking here of a morality of public outcomes, rather than one of private intentions. By supporting Iraq, the Reagan administration succeeded in preventing Iran in the last years of the Cold War from becoming a regional hegemon. That was an outcome convenient to U.S. interests, even if the morality of the affair was ambiguous, given that Iraq's regime was at the time the more brutal of the two.

In seeking good outcomes, policy makers are usually guided by constraints: a realistic awareness of what, for instance, the United States should and should not do, given its finite resources. After all, the United States had hundreds of thousands of troops tied down in Europe and Northeast Asia during the Cold War, and thus had to contain Iran through the use of a proxy, Saddam's Iraq. That was not entirely cynical: It was an intelligent use of limited assets in the context of a worldwide geopolitical struggle.

The problem with a foreign policy driven foremost by *Never Again!* is that it ignores limits and the availability of resources. World War II had the secondary, moral effect of saving what was left of European Jewry. Its primary goal and effect was to restore the European and Asian balance of power in a manner tolerable to the United States—something that the Nazis and the Japanese fascists had overturned. Of course, the Soviet Union wrested control of Eastern Europe for nearly half a century following the war. But again, limited resources necessitated an American alliance with the mass murderer Stalin against the mass murderer Hitler. It is because of such awful choices and attendant compromises—in which morality intertwines with amorality—that humanitarians will frequently be disappointed with the foreign policy of even the most heroic administrations.

World War II certainly involved many hideous compromises and even mistakes on President Franklin D. Roosevelt's part. He got into the war in Europe very late, he did not bomb the rail tracks leading to the concentration camps, he might have been more aggressive with the Soviets on the question of Eastern Europe. But as someone representing the interests of the millions of strangers who had and had not voted for him, his aim was to defeat Nazi Germany and Imperial Japan in a manner that cost the fewest American soldiers' lives and utilized the least amount of national resources. Saving the remnants of European Jewry was a moral consequence of his actions, but his methods contained tactical concessions that had fundamental amoral elements. Abraham Lincoln, for his part, brought mass suffering upon southern civilians in the last phase of the Civil War in order to decisively defeat the South. The total war waged by Generals William Tecumseh Sherman and Ulysses S.

Grant was evidence of that. Simply put, there are actions of state that are the right things to do, even if they cannot be defined in terms of conventional morality.

Amoral goals, properly applied, do have moral effects. Indeed, in more recent times, President Richard Nixon and his secretary of state, Henry Kissinger, rushed arms to Israel following a surprise attack by Arab armies in the fall of 1973. The two men essentially told the American defense establishment that supporting Israel in its hour of need was the right thing to do, because it was necessary to send an unambiguous message of resolve to the Soviets and their Arab allies at a critical stage in the Cold War. Had they justified the arms transfers purely in terms of helping embattled post-Holocaust Jewry—rather than in terms of power politics as they did—it would have made for a much weaker argument in Washington, where officials rightly had American interests at heart more than Israeli ones. George McGovern was possibly a more ethical man than either Nixon or Kissinger. But had he been elected president in 1972, would he have acted so wisely and so decisively during the 1973 Middle East war? The fact is, individual perfection, as Machiavelli knew, is not necessarily synonymous with public virtue.

Then there is the case of Deng Xiaoping. Deng approved the brutal suppression of students at Beijing's Tiananmen Square in 1989. For that he is not respected among humanitarians in the West. But the consolidation of Communist Party control that followed the clampdown allowed for Deng's methodical, market-oriented reforms to continue for a generation in China. Perhaps never before in recorded economic history have so many people seen such a dramatic rise in living standards, with an attendant rise in personal (if not political) freedoms, in so short a time frame. Thus, Deng might be considered both a brutal communist and the greatest man of the twentieth century. The morality of his life is complex.

The Bosnia and Kosovo interventions of 1995 and 1999 are frequently held out as evidence that the United States is most effective when it acts according to its humanitarian values—never mind its amoral interests. But those who make that argument neglect to mention that the two successful interventions were eased by the fact that America operated in the Balkans with the balance of power strongly in its favor. Russia in the 1990s was weak and chaotic under Boris Yeltsin's incompetent rule, and thus temporarily less able to challenge the United States in a region where historically the czars and commissars had exerted considerable sway. However, Russia, even in the 1990s, still exerted considerable sway in the Caucasus, and thus a Western response to halt ethnic cleansing there during the same decade was not even considered. More broadly, the 1990s allowed for ground interventions in the Balkans because the international climate was relatively benign: China was only just beginning its naval expansion (endangering our Pacific allies) and September 11 still lay in the future. Truly, beyond many a moral response lies a question of power that cannot be explained wholly in terms of morality.

Thus, to raise morality as a sole arbiter is ultimately not to be serious about foreign policy. R2P must play as large a role as realistically possible in the affairs of state. But it cannot ultimately dominate. Syria is the current and best example of this. U.S. power is capable of many things, yet putting a complex and war-torn Islamic society's house in order is not one of them. In this respect, our tragic experience in Iraq is indeed relevant. Quick fixes like a no-fly zone and arming the rebels may topple Syrian dictator Bashar al-Assad, but that might only make President Barack Obama culpable in mid-wifing to power a Sunni-jihadist regime, even as ethnic cleansing of al-Assad's Alawites commences. At least at this late juncture, without significant numbers of Western boots on the ground for a significant period—something for which there is little public support—the likelihood of a better, more stable regime emerging in Damascus is highly questionable. Frankly, there are just no easy answers here, especially as the pro-Western regime in Jordan is threatened by continued Syrian violence. R2P applied in 2011 in Syria might actually have yielded a better strategic result: It will remain an unknowable.

Because moralists in these matters are always driven by righteous passion, whenever you disagree with them, you are by definition immoral and deserve no quarter; whereas realists, precisely because they are used to conflict, are less likely to overreact to it. Realists know that passion and wise policy rarely flow together. (The late diplomat Richard Holbrooke was a stunning exception to this rule.) Realists adhere to the belief of the mid-twentieth-century University of Chicago political scientist Hans Morgenthau, who wrote that "one must work with" the base forces of human nature, "not against them." Thus, realists accept the human material at hand in any given place, however imperfect that material may be. To wit, you can't go around toppling regimes just because you don't like them. Realism, adds Morgenthau, "appeals to historical precedent rather than to abstract principles [of justice] and aims at the realization of the lesser evil rather than of the absolute good."

No group of people internalized such tragic realizations better than Republican presidents during the Cold War. Dwight Eisenhower, Richard Nixon, Ronald Reagan and George H. W. Bush all practiced amorality, realism, restraint, and humility in foreign affairs (if not all the time). It is their sensibility that should guide us now. Eisenhower represented a pragmatic compromise within the Republican Party between isolationists and rabid anticommunists. All of these men supported repressive, undemocratic regimes in the third world in support of a favorable balance of power against the Soviet Union. Nixon accepted the altogether brutal regimes in the Soviet Union and "Red" China as legitimate, even as he balanced one against the other. Reagan spoke the Wilsonian language of moral rearmament, even as he awarded the key levers of bureaucratic power to realists like Caspar Weinberger, George Shultz, and Frank Carlucci, whose effect regarding policy was to temper Reagan's rhetoric. The elder Bush did not break relations with China after the Tiananmen uprising; nor did he immediately pledge support for Lithuania after that brave little country declared its independence—for fear of antagonizing the Soviet military. It was caution and restraint on Bush's part that helped bring the Cold War to a largely peaceful—and, therefore, moral—conclusion. In some of these policies, the difference between amorality and morality was, to paraphrase Joseph Conrad in *Lord Jim,* no more than "the thickness of a sheet of paper."

And that is precisely the point: Foreign policy at its best is subtle, innovative, contradictory, and truly bold only on occasion, aware as its most disciplined practitioners are of the limits of American power. That is heartrending, simply because calls to alleviate suffering will in too many instances go unanswered. For the essence of tragedy is not the triumph of evil over good, so much as the triumph of one good over another that causes suffering.

4.

Elegant Decline: The Navy's Rising Importance

THE ATLANTIC, NOVEMBER 2007

Beware pendulum swings. Before 9/11, not enough U.S. generals believed that the future of war was unconventional and tied to global anarchy. They insisted on having divisions to fight against, not ragtag groups of religious warriors who, as it turned out, fought better than state armies in the Muslim world ever did. Now the Pentagon is consumed by a focus on urban warfare and counterinsurgency; inside military circles, the development of culturally adroit foreign-area officers (FAOs) and the learning of exotic languages have become the rage. My own warnings about anarchy ("The Coming Anarchy," February 1994 *Atlantic*) and my concentration on FAOs and Army Special Forces in recent books may have helped this trend. But have we pushed it too far? We may finally master the art of counterinsurgency just in time for it to recede in importance.

History suggests that the wars in Iraq and Afghanistan will be imperfect guideposts to conflicts ahead. The quaint Franco-Prussian War of 1870–71 gave no intimation of World War I. Neither World War II nor Korea prepared us for Vietnam, which was more similar to the Philippine War of 1899–1902 than to its immediate predecessors. The ease of the Gulf War provided no hint of what an ordeal the Iraq War would be. Today, while we remain fixated on street fighting in Baghdad, the militaries of China, India, South Korea, and Japan are modernizing, and Russia has maintained and subsidized its military research-and-development base by selling weapons to China and others. Though counterinsurgency will remain a core part of our military doctrine, the Pentagon does not have the luxury of planning for one military future; it must plan for several.

"Regular wars" between major states could be as frequent in the twenty-first century as they were in the twentieth. In his 2005 book, *Another Bloody Century,* the British scholar Colin Gray, a professor of international politics and strategic studies at the University of Reading, explains convincingly that these future wars will not require any "manifestation of insanity by political leaders," nor even an "aberration from normal statecraft," but may come about merely because of what Thucydides recognized as "fear, honour, and interest." Wars between the United States and a Sino-Russian axis or between the United States and a coalition of rogue states are just two of the scenarios Gray imagines.

Are we prepared to fight these wars? Our Army and Marine Corps together constitute the most battle-hardened regular land force in the world. But it has been a long time since our Navy has truly fought another navy, or our Air Force another air force. In the future they could be tested to the same extent that the Army and Marine Corps have been. The current catchphrase is *boots on the ground;* in the future it could be *hulls in the water.*

Democracy and supremacy undermine the tragic sense required for long-range planning. A "peaceful, gain-loving nation" like the United States "is not far-sighted, and far-sightedness is needed for adequate military preparation, especially in these days," warned Navy Captain Alfred Thayer Mahan in 1890, a time when— although the Panama Canal was soon to be built and World War I lay just over the horizon—America was still preoccupied with land-based westward expansion (Wounded Knee, the last battle of the Indian Wars, was fought that year). Mahan notwithstanding, too few strategists at the time were thinking seriously about sea power. Today we are similarly obsessed with dirty land wars, and our three-hundred-ship Navy is roughly half the size it was in the mid-1980s.

A great navy is like oxygen: You notice it only when it is gone. But the strength of a nation's sea presence, more than any other indicator, has throughout history often been the best barometer of that nation's power and prospects. "Those far-distant storm-beaten ships upon which [Napoleon's] Grand Army never looked, stood between it and the dominion of the world," Mahan wrote, describing how the British Royal Navy had checked Napoleon's ambitions. In our day, carrier strike groups, floating in international waters only a few miles off enemy territory, require no visas or exit strategies. Despite the quagmire of Iraq, we remain the greatest outside power in the Middle East because of our ability to project destructive fire from warships in the Indian Ocean and its tributary waters such as the Persian Gulf. Our sea power allows us to lose a limited war on land without catastrophic consequences. The Navy, together with the Air Force, constitutes our insurance policy. The Navy also plays a crucial role as the bus driver for most of the Army's equipment whenever the Army deploys overseas.

Army units can't forward-deploy anywhere in significant numbers without a national debate. Not so the Navy. Forget the cliché about the essence of the Navy being tradition; I've spent enough time with junior officers and enlisted sailors on Pacific deployments to know that the essence of our Navy is *operations:* disaster relief, tracking Chinese subs, guarding sea-lanes, and so forth. American sailors don't care what the mission is, as long as there is one, and the farther forward the better. The seminal event for the U.S. Navy was John Paul Jones's interdiction of the British during the Revolutionary War—which occurred off Yorkshire, on the other side of the Atlantic. During the quasi-war that President John Adams waged against France from 1798 to 1800, U.S. warships protected American merchant vessels off what is today Indonesia. American warships operated off North Africa in the First Barbary War of 1801 to 1805. The War of 1812 found the Navy as far down the globe as the coast of Brazil and as far up as the North Cape of Scandinavia. Peter Swartz, an expert at the Center for Naval Analyses, observes that because operating thousands of miles from home ports is so ingrained in U.S. naval tradition, no one thinks it odd that even the Coast Guard has ships in service from Greenland to South America.

Great navies help preserve international stability. When the British navy began to decline, the vacuum it left behind helped engender the competition among major powers that led to World War I. After the U.S. Navy was forced to depart Subic Bay in the Philippines in 1992, piracy quintupled in the Southeast Asian archipelago—which includes one of the world's busiest waterways, the Strait of Malacca. In an age when 90 percent of global commerce travels by sea, and 95 percent of our imports and exports from outside North America do the same (even as that trade volume is set to double by 2020), and when 75 percent of the world's population is clustered within two hundred miles of the sea, the relative decline of our Navy is a big, dangerous fact to which our elites appear blind.

The End of the Mahanian Century?

The best way to understand the tenuousness of our grip on "hard," military power (to say nothing of "soft," diplomatic power) is to understand our situation at sea. This requires an acquaintance with two books published a century ago: Mahan's *The Influence of Sea Power Upon History, 1660–1783*, which was written in 1890, and Julian S. Corbett's *Some Principles of Maritime Strategy*, which came out in 1911.

Few books have had more influence on military policy than Mahan's. It affected the thinking of Presidents William McKinley and

Theodore Roosevelt—as well as that of Germany's Kaiser Wilhelm II—and it helped prompt the naval buildup before World War I. Mahan showed that because the sea is the great "commons" of civilization, naval power—to protect merchant fleets—had always been the determining factor in European political struggles. The strength of his argument lay less in its originality than in its comprehensiveness, achieved by numerous examples. He pointed out that there were no great sea battles in the Second Punic War, because Rome's mastery of the Mediterranean was a deciding factor in Carthage's defeat. He noted that George Washington partly attributed America's victory in its war for independence to France's control of the seas—even as several decades earlier France had lost the Seven Years' War partly because of its neglect of sea power.

Mahan believed in concentrating national naval forces in search of the decisive battle: For him, success was about sinking the other fleet. Mahan's aggressive sensibility perfectly matched the temperament of Theodore Roosevelt. As a result, it was in the quiet years before World War I that America became a great sea power—and consequently a Great Power.

Julian Corbett, a British historian, did not so much disagree with Mahan as offer a subtler approach, placing greater emphasis on doing more with less. Corbett asserted that just because one nation has lost control of the sea, another nation has not necessarily gained it. A naval coalition that may appear weak and dispersed can, if properly constituted, have "a reality of strength." He called this a "fleet in being"—a collection of ships that can quickly coalesce into a unified fleet when necessary. This fleet-in-being wouldn't need to dominate or sink other fleets; it could be effective by seizing bases and policing choke points. Such a deceptively able fleet, Corbett argued, should pursue an "active and vigorous life" in the conduct of limited defense, by, for example, carrying out harassing operations. As it happened, Corbett's book came out after the British

Royal Navy had reduced its worldwide presence by leveraging the growing sea power of its allies Japan and the United States.

A hundred years later, the Mahanian Century has ended. The period of 1890 to 1989 was about dominance: controlling vast oceanic spaces by making sure your national navy had more ships than those of your competitors. This era reached its zenith in 1945, when the U.S. Navy and its vast fleet of supply ships numbered 6,700. With no peer competitor in sight, the president and Congress moved quickly to cut that Navy, along with the standing Army, considerably. By 1950 the United States had only 634 ships. The drawdown helped set the stage for the "Revolt of the Admirals," when a group of officers warned the nation of calamities ahead. (Indeed, two decades later the Soviet navy would be a near-peer competitor.) But in a 1954 article in *Proceedings,* the journal of the U.S. Naval Institute, in Annapolis, Maryland, a young Harvard academic named Samuel P. Huntington told the Navy not to feel sorry for itself:

> The resources which a service is able to obtain in a democratic society are a function of the public support of that service. The service has the responsibility to develop this necessary support, and it can only do this if it possesses a strategic concept which clearly formulates its relationship to the national security.

Huntington recommended that the Navy emphasize its ability to support ground troops *from the sea:* Any battles with the Soviet Union were likely to be on land, so the Navy needed to play up the job it could do in a war with a great land power. The Navy took Huntington's advice, and it worked: For the remainder of the Cold War, the Navy was able to hold the line at roughly six hundred ships, in part by arguing for its importance in supporting a ground war against the Soviet Union and its allies—it would be the Navy's job to get soldiers to the fight, and to soften up the battlefield with offshore firepower.

In 1991, the Gulf War provided a live-action demonstration of this capacity. Even so, by 1997, Post Cold War budget cuts had reduced the Navy to 365 ships. (In the Quadrennial Defense Review of that year, the Pentagon established a "red line" of 300 ships, below which the Navy would not go.) Of course the three-hundred-ship Navy could still, in the words of Robert O. Work, vice president for strategic studies at the Center for Strategic and Budgetary Assessment, in Washington, "pound the snot" out of primitive challengers like Iraq, Iran, and North Korea, because the precision revolution in weaponry enabled, for instance, a single wire-guided missile from a U.S. destroyer to accomplish what in Vietnam had required wave after wave of carrier-based planes.

Still, the fewer vessels you have, the riskier each deployment, because a ship can't be in two places at once. Due to the rapid increase in shipborne trade, globalization favors large navies that protect trade and tanker routes. Additionally, while the United States remains a great naval power, it is no longer a maritime power; that is, we don't have much of a merchant fleet left to support our warships in an emergency. We've been priced out of the shipbuilding market by cheap-labor countries in Asia.

All of this puts us in a precarious position. History shows that powerful competitor navies can easily emerge out of nowhere in just a few decades. The vast majority of American ships that saw combat in World War II had not even been planned before the spring of 1941. The Indian navy, which may soon be the third largest in the world, was not on many people's radar screens at the close of the Cold War. Nor, for that matter, was the now-expanding Chinese submarine fleet. Robert Work told me that he believes the eventual incorporation of Taiwan into China will have the effect that the Battle of Wounded Knee had on the United States: It will psychologically close an era of national consolidation for the Chinese, thereby dramatically redirecting their military energies outward, beyond their coastal waters. Tellingly, whereas the U.S. Navy pays homage to Mahan by naming buildings after him, the Chinese avidly read him; the Chinese are the Mahanians now.

Then there is the Japanese navy, which now operates 117 warships, including 16 submarines. In a sense, we're back to 1890, when a spark of naval competition among rising powers like Japan, Germany, and the United States left Britain unable to maintain its relative advantage.

The Thousand-Ship Navy

By necessity, the American navy is turning from Mahan to Corbett. "Where the old 'Maritime Strategy' focused on sea control," Admiral Michael Mullen, the chief of naval operations (recently promoted to chairman of the Joint Chiefs of Staff), said last year, "the new one must recognize that the economic tide of all nations rises not when the seas are controlled by one [nation], but rather when they are made safe and free for all."

He went on: "I'm after that proverbial thousand-ship Navy—a fleet-in-being, if you will, comprised of all freedom-loving nations, standing watch over the seas, standing watch over each other." Subtract the platitudes and it's clear that Admiral Mullen is squaring a number of circles to contend with the difficult reality he's up against.

A grand maritime coalition that policed the seas and provided disaster relief would allow for such possibilities as joint American-Chinese antipiracy patrols in MALSINDO (the Malaysia-Singapore-Indonesia archipelagic region, as an American Navy acronym labels it). In fact, national navies tend to cooperate better than national armies, partly because sailors are united by a kind of fellowship-of-the-sea born of their shared experience facing violent natural forces. Such coalitions would likely get along better than the land-based ones we have seen in Iraq, Afghanistan, and Kosovo. Requirements for membership would be minimal: Any navy could join, provided it were willing to share information. Leading a cooperative international enterprise like this to interdict terrorists, pirates, and smugglers in coastal waters and to deter rogue states would help the United States improve its deteriorating reputation in the wake of Iraq.

Mullen's emphasis on a coalition of freedom-loving nations is itself an indication of diminished resources. During the Cold War, we had crucial naval allies whose bases could always be depended upon—Japan, Great Britain, Denmark, Norway, Iceland, and several others. With their help, we held the Soviet navy in check under the polar ice. But given current public opinion in Europe, perhaps the only one of these allies we can rely on in the future is Japan, which, as an island civilization still hated throughout Asia and beset with security dilemmas of limited interest to Europeans, may be the loneliest country in the world except for Israel. (Experts I spoke to for this article worried about the prospective loss of allied basing and advocated sea basing. One of the Navy's earliest proposed designs was a device resembling a self-powered oil rig with massive platforms for UAVs—unmanned aerial vehicles—and other air assets.)

With no core group of allies, commerce has to be protected by all, for all. That's no easy challenge. Whereas airplanes are monitored and regulated from takeoff to landing, merchant ships are on their own in the anarchic seas. But in a post-9/11 world, with the possibility of nuclear terrorism abetted by ocean-based piracy and smuggling, the anarchy needs to be quelled, and the seas and the ports policed. Hence the benefits of a multination piracy patrol.

Stanley Weeks is a Washington-based naval and defense-policy analyst for a Fortune 500 commercial consulting company. Over the course of his career, he has done everything from mentoring the new Albanian navy to advising U.S. combatant commanders about how to defend against missiles. When I spoke to him in his office in

McLean, Virginia, he told me about other possibilities for Admiral Mullen's thousand-ship fleet-in-being. "Boots on the ground in most cases is a loser," Weeks said. "On land, we're not playing to our advantage, because there is an endless demographic supply of young male religious fanatics." He emphasized that naval operations can lower America's profile, since they attract less attention than Army operations, making our military less vulnerable to media attacks—and therefore also making it easier to carry out operations that might otherwise become lightning rods for criticism. Offshore maritime capability also enables us to "take out selected individuals and insert small groups of special forces," Weeks says, adding that leveraging other powers by operating as part of an international thousand-ship navy would certainly help with all this.

A multinational fleet-in-being would also lead to greater intelligence sharing and allow us greater forward presence, closer to enemy shores. This would make it easier to identify key targets. In fact, the thousand-ship multinational navy is essentially the seagoing equivalent of counterinsurgency.

But while the thousand-ship navy would help cut down on smuggling and piracy, and possibly terrorism, it doesn't really deal with the basic strategic function of the U.S. Navy: the need to offer a serious, inviolable instrument for inflicting great punishment— a stare-down capability. Nor does it address the need to quickly transport troops and equipment to distant conflicts.

"The Navy is not primarily about low-level raiding, piracy patrols, and riverine warfare," Jim Thomas, a former deputy assistant secretary of defense, told me. "If we delude ourselves into thinking that it is, we're finished as a great power." Piracy, for example, has been a scourge for hundreds of years in some of the very same places we say it cannot be tolerated, like off the Horn of Africa or in archipelagic Southeast Asia. As the late vice admiral and Navy futurist Arthur Cebrowski once told me, with a dismissive wave of his arm, "Piracy is just part of the noise." No matter how the Pentagon spins it, the reality is that development of a thousand-ship international navy is not a way of maintaining our current strength; rather, it's a way of elegantly managing American decline.

But let's remember that while the relative decline of the British Royal Navy helped produce World War I, Britain and its allies still won that war, thanks in some measure to sea power—and that Britain would go on to triumph in an even greater world war two decades later. Our own growing relative weakness need not mean that our adversaries gain advantage. Decline can be overrated.

The Weary Titan

As noted, today we have only half the nearly six hundred ships that the U.S. Navy had in the 1980s, when it was directed by Secretary of the Navy John Lehman; he observes that now, because we are building only five ships per year, "we're on the way to a 150-ship Navy."

This attrition is partly a result of the high cost of the war in Iraq and the shrinkage of discretionary funds in the national budget, but it's also a function of the procurement process itself. The building of naval platforms offers a case study in how a vast and aged bureaucratic system is subject to disease and calcification—which are in part what doomed Pharaonic Egypt, Mayan Central America, and Soviet Russia.

To get this bureaucracy to agree on a new class of ship can take years—even decades—of studies and committee meetings, in which slowing down the process is easy and taking even the smallest risk is hard. Consequently, by the time a ship is launched, it is already dated. Yet because the ship must be equipped with every weapons system conceivable, the cost remains high. (To leave any weapon system out is to make the ship, to some degree, more vulnerable—and that means risk.) The *Arleigh Burke*–class guided-missile destroyer on which I was embedded in 2005 cost nearly $1 billion.

The new DDG-1000 *Zumwalt*-class destroyer, envisioned in one form or another for twelve years and beset with delays, could end up costing $3 billion a ship—if any get built. The new *Gerald R. Ford*–class aircraft carriers could cost a whopping $8 billion each—not including $6 billion of research-and-development costs.

History can be cruel to such a geologic pace; this slowness is a recipe for vulnerability and nasty strategic surprise. We have a capital-intensive Navy consisting of vessels that cost tens of billions of dollars, and that must therefore each deploy for decades if they are to return the investment. Yet all a future peer competitor like China need do to greatly devalue our fleet is to improve its ballistic missile technology to the point where we're forced to move our carriers, say, one hundred miles east of their present positions off the Asian mainland, to keep them out of missile range. Worse, a nuclear radiation device arriving in a container in the harbor at, say, Norfolk, Virginia, could render these multibillion-dollar platforms suddenly unusable.

The coming technological era of precision and stealth will not be friendly to gargantuan objects like carriers. Consider the "supercavitation" torpedo, a torpedo that launches from a small boat and, by its ability to create a cushion of air between it and the surrounding water, can travel at 200 knots (regular torpedoes can travel at only 35 knots) and immobilize a carrier on detonation.

Fortunately, our defense bureaucracy is slowly rising to the challenge—not by eliminating such threats but by diminishing them. For instance, the new *Ford*-class carriers will be built with laser guns to kill incoming missiles, anti-torpedo torpedoes to deal with supercavitation technology, and electric catapults for launching UAVs in case fighter jets, with their human pilots, give way to enhanced remote-controlled Predators that can be refueled in the air.

Decline can be imperceptible. But if you think that what I have been describing does not constitute decline, consider the financial burden of sustaining this Navy. Admiral Mullen was "hanging on by his fingernails" trying to keep current projects going, according to one expert. "It would take a Chinese-perpetrated 9/11 to give us the budget we need," the same expert told me, "and the Chinese would never be that stupid. They will bleed us slowly, by just doing what they're doing." On October 26, 2006, a Chinese *Song*-class attack submarine, equipped with Russian-made wake-homing torpedoes, reportedly stalked the USS *Kitty Hawk* Carrier Strike Group in the Pacific. The sub boldly surfaced within firing range before being detected only five miles from the carrier itself.

That incident might prove to be a better harbinger of the future than anything going on in Iraq. A second incident, this past January, provided another augury. When the Chinese destroyed an aging weather satellite with a missile-launched interceptor, "they ended two decades of restraint over the militarization of space," as Vice Admiral John G. Morgan, Jr., deputy chief of naval operations for information, plans, and strategy, told me. According to Stratfor, a consulting company that analyzes intelligence, the Chinese are developing a space-warfare capability that could allow them to limit U.S. naval power without a massive naval buildup of their own, by threatening our satellite-based intelligence-gathering and weapons systems.

The danger isn't China per se. China's actions are merely a premonition of a future that will favor nations with dynamic start-up defense bureaucracies less careful and doubt-ridden than our own, unburdened by layers of committees and commissions, and willing to buy—or steal—cutting-edge technology.

To grasp what our military is up against, think of our defense bureaucracy as a great metropolitan newspaper, proud of its editorial oversight, accuracy, and formal English usage, yet besieged and occasionally humiliated by bloggers, whose usage is sloppy and whose fact-checking is weak, sometimes nonexistent. The paper soldiers on, winning awards and affecting the national debate, even as each half decade its opinion carries less weight. Now think of an

$8 billion *Ford*-class carrier surprised by dozens of jet-skis ridden by Iranians armed with shoulder-fired missiles—a scenario one expert described to me. Such an attack wouldn't destroy the carrier, but it might kill sailors and damage some of the radar and planes on deck, worth millions of dollars. Imagine the headlines. Riding through the Strait of Malacca with a carrier strike group not long ago, I saw how easy it is for small fishing boats to draw suddenly alongside.

Another likely future scenario our Navy may have to confront, described to me by Ronald O'Rourke of the Congressional Research Service, is so distributive and networked that it's reminiscent of the Borg aliens in *Star Trek: The Next Generation* episodes, who are able, because of their collective mind, to simultaneously experience what only one of them witnesses. Instead of one big sonar device on a warship, there would be hundreds or thousands of hydrophones floating all over the ocean, each the size of a soda can, listening to submarines and sending information simultaneously.

And if the United States develops such technology, there is no guarantee that we could keep it from the open market. "Because of new surveillance measures, you could have whole zones of the ocean where you are unable to operate safely on the surface," Donald Henry, special assistant to the director of the Pentagon's Office of Net Assessment, told me. Technology and the risk of unconventional attacks "could drive navies underwater, unless carrier strike groups are protected by something we don't have yet." The faster technology progresses, the less likely that people will play by our rules.

Meanwhile, as costs drive us toward that 150-ship Navy, we may need to delegate some tasks to private naval companies, in the same way that private contractors have been used on land in Iraq and Afghanistan. According to Navy Lieutenant Commander Claude Berube, who teaches at the U.S. Naval Academy, in an emergency we might even issue letters of marque, the way we did during the Revolutionary War, giving privateers the legal authority to act in our defense. Allowing privateers to help with, say, the drug interdiction effort in the Caribbean would enable uniformed sailors to concentrate on the Pacific and Indian oceans.

More submarines might seem like a quick fix for many of these challenges. They operate under the surface. They are moving, underwater intelligence factories, able to listen to cellphone conversations on land. They can launch missiles at targets onshore. Some are now being refitted so that they can clandestinely deliver Special Operations teams onto beaches. But the catch is that they are expensive. Each fast-attack, *Los Angeles*–class submarine costs easily more than $1 billion in today's dollars, despite having much less general firepower than a comparably priced *Arleigh Burke*–class destroyer.

Today the United States devotes 4.38 percent of its annual gross domestic product to defense. Before the Iraq War, it was 3.5 percent. Although two dozen or so countries spend more on defense than we do relative to GDP, we still spend more in absolute terms than much of the rest of the world combined. But if we are to maintain our current relative military advantage, we will have to spend at even higher rates. Admiral Morgan, the deputy chief of naval operations for information, plans, and strategy, told me that to maintain our naval primacy, we may need to devote close to 5 percent of gross domestic product (assuming a growing economy) to defense. Yet it's unclear whether the American public will abide that.

During the Cold War, our six-hundred-ship Navy needed to be in only three places in force—the Atlantic and Pacific flanks of the Soviet Union and the Mediterranean; we sometimes subcontracted out less important tropical sea-lanes to other free-world navies (in this, Admiral Mullen's thousand-ship fleet-in-being does have a recent precedent). Now we need to cover the earth with less than half that number of ships. Decline can never be admitted as such until a rival makes demonstrable inroads into your power. But naval trends now appear to buttress political and economic ones that suggest we are indeed headed for a world with multiple competing powers.

Of course, admirals will continue to march to Capitol Hill and declare that no matter the size of the budget, they will succeed in every mission. Managing decline requires "a degree of self-delusion," as Aaron Friedberg put it in his 1988 book, *The Weary Titan: Britain and the Experience of Relative Decline, 1895–1905.* "British statesmen," Friedberg observed, "continued to talk as if nothing of any significance" had occurred, even as they abandoned worldwide sea supremacy. Abandoning supremacy was, in Friedberg's view, a "prudent" and "sensible" strategy, given the economic and political realities of the time. And it didn't stop Britain from helping to save the world in succeeding decades.

We could do much worse.

5.

When North Korea Falls

THE ATLANTIC, OCTOBER 2006

The abbreviation for North Korea used by American military officers says it all: KFR, the Kim Family Regime. It is a regime whose demonization by the American media and policy makers has obscured some vital facts. North Korea's founder, Kim Il Sung, was not merely a dreary Stalinist tyrant. As defectors from his country will tell you, he was also a popular anti-Japanese guerrilla leader in the mold of Enver Hoxha, the Stalinist tyrant of Albania who led his countrymen in a successful insurgency against the Nazis. Nor is his son Kim Jong Il anything like the childish psychopath parodied in the film *Team America: World Police*. It's true that Kim Jong Il was once a playboy. But he has evolved into a canny operator. Andrei Lankov, a professor of history at South Korea's Kookmin University, in Seoul, says that under different circumstances Kim might have actually become the successful Hollywood film producer that regime propaganda claims he already is.

Kim Jong Il's succession was aided by the link that his father had established in the North Korean mind between the Kim Family Regime and the Choson Dynasty, which ruled the Korean Peninsula for five hundred years, starting in the late fourteenth century. Expertly tutored by his father, Kim consolidated power and manipulated the Chinese, the Americans, and the South Koreans into subsidizing him throughout the 1990s. And Kim is hardly impulsive: He has the equivalent of think tanks studying how best to respond to potential attacks from the United States and South Korea—attacks that themselves would be reactions to crises cleverly instigated by the North Korean government in Pyongyang. "The regime constitutes an extremely rational bunch of killers," Lankov says.

Yet for all Kim's canniness, there is evidence that he may be losing his edge. And that may be reason to worry: Totalitarian regimes close to demise are apt to get panicky and do rash things. The weaker North Korea gets, the more dangerous it becomes. The question that should be of greatest concern to the U.S. military in the Pacific—and the question that will likely determine the global balance of power in Asia for generations—is, What happens when North Korea collapses?

The Nightmare After Iraq

On the Korean Peninsula, the Cold War has never ended. On the somber, seaweed-toned border dividing the two Koreas, amid the cries of egrets and Manchurian cranes, I observed South Korean soldiers standing frozen in tae kwon do ready positions, their fists clenched and forearms tightened, staring into the faces of their North Korean counterparts. Each side picks its tallest, most intimidating soldiers for the task (they are still short by American standards).

In the immediate aftermath of the Korean War, the South raised a 328-foot flagpole; the North responded with a 525-foot pole, then put a flag on it whose dry weight is 595 pounds. The North built a two-story building in the Joint Security Area at Panmunjom; the South built a three-story one. The North then added another story to its building. "The land of one-upmanship," is how one U.S. Army sergeant describes the DMZ, or demilitarized zone. The two sides once held a meeting in Panmunjom that went on for eleven hours. Because there was no formal agreement about when to take a bathroom break, neither side budged. The meeting became known as the "Battle of the Bladders."

In other divided countries of the twentieth century—Vietnam, Germany, Yemen—the forces of unity ultimately triumphed. But history suggests that unification does not happen through a calibrated political process in which the interests of all sides are respected. Rather, it tends to happen through a cataclysm of events that, piles of white papers and war-gaming exercises notwithstanding, catches experts by surprise.

Given that North Korea's army of 1.2 million soldiers has been increasingly deployed toward the South Korean border, the Korean Peninsula looms as potentially the next American military nightmare. In 1980, 40 percent of North Korean combat forces were deployed south of Pyongyang near the DMZ; by 2003, more than 70 percent were. As the saying goes among American soldiers, "There is no peacetime in the ROK." (ROK, pronounced "rock," is militaryspeak for the Republic of Korea.) One has merely to observe the Patriot missile batteries, the reinforced concrete hangars, and the blast barriers at the U.S. Air Force bases at Osan and Kunsan, south of Seoul—which are as heavily fortified as any bases in Iraq—to be aware of this. A marine in Okinawa told me, "North Korea is not some third-rate, Middle Eastern conventional army. These brainwashed Asians"—as he crudely put it—"will stand and fight." American soldiers in Korea refer to the fighting on the peninsula between 1950 and 1953 as "the first Korean War." The implicit assumption is that there will be a second.

This helps explain why Korea may be the most dismal place in the world for U.S. troops to be deployed—worse, in some ways, than Iraq. While I traveled on the peninsula, numerous members of the combat-arms community, both air and infantry, told me that they would rather be in Iraq or Afghanistan than in Korea, which constitutes the worst of all military worlds. Soldiers and airmen often live on a grueling wartime schedule, with constant drills, and yet they also have to put up with the official folderol that is part of all peacetime bases—the saluting and inspections that fall by the wayside in war zones, where the only thing that matters is how well you fight. The weather on the peninsula is lousy, too: the winds charging down from Siberia make the winters unbearably frigid, and the monsoons coming off the Pacific Ocean make the summers hot and humid. The dust blowing in from the Gobi Desert doesn't help.

The threat from north of the DMZ is formidable. North Korea boasts 100,000 well-trained special-operations forces and one of the world's largest biological and chemical arsenals. It has stockpiles of anthrax, cholera, and plague, as well as eight industrial facilities for producing chemical agents—any of which could be launched at Seoul by the army's conventional artillery. If the governing infrastructure in Pyongyang were to unravel, the result could be widespread lawlessness (compounded by the guerrilla mentality of the Kim Family Regime's armed forces), as well as mass migration out of and within North Korea. In short, North Korea's potential for anarchy is equal to that of Iraq, and the potential for the deployment of weapons of mass destruction—either during or after precollapse fighting—is far greater.

For a harbinger of the kind of chaos that looms on the peninsula, consider Albania, which was for some years the most anarchic country in post-communist Eastern Europe, save for war-torn Yugoslavia. On a visit to Albania before the Stalinist regime there finally collapsed, I saw vicious gangs of boys as young as eight harassing people. North Korea is reportedly plagued by the same phenomenon outside of its showcase capital. That may be an indication of what lies ahead. In fact, what terrifies South Koreans more than North Korean missiles is North Korean refugees pouring south. The

Chinese, for their part, have nightmare visions of millions of North Korean refugees heading north over the Yalu River into Manchuria.

Obviously, it would be reckless not to worry about North Korea's missile and WMD technologies. In August, there were reports yet again that Kim Jong Il was preparing an underground nuclear test. And the North test-fired seven missiles in July. According to U.S. data, three of the missiles were Scud-Cs, and three were No-dong-As with ranges of 300 to 1,000 miles; all were capable of carrying a nuclear warhead. (Whether North Korea has such warheads is not definitively known, but it is widely believed to have in the neighborhood of ten—and the KFR certainly has the materials and technological know-how to build them.) The third type of missile, a Taep'o-dong-2, has a range of 2,300 to 9,300 miles, which means it could conceivably hit the continental United States. Though the Taep'o-dong-2 failed after takeoff during the recent testing, it did so at the point of maximum dynamic pressure—the same point where the space shuttle *Challenger* exploded, and the moment when things are most likely to go wrong. So this is likely not an insoluble problem for the KFR.

The Seven Stages of Collapse

Kim Jong Il's compulsion to demonstrate his missile prowess is a sign of his weakness. Contrary to popular perception in the United States, Kim doesn't stay up at night worrying about what the Americans might do to him; it's not North Korea's weakness relative to the United States that preoccupies him. Rather, if he does stay up late worrying, it's about China. He knows the Chinese have always had a greater interest in North Korea's geography—with its additional outlets to the sea close to Russia—than they have in the long-term survival of his regime. (Like us, even as they want the regime to survive, the Chinese have plans for the northern half of the Korean Peninsula that do not include the "Dear Leader.") One of Kim's main goals in so aggressively displaying North Korea's missile capacity is to compel the United States to deal directly with him, thereby making his otherwise weakening state seem stronger. And the stronger Pyongyang appears to be, the better off it is in its crucial dealings with Beijing, which are what really matter to Kim.

To Kim's sure dismay, the American response to his recent missile tests was a shrug. President George W. Bush dispatched Christopher Hill, his assistant secretary of state for East Asian and Pacific affairs, to the region rather than Secretary of State Condoleezza Rice. I was in South Korea during the missile firings, and there were few signs of alert on any of the U.S. bases in Korea. Pilots in several fighter squadrons were told not to drink too much on their days off, in case they had to be called in, but that was about the extent of it.

What should concentrate the minds of American strategists is not Kim's missiles per se but rather what his decision to launch them says about the stability of his regime. Middle- and upper-middle-level U.S. officers based in South Korea and Japan are planning for a meltdown of North Korea that, within days or even hours of its occurrence, could present the world—meaning, really, the American military—with the greatest stabilization operation since the end of World War II. "It could be the mother of all humanitarian relief operations," Army Special Forces Colonel David Maxwell told me. On one day, a semi-starving population of 23 million people would be Kim Jong Il's responsibility; on the next, it would be the U.S. military's, which would have to work out an arrangement with the Chinese People's Liberation Army (among others) about how to manage the crisis.

Fortunately, the demise of North Korea is more likely to be drawn out. Robert Collins, a retired Army master sergeant and now a civilian area expert for the American military in South Korea, outlined for me seven phases of collapse in the North:

Phase One: resource depletion;

Phase Two: the failure to maintain infrastructure around the country because of resource depletion;

Phase Three: the rise of independent fiefs informally controlled by local party apparatchiks or warlords, along with widespread corruption to circumvent a failing central government;

Phase Four: the attempted suppression of these fiefs by the KFR once it feels that they have become powerful enough;

Phase Five: active resistance against the central government;

Phase Six: the fracture of the regime;

Phase Seven: the formation of new national leadership.

North Korea probably reached Phase Four in the mid-1990s, but was saved by subsidies from China and South Korea, as well as by famine aid from the United States. It has now gone back to Phase Three.

Kim Jong Il learned a powerful lesson by watching the fall of the Ceauşescu Family Regime, in Romania: Take utter and complete control of the military. And so he has. The KFR now rules through the army. There have been only individual defections of North Korean soldiers to the South. Even small, unit-level defections—which would indicate that soldiers are talking to one another and are no longer afraid of exposure by comrades—have not yet occurred. One defector from the North's special operations forces told me that soldiers in the ranks are afraid to discuss politics with one another.

The North Korean People's Army is simply too big to be kept happy and well fed, so the regime concentrates on keeping the elite units comfortable. The defector I spoke to—a scout swimmer—told me that while the special operations forces live well, the extreme poverty of conventional soldiers would make their loyalty to Kim Jong Il in a difficult war questionable. Would they fight to defend the KFR if there were an unforeseen rebellion? The Romanian example suggests that it depends on the circumstances: When workers revolted in 1987 in Braşov, the Romanian military crushed them; when ethnic Hungarians did so two years later in Timişoara, the military deserted the regime.

How to Prevent Another Iraq

Stephen Bradner, a civilian expert on the region and an advisor to the military in South Korea, has thought a lot about the tactical and operational problems an unraveling North Korean state would present. So has Colonel Maxwell, the chief of staff of U.S. Special Operations in South Korea. "The regime in Pyongyang could collapse without necessarily its army corps and brigades collapsing," Maxwell says. "So we might have to mount a relief operation at the same time that we'd be conducting combat ops. If there is anybody in the UN who thinks it will just be a matter of feeding people, they're smoking dope."

Maxwell has conducted similar operations before: He was the commander of a U.S. Army Special Forces battalion that landed on Basilan Island, in the southern Philippines, in early 2002, part of a mission that combined humanitarian assistance with counterinsurgency operations against Jemaah Islamiyah and the Abu Sayyaf Group, two terrorist organizations. But the Korean Peninsula presents a far vaster and more difficult challenge. "The situation in the North could become so messy and ambiguous," Maxwell says, "that the collapse of the chain of command of the KFR could be more dangerous than the preservation of it, particularly when one considers control over WMD."

In order to prevent a debacle of the sort that occurred in Iraq—but with potentially deadlier consequences, because of the free-floating weapons of mass destruction—a successful relief operation would require making contacts with KFR generals and various factions of the former North Korean military, who would be vying for control in different regions. If the generals were not absorbed into the operational command structure of the occupying force, Maxwell says, they might form the basis of an insurgency. The Chinese, who have connections inside the North Korean military, would be best positioned to make these contacts—but the role of U.S. Army Special Forces in this effort might be substantial. Green Berets and the CIA would be among the first in, much like in Afghanistan in 2001.

Obviously, the United States could not unilaterally insert troops into a dissolved North Korea. It would likely be a four-power intervention force—the United States, China, South Korea, and Russia—officially sanctioned by the United Nations. Japan would be kept out (though all parties would gladly accept Japanese money for the endeavor).

Although Japan's proximity to the peninsula gives it the most to fear from reunification, Korean hatred of the Japanese makes participation of Japanese troops in an intervention force unlikely. Between 1910 and 1945, Japan brutally occupied not only Korea but parts of China too, and it defeated Russia on land and at sea in the early twentieth century. Tokyo may have more reason than any other government for wanting to put boots on the ground in a collapsed North Korea, but it won't be able to, because both China and South Korea would fight tooth and nail to prevent it from doing so.

Whereas Japan's strategic position would be dramatically weakened by a collapsed North Korean state, China would eventually benefit. A post-KFR Korean Peninsula could be more or less under Seoul's control—and China is now South Korea's biggest trading partner. Driving along the coast, all I saw at South Korean ports were Chinese ships.

Other factors also work in Beijing's favor. China harbors thousands of North Korean defectors that it would send back after a collapse, in order to build a favorable political base for China's gradual economic takeover of the Tumen River region—the northeast Asian river valley where China, Russia, and North Korea intersect, with good port facilities on the Pacific. De facto control of a future Tumen Prosperity Sphere would bolster China's fiscal strength, helping it to do economic battle with the United States and Japan. If China's troops could carve out a buffer zone in the part of North Korea near Manchuria—where China is now developing massive infrastructure projects, such as roads and ports—Beijing might then sanction the installation of an international coalition elsewhere in the North.

Russia's weakness in the Far East is demonstrated by its failure to prevent the creeping demographic conquest of its eastern territories by ethnic Chinese. It will be truculent in guarding its interests on the Korean Peninsula. And Russia does have a historical legacy here: North Korea was originally a Soviet creation and client state. Keeping Russian troops out of Korea would probably be more trouble for the other powers than letting some in.

Of course, South Korea would bear the brunt of the economic and social disruption in returning the peninsula to normalcy. No official will say this out loud, but South Korea—along with every other country in the region—has little interest in reunification, unless it were to happen gradually over years or decades. The best outcome would be a South Korean protectorate in much of the North, officially under an international trusteeship, that would keep the two Koreas functionally separate for a significant period of time. This would allow each country time to prepare for a unified Korean state, without the attendant chaos.

Following the communist regime's collapse, the early stabilization of the North could fall unofficially to the U.S. Pacific Command (PACOM) and U.S. Forces Korea (which is a semiautonomous subcommand of PACOM), also wearing blue UN helmets. But while the U.S. military would have operational responsibility, it would not have sole control. It would have to lead an unwieldy regional coalition that would need to deploy rapidly in order to stabilize the

North and deliver humanitarian assistance. A successful relief operation in North Korea in the weeks following the regime's collapse could mean the difference between anarchy and prosperity on the peninsula for years to come.

If North Korea Attacks

But what if rather than simply unraveling, the North launched a surprise attack on the South? This is probably less likely to happen now than it was, say, two decades ago, when Kim Il Sung commanded a stronger state and the South Korean armed forces were less mature. But Colonel Maxwell and others are preparing for this possibility.

Simply driving through Seoul, one of the world's great and congested megacities, makes it clear that a conventional infantry attack on South Korea's capital is something that not even a fool would contemplate. So if the North were to attack, it would likely resort instead to a low-grade demonstration of "shock and awe," using its 13,000 artillery pieces and multiple-rocket launchers to fire more than 300,000 shells per hour on the South Korean capital, where close to half the nation's 49 million people live. The widespread havoc this would cause would be amplified by North Korean special operations forces, which would infiltrate the South to sabotage water plants and train and bus terminals. Meanwhile, the North Korean People's Army would march on the city of Uijongbu, north of Seoul, from which it could cross over the Han River and bypass Seoul from the east.

But this strategy would fail. While American A-10 Warthogs, F-16 Vipers, and other aircraft would destroy enemy missile batteries and kill many North Korean troops inside South Korea, submarine-launched missiles and B-2 Spirit bombers sent from Guam and Whiteman Air Force Base in Missouri would take out strategic assets inside North Korea. In the meantime, the South Korean army would quickly occupy the transport hubs, while unleashing its own divisions and special operations forces on the marauding People's Army. The KFR knows this; thus any such invasion would have to be the act of a regime in the latter phases of disintegration. North Korea's lone hope would be that the hourly carnage it could produce—in the time between the first artillery barrage on Seoul and the beginning of a robust military response by South Korea and the United States—would lead the South Korean left, abetted by the United Nations and elements of the global media, to cry out for diplomacy and a negotiated settlement as an alternative to violence.

And there is no question: The violence would be horrific. Iraq and Afghanistan would look clean by comparison. A South Korea filled with North Korean troops would be (in military parlance) a "target-rich environment," in which the good guys and the bad guys would always be close to each other. "Gnarly chaos," is how one F-16 Viper pilot described it to me. "The ultimate fog of war." The battlefield would be made more confusing by the serious language barrier that exists between American pilots and South Korean JTACs, or Joint Tactical Air Controllers, who would have to guide the Americans to many of their targets. A-10 and F-16 pilots in South Korea have complained to me that this weak link in the bilateral military relationship would drive up the instances of friendly-fire and collateral civilian deaths—on which the media undoubtedly would then concentrate. As part of a deal to halt the bloodbath, members of the KFR might be able to negotiate their own post-regime survival.

What Now, Lieutenant?

But middle and upper-middle levels of the American military worry less about an indiscriminate artillery attack on the South than about a very discriminate one. My sources feared that in the aftermath of the KFR's missile launches in July, the Bush administration might actually have been foolish enough to react militarily—which might have been exactly what Kim Jong Il was hoping for, since it would have allowed him to achieve a primary strategic goal: splitting the alliance between South Korea and the United States. How would that happen? After the United States responded in a targeted fashion to the missile launches or some other future outrage, the North would initiate an intensive five- or ten-minute-long artillery barrage on Seoul, killing some Americans and South Koreans near Yongsan Garrison ("Dragon Mountain"), the American military's Green Zone in the heart of the city. Then the North would simply stop. And after the shell fire halted, the proverbial question among American officers in a quandary would arise: *What now, Lieutenant?*

Politically speaking, we would be trumped. The South Korean left—which has been made powerful by an intrusively large American troop presence and by decades of manipulation by the North— would blame the United States for the carnage in Seoul, pointing out that it had been provoked by the Americans' targeted strike against North Korea. The United Nations and the global media would subtly blame Washington for the crisis—and call not so subtly for peace talks. With that, the KFR would get a new lease on life, with more aid forthcoming from the international community to keep it afloat.

Which is why some of the military and civilian experts I spoke with argue for economic warfare against the North. Stop helping the regime with humanitarian aid, they say. The North Korean population has been on the brink of starvation for decades. The forests are denuded. People are eating tree bark. Stop prolonging the agony. Help the KFR collapse.

Of course, one problem with this strategy is that it could end up making North Korea's direst military options more likely; as noted, regimes like this one, in the latter stages of collapse, are apt to behave irresponsibly, possibly resorting to WMD. Another problem is that we can't do much to squeeze the North Koreans economically; it's China, not the United States, that is really keeping the regime alive. The Chinese are already in the process of gaining operational control over anything in North Korea that has strategic economic and military value: mines, railways, and so on. Thus, any soft landing for the KFR would more likely be orchestrated by Beijing than by Washington, even though the Chinese might not mind saddling the Americans with the short-term military responsibility of stabilizing a collapsed North Korea.

After Reunification

If the peninsula could be stabilized after the fall of the KFR, this Greater Korea would have an instant, undisputed enemy: Japan. Any Korean politician would be able to stand up in parliament and get political mileage out of an anti-Japanese tirade. The Japanese know this, and it's helping fuel their remilitarization. (The Japanese navy, in particular, has been emphasizing the latest diesel submarines and Aegis destroyers.) In July, there was a saber-rattling contest between Tokyo and Seoul over disputed islets that South Koreans call Tokdo and the Japanese Takeshima, in what the Koreans refer to as the East Sea and the Japanese the Sea of Japan. Harsh words were exchanged after South Korea sent a survey ship to the area. The United States has a history of underestimating historical-ethnic disputes: In the 1980s, it paid insufficient attention to ethnic tensions in Yugoslavia; more recently, it mistakenly downplayed Sunni-Shiite tensions in Iraq. It should not make the same mistake in Asia.

Here it is useful to review Korean history. In the medieval era, the Koreans fought wars against Chinese dynasties like the Sui and the Tang. But later on, following the rise to power of Korea's own Choson Dynasty in 1392, Japan gradually caught up with China as Korea's principal adversary. There was a brutal Japanese violation of the peninsula at the end of the sixteenth century, culminating in an orgy of rape and murder, and a savage occupation at the beginning of the twentieth, which ended only with the Soviet and American conquests. (The Japanese effect on the peninsula has not been all negative: South Koreans may have trouble admitting it, but Japanese colonialism in the early twentieth century nearly doubled the life expectancy of the average Korean.)

Reunification would provide at least one benefit to Japan. As Park Syung Je, an analyst at the Asia Strategy Institute in Seoul, explained to me, a unified Greater Korea might serve to balance against an even more significant threat to Japan: a rising China. But this Greater Korea would still be a linchpin of China's twenty-first-century Asian economic-prosperity sphere, a more benign version of Imperial Japan's Co-Prosperity Sphere of the 1940s. America could be pushed to the margins. Although Korean businessmen would resist economic domination by China, lingering anti-Americanism in South Korea might outweigh that resistance—especially once the generation that still remembers the sacrifices of American servicemen during the 1950s disappears entirely. America's large troop presence will have granted Korea a free society, just as a similar American presence helped to make Germany a free society. But younger generations of South Koreans may remember U.S. troops only negatively—and what is more indelibly inscribed in the Korean national memory is America's support for the Japanese occupation of Korea following the Russo-Japanese War of 1904 and 1905. (This was in exchange for Imperial Japan's support of America's occupation of the Philippines a few years earlier.)

Greater Korea's troubled relationship with China may ultimately be determined by what America does, and specifically by the degree to which the United States can get Japan to recognize its war guilt. If Washington continues to maintain a military alliance with Tokyo without Japan's publicly coming to terms with its past, Greater Korea will move psychologically toward China. President Bush's recent lovefest with Japanese prime minister Junichiro Koizumi at Graceland may have played well in the United States, but it was seen as an insult in South Korea because of Koizumi's earlier visit to the Yasukuni Shrine, which honors the Japanese war dead—including war criminals. If the United States continues to treat Japan as a golden stepchild, then China and its implicit ally, Greater Korea, will have a tense relationship with Japan and its implicit allies, the United States and India. But because of its own manifold business interests in China, America could only balance against China very delicately.

China Versus America

With so many complex and subtle interests to weigh here, what should the American strategy be over the long term? South Korean army colonel Chung Kyung Yung, a professor at Seoul's National Defense University, says that after the KFR collapses and the North is stabilized, the wisest thing for the United States to do would be to keep 10,000 troops or so on the peninsula. Such a contingent, he told me, would serve as a statement that the United States is not abandoning Korea to a militarily resurgent Japan. The best way to stabilize Asia, Chung emphasizes, would be to prevent Greater Korea—which would be fragile in the period after the North's collapse—from becoming a source of contention between China and Japan. Peter Beck, the director of the International Crisis Group's North East Asia Project, agrees. "Because the United States is the furthest away of all these powers," he told me, "it should be perceived as the least dangerous—the one power without territorial ambitions."

Unfortunately, South Korean politics might make it more difficult to keep American troops on the peninsula long-term. Yes, it's true that of the few prominent statues of foreigners in the country, two are of Americans (General Douglas MacArthur and General James Van Fleet, the father of the South Korean armed forces). And it is also true that, because of late-nineteenth-century missionary activity, American-style Protestantism is practically the dominant religion in South Korea. (If North Korea collapses, expect Christian evangelism to quickly replace the communist regime's Juche ethos of self-reliance: Pyongyang was once the "Jerusalem of Asia" for missionaries.) And yet, despite all this, the South Koreans have largely convinced themselves that they need to be as worried about the Americans as they are about the Chinese—just as they have convinced themselves that they should be as afraid of the Japanese as they are of the North Koreans. The fact is that South Koreans may not want *any* American troops in their country.

Already the American air and ground troops who would defend the South if the KFR were to attack are facing increasing restrictions on their training, because of South Korean political pressures. The A-10 squadron that would be flying nonstop sorties near the DMZ in the event of a war had to train in Thailand this past winter, because of limitations Seoul placed on its flight patterns. This is all part of yet another frustration that U.S. troops in South Korea must endure: having to be on a war footing in order to defend a government that wants to be defended but publicly pretends otherwise.

The truth is, many South Koreans have an interest in the perpetuation of the Kim Family Regime, or something like it, since the KFR's demise would usher in a period of economic sacrifice that nobody in South Korea is prepared for. A long-standing commitment by the American military has allowed the country to evolve into a materialistic society. Few South Koreans have any interest in the disruption the collapse of the KFR would produce.

Meanwhile, China's infrastructure investments are already laying the groundwork for a Tibet-like buffer state in much of North Korea, to be ruled indirectly through Beijing's Korean cronies once the KFR unravels. This buffer state will be less oppressive than the morbid, crushing tyranny it will replace. So from the point of view of the average South Korean, the Chinese look to be offering a better deal than the Americans, whose plan for a free and democratic unified peninsula would require South Korean taxpayers to pay much of the cost. The more that Washington thinks narrowly in terms of a democratic Korean Peninsula, the more Beijing has the potential to lock the United States out of it. For there is a yawning distance between the Stalinist KFR tyranny and a stable, Western-style democracy: in between these extremes lie several categories of mixed regimes and benign dictatorships, any of which might offer the North Koreans far more stability as a transition mechanism than anything the United States might be able to provide. No one should forget that South Korea's prosperity and state cohesion were achieved not under a purely democratic government but under Park Chung Hee's benign dictatorship of the 1960s and '70s. Furthermore, North Koreans, who were never ruled by the British, have even less historical experience with democracy than Iraqis. Ultimately, victory on the Korean Peninsula will go to the side with the most indirect and nuanced strategy.

The long-term success of America's basic policy on the peninsula hinges on the willingness of South Koreans to make a significant sacrifice, at some point, for the sake of freedom in the North. But "sacrifice" is not a word that voters in free and prosperous societies tend to like. If voters in Western-style democracies are good at anything, it's rationalizing their own selfishness—and it may turn out that the authoritarian Chinese understand the voters of South Korea's free and democratic society better than we do. If that's the case, there may never actually be a Greater Korea in the way that we imagine it. Rather, the North's demise will be carefully managed by Beijing in such a way that the country will go from being a rogue nation to a de facto satellite of the Middle Kingdom—but one with sufficient contact with the South that the Korean yearning for a measure of reunification will be satisfied.

Keep in mind that Asia—largely because it is so economically dynamic—is politically and militarily volatile. Its alliance structures are not nearly as developed as those in Europe, which has NATO and the European Union. Conflicting nationalisms are expressed in

Asia through more than just soccer games. Thus, the question of whether it's to be the American or the Chinese vision of North Korea's future that gets realized may hinge on political-military decisions made in the midst of an opaque and confusing crisis.

North Korea and the Future of Asia

Before I left Seoul, I met with a local military legend. Retired general Paik Sun Yup, now eighty-six years old, was the First Infantry Division commander during the Korean War and worked hand in hand with General MacArthur. When we spoke, Paik insisted that crisis-driven political-military decisions here will ultimately determine the balance of power throughout Asia, the most important region for the world's economy. "This peninsula is the pivot," he said.

When I reflected on Paik's words later, it occurred to me that while the United States is in its fourth year of a war in Iraq, it has been on a war footing in Korea for fifty-six years now. More than ten times as many Americans have been killed on the Korean Peninsula as in Mesopotamia. Most Americans hope and expect that we will withdraw from Iraq within a few years—yet we still have 32,000 troops in South Korea, more than half a century after the armistice. Korea provides a sense of America's daunting, imperial-like burdens.

But South Korea also provides a lesson in what can be accomplished with patience and dogged persistence. The drive from the airport at Inchon to downtown Seoul goes through the heart of a former urban war zone. South Korea's capital was taken and retaken four times in some of the most intense fighting of the Korean War. Korean men and women who lived through that time will always be grateful for what retired U.S. Army Colonel Robert Killebrew has called American "stick-to-itiveness," without which we would have little hope of remaining a great power.

In the heart of Seoul lies Yongsan Garrison, a leafy, fortified

Little America, guarded and surrounded by high walls. Inside these 630 acres, which closely resemble the Panama Canal Zone before the Americans gave it up, are 8,000 American military and diplomatic personnel in manicured suburban homes surrounded by neatly clipped hedges and backyard barbecue grills. I drove by a high school, baseball and football fields, a driving range, a hospital, a massive commissary, a bowling alley, and restaurants. U.S. Forces Korea and its attendant bureaucracies are located in redbrick buildings that the Americans inherited in 1945 from the Japanese occupiers. Korea is so substantial a military commitment for us that it merits its own semiautonomous subcommand of PACOM—just as Iraq, unofficially anyway, merits its own four-star subcommand of CENTCOM.

The United States hopes to complete a troop drawdown in South Korea in 2008. Having moved into Yongsan Garrison when Korea's future seemed highly uncertain, American troops plan to give up this prime downtown real estate and relocate to Camp Humphreys, in Pyeongtaek, thirty miles to the south. The number of ground troops will drop to 25,000, and will essentially comprise a skeleton of logistical support shops, which would be able to acquire muscles and tendons in the form of a large invasion force in the event of a war or a regime collapse that necessitated a military intervention.

Patience and dogged persistence are heroic attributes. But while military units can be expected to be heroic, one should not expect a home front to be forever so. And while in the fullness of time patience and dogged persistence can breed success, it is the kind of success that does not necessarily reward the victor but, rather, the player best able to take advantage of the new situation. It is far too early to tell who ultimately will benefit from a stable and prosperous Mesopotamia, if one should ever emerge. But in the case of Korea, it looks like it will be the Chinese.

WAR AND
ITS COSTS

6.

Rereading Vietnam

THE ATLANTIC, AUGUST 2007

In 1943, at the age of eighteen, George Everette "Bud" Day of Sioux City, Iowa, enlisted in the Marines. He served in the Pacific during World War II and later became a fighter pilot. He flew the F-84F Thunderstreak during the Korean War and the F-100F Super Sabre in Vietnam. Bud Day, a legendary "full-blooded jet-jock," as one recent account dubbed him, would see service in all three wars as a sanctified whole: For him the concept of the "long war" was something he had built his life around in the middle decades of the twentieth century. As an Air Force major, he was the first commander of the squadron of fast FACs (forward air controllers), who loitered daily for hours over North Vietnamese airspace, seeking out targets for other fighter bombers. With the most dangerous air mission in the Vietnam War, Day and the other fast FACs were known as "Misty warriors." Misty was the radio call sign that Day himself had chosen for the squadron, inspired by his favorite Johnny Mathis song. The Mistys were "an aggressive bunch of bastards who pressed the fight; they got down in the weeds" and "trolled for trouble," writes Robert Coram in a recently published book about

Bud Day, *American Patriot*. On August 26, 1967, Bud Day's luck ran out. He was shot down over North Vietnam.

The Military Code of Conduct "required that escape take priority over personal fears and concerns," Day writes in his own memoir, *Duty Honor Country*, published in 1989 by American Hero Press, Fort Walton Beach, Florida. Not ranked on Amazon, it is among the most amazing personal stories of any war. His eardrums ruptured, his face crusted with blood from beatings, one arm broken and both knees badly injured from the ejection, Bud Day was hung by the feet "like a side of butchered beef for many hours" by his captors after he refused to answer their questions. A week into his captivity he escaped. He then hiked twelve days alone in the jungle back to South Vietnam, eating frogs, nauseous from pain, only to be recaptured.

With all of his limbs now broken or shot up, he spent the next six years in captivity, undergoing mock executions, hung again repeatedly by his feet, often not permitted to urinate, beaten senseless in scenes "out of the Mongol Hordes" with whips that made his testicles like charred meat. When prison guards burst in on him and other POWs during a clandestine Christian service, Day stared into their muzzles and sang "The Star-Spangled Banner."

A recipient of the Congressional Medal of Honor, Day took the greatest pride in never revealing information to his captors about the Misty program. "If I were to divulge our secrets and tactics, it was highly likely that many of my fine, young, loyal pilots would die as a result. . . ."

I met Bud Day in September 2005 at the Jacksonville Naval Air Station, where Navy flyers had lined up to buy his book, for which he had to take payments in cash. I thought it demeaning that he had to sell his book this way. It says something about the blind spots of a Manhattan-based publishing industry that Day had to go to what is essentially a vanity press. The publication of Coram's book is, therefore, a welcome event.

The relative obscurity of Day's autobiography and other books like it about Vietnam constitute a lesser-known aspect of our civilian-military divide. The books to which I refer should be part of our recollection of Vietnam, but they generally aren't. They aren't so much stories that soldiers tell civilians as those that soldiers tell each other. Of course, there are exceptions, most famously James Webb's *Fields of Fire* (1978), a book that overlaps with this category and in fact did become a bestseller. But there is a range of books of lesser literary merit, yet of equal historical worth, that either have small readerships or readerships consisting overwhelmingly of military personnel, active duty and retired. The authors of these lesser-known books include Marines and Green Berets (Army Special Forces) who were involved in counterinsurgency operations. Their writing reveals a second divide—that between professional warriors and conventional, citizen soldiers—which is but another facet of the warrior's alienation from the civilian world. To explore this second divide, I must also bring into the discussion a French writer and a British soldier, whose legacies include not only Indochina, but Algeria and pre–World War II Palestine—scenes, too, of messy, irregular warfare. Thus, my notion of another Vietnam library goes beyond the subject at hand.

Reading habits are influenced by the people you meet. If I hadn't had the opportunity to embed with professional warriors, I would never have heard of some of these books. For example, I learned a great deal about Bud Day and *Duty Honor Country* from Air Force Captain Jeremiah Parvin of Rocky Mount, North Carolina, a young A-10 Warthog pilot with a "Misty" patch on his arm. The A-10 is essentially a flying Gatling gun. Its pilots hover low to the ground and loiter over the battlefield at great risk. Even as they disdain the rest of the Air Force, Marines and Green Berets consider A-10 pilots true warriors. A-10 pilots feel the same bond toward combat infantry. It is a trait of professional warriors that they feel closer to those in other armed services who take similar risks than toward men and women in their own service who don't. Being in the military is not enough for these men: To earn their respect, you had to have joined in order to fight—not to better your career, or your station in life.

Captain Parvin was serving in South Korea when I met him. He hoped soon to be deployed to Iraq or Afghanistan. He told me all about the Misty FACs in Vietnam. He showed me a coin that he always carried in his pocket, commemorating the Mistys, with Bud Day's name inscribed on it. It was a tradition in his squadron that the youngest and oldest members always carried the coin on their person. Whenever there is a reunion of Misty warriors from Vietnam, held usually in the Florida Panhandle—where Day now lives—the pilots of Parvin's A-10 squadron, two generations removed, send a representative.

Bud Day's memoir is riveting. But it is also a raw manuscript in need of an editor. His tirades against the likes of Lyndon Johnson and the "ding-bat traitor" Jane Fonda get tiresome. To be sure, Day's address to the Navy flyers the morning I met him was laced with colorful profanities. But it was his very rage and aggression against communism, against the Democratic Party of the era, against those whom he considered weak soldiers in America's own ranks, against many things, that allowed him to survive more than half a decade of sustained torture.

Among the persons he dedicates his book to is "President Richard M. Nixon," for ordering "Linebacker I and Linebacker II," the 1972 bombings of North Vietnam (the latter known as the Christmas bombings), and for giving the go-ahead to the Son Tay Raiders, the Green Berets out of Fort Bragg, North Carolina, who in November 1970 stormed the Son Tay prison west of Hanoi, where POWs were believed to have been held.

Because the prisoners had been moved from Son Tay nearly four months earlier, the raid was harshly criticized by major newspapers and some Democratic senators, notably William Fulbright, who questioned the "real purpose" of the mission, beyond freeing the prisoners. A *New York Times* editorial said the raid was "likely to widen the home-front credibility gap." Yet as Day recounts, the raid—along with the bombing campaigns that followed—constituted enormous morale boosts for the prisoners and led to improved treatment for them. Today among Green Berets, the Son Tay Raiders are looked upon as though mythical heroes from a bygone age.

What Bud Day and other POWs specifically admired about Nixon was his willingness to strike back in a way that Johnson hadn't. Johnson's bombing halt in 1968 was seen as a betrayal by POWs, and caused disappointment and anger even throughout the U.S. military. Remember that these POWs were often combat pilots—professional warriors and volunteers, that is, not citizen soldiers who were drafted. Professional warriors are not fatalists. In their minds, there is no such thing as defeat so long as they are still fighting, even from prison. That belief is why true soldiers have an affinity for seemingly lost causes.

In December 1967, a prisoner was dumped in Day's cell on the outskirts of Hanoi, known as the Plantation. This prisoner's legs were atrophied and he weighed under 100 pounds. Day helped scrub his face and nurse him back from the brink of death. The fellow American was Navy Lieutenant Commander John Sidney McCain III, of the Panama Canal Zone. As his health improved, McCain's rants against his captors were sometimes as ferocious as Day's. The North Vietnamese tried and failed, through torture, to get McCain to accept a release for their own propaganda purposes: The lieutenant commander was the son of Admiral John McCain, Jr., the commander of all American forces in the Pacific. "Character," writes the younger McCain, quoting the nineteenth-century evangelist Dwight Moody, "is what you are in the dark," when nobody's looking and you silently make decisions about how you will act the next day.

In early 1973, during a visit to Hanoi, North Vietnamese officials told Secretary of State Henry Kissinger that they would be willing to free McCain into his custody. Kissinger refused, aware that there were prisoners held longer than McCain ahead of him in the line for release. McCain suffered awhile longer in confinement, then, once freed, thanked Kissinger for "preserving my honor." The two have been good friends since. McCain blurbs with gusto Bud Day's memoir. The senator writes: "I recommend this book to anyone who wants to understand the dimensions of human greatness."

The term "professional warrior" is explicitly used by Navy Vice Admiral James Bond Stockdale of Abingdon, Illinois, to describe himself, in *A Vietnam Experience: Ten Years of Reflection* (Hoover Institution Press, 1984). I learned in depth about Vice Admiral Stockdale's writings in this and a second book, *Thoughts of a Philosophical Fighter Pilot* (Hoover, 1995), from midshipmen at the United States Naval Academy in Annapolis, where I teach. One "mid" told me that the moral lessons Stockdale provides helped inspire him to go to the academy.

Stockdale himself is a symbol of a civilian-military divide. The very way you recall him upon hearing his name shows on what side of the divide you fall. Most civilians remember Stockdale as H. Ross Perot's seemingly dazed vice presidential candidate, who in the 1992 debate with Al Gore and Dan Quayle asked aloud, "Who am I? Why am I here?" and later requested that a question be repeated, since he had not turned on his hearing aid. In fact, Stockdale, a lifelong student of philosophy, had meant his questions to be rhetorical, a restatement of the most ancient and essential of questions. Because of television's ability to ruin people's lives by catching them in an embarrassing moment in time, too few are aware that Stockdale's vice presidential bid was insignificant compared with almost everything else he did.

Those on the other side of the divide remember him as among the most selfless and self-reflecting heroes the armed services have ever produced. In September 1965, then–Navy Commander Stockdale (the equivalent of a lieutenant colonel) was forced to eject from his A-4 Skyraider over North Vietnam. He spent the next seven years in prison, undergoing the usual barbaric treatment that the North Vietnamese communists meted out to Americans who did not provide information. Told that he was going to be shown to foreign journalists, Stockdale, a Medal of Honor winner, slashed his scalp with a razor and beat himself in the face with a wooden stool to prevent being used for propaganda purposes. "When George McGovern said he would go to Hanoi on his knees, we prisoners . . . were humiliated," Stockdale writes. "We did not go anywhere on our knees, least of all home. . . . Most of us would be there now rather than knuckle under," he writes in 1984.

Unlike in World War II, when the Japanese and Germans considered POWs to be liabilities and a drain on resources, the North Vietnamese considered captured American pilots as prime political assets. For POWs, not allowing themselves to be used as such meant being able to withstand years of torture. Rather than victims, men like Day, McCain, and Stockdale, once incarcerated, continued to see themselves as warriors, fighting on the most difficult of fronts.

Moral philosophy, in particular the Stoics, helped Stockdale survive. As he puts it, after he ejected from his plane, "I left my world of technology and entered the world of Epictetus." Epictetus was a Greek-born philosopher in first-century Rome, whose Stoic beliefs arose from his brutal treatment as a slave. Stockdale explains, "Stoics belittle physical harm, but this is not braggadocio. They are speaking of it in comparison to the devastating agony of shame they fancied good men generating when they knew in their hearts that they had *failed* to do their duty. . . ." When Stockdale writes about Epictetus, Socrates, Homer, Cervantes, Calvin, and other writers and philosophers, their work achieves a soaring reality because he relates them to his own, extraordinary experiences as a prisoner in one of the twentieth century's most barbaric penal programs. Stockdale reminds us about something that much scholarship, with its obsession for textual subtleties, obscures: The real purpose of reading the classics is to develop courage and leadership.

Stockdale explains—drawing on Napoleon, Clausewitz, and other military strategists—that "the word *moral*" bears an "unmistakably *manly, heroic* connotation." (Virtue, or *virtu* in Machiavelli's Italian, derives ultimately from *vir*, Latin for "man.") He says that while we think of immorality in terms of categories like sexual abandon and fiscal irresponsibility, such vices, as serious as they may seem to civilians, are not in the same category as failure of *nerve* (his italics) in war. For a professional warrior, "doing your duty" is not to be confused with "following orders." The latter implies routine and mechanistic repetition, the former an act of potentially painful and devastating consequences, in which serving a larger good may mean something worse than death even.

The implications of "doing your duty" are spelled out further in *Bury Us Upside Down: The Misty Pilots and the Secret Battle for the Ho Chi Minh Trail* (Ballantine, 2006), by Rick Newman, a journalist at *U.S. News & World Report*, and Don Shepperd, a former Misty. They write that in November 1967, in order to rescue Captain Lance Sijan of Milwaukee, a smoke screen of cluster bombs was dropped near North Vietnamese antiaircraft guns so that the guns could be taken out by low-flying F-4 Phantoms, throwing enemy air defenses into enough chaos to allow a helicopter to pick up the downed pilot. The operation failed. Captain Sijan, injured worse than Bud Day during ejection, evaded the North Vietnamese for six weeks. After he was captured, he escaped again, then was recaptured, and died of torture and pneumonia. He was awarded the Medal of Honor posthumously.

This occurred while the pilots were operating under extremely restrictive ROEs (rules of engagement). Stockdale describes bombing runs over Hanoi in which each plane had to follow the other in exactly the same path, with almost no unscheduled maneuvering permitted—significantly increasing the chance of a plane being shot down—in order to reduce the chances of errant bombs hitting civilians. He and other pilots rage over how restrictive rather than wanton were the so-called Christmas bombings (which, incidentally, were called off on Christmas Day). Few other air campaigns in history were fought under such limited ROEs and yet achieved such an immediate and desired political impact: the return of the North Vietnamese to the negotiating table, the release of the POWs, and the end of America's military involvement in the war. The equivalent would have been if the pinprick bombings ordered by President Bill Clinton on Iraq in 1998 had led to a regime change in Baghdad, or a change of heart by Saddam Hussein that opened the country unambiguously to United Nations weapons inspections.

Bury Us Upside Down documents the lives of men who, like Bud Day, served in World War II, Korea, and Vietnam—a fact that inspires envy among professional warriors I know. "If I had the choice I would have been born before the Great Depression," Army Special Forces Master Sergeant Mark Lopez of Yuba City, California, told me recently. "That way I could have enlisted at eighteen and fought in World War II and Korea, and still be young enough to have seen action in Vietnam."

Yet my favorite story in *Bury Us Upside Down* is about a different sort of serviceman: Air Force flight surgeon Dean Echenberg of San Francisco—a former hippie who helped start a free clinic in Haight-Ashbury, did drugs, went to the great rock concerts, and then volunteered for service in Vietnam, more or less out of sheer adventure. He ended up with the Mistys, billeted among men whom Bud Day had trained. If anyone lived the American experience of the 1960s in its totality, it was Echenberg. One day in 1968, his medical unit was near Phu Cat, just as it was attacked by Viet Cong. "The dispensary quickly filled with blood and body parts," write the authors. "Parents and family members staggered around in a daze, desperate for their children to be saved." Echenberg worked almost the entire night with a pretty American nurse. Near dawn, emotionally overwrought, the two lay down to rest near the end of the runway on the American base and "made love in the grass while artillery boomed in the distance."

"Echenberg struggled to understand how anybody could be so savage as to murder children." The authors continue:

> The young doctor had been ambivalent about the war when he first showed up in Vietnam. But he could no longer humor the anti-war protestors he knew. Yes, combat was inhumane, and atrocities happened on both sides, especially during the heat of battle. But he didn't see the communists as "freedom fighters" or "revolutionaries" like the crowd back in San Francisco. To him the communists were savages who terrorized civilians. . . .

It was another young A-10 pilot, Air Force Captain Brandon Kelly of Cairo, Georgia, a forward air controller on the ground in Iraq, one of the most dangerous jobs there, who told me about *Bury Us Upside Down,* which was not reviewed prominently. Captain Kelly told me that to fully understand what motivated people like him, I had to read this book.

"Protests against the war spawned ideologies . . . *everything* about Vietnam had to be rejected. The result was a shunning of this excellent book. Fashionable journals declined to review it," writes former defense secretary James Schlesinger in the preface to a reissue of Bing West's *The Village* (1972). While the battle in Mark Bowden's *Black Hawk Down* (1999) lasted a day, and the one in Harold Moore and Joe Galloway's *We Were Soldiers Once . . . and Young* (1992) lasted three days, *The Village* is about a Marine squad that fought in the same place for 495 days. Half of them died, seven out of fifteen.

All of them had volunteered to go to "the village," a job they knew would likely get them killed. Their reason? As the commanding sergeant tells the author: "you have a sense of independence down here. There's no . . . paperwork. You're always in contact with the Viet Cong. You know you have a job to do. You go out at night and you do it." And so, these Marines left their base camp, with its "canvas cots, solid bunkers . . . ice cream and endless guard rosters, and went to live with some Vietnamese. . . ."

In West's story there is no sense of defeat and doom and perversion as in classic Hollywood movies about Vietnam; no beautiful, ingeniously constructed, and introspective narration about soldiers and their vulnerabilities, beset with moral complexities, as in a work like Tim O'Brien's *The Things They Carried* (1990), a favorite of high school and college literature courses. West has not written a better book than O'Brien, himself a twice-wounded veteran of the war. But he has written a very different, equally worthy kind that, outside of the members of the military who have regularly recommended it to me over the years, is still relatively little known.

The Village is a story of interminable, deadly, monotonous life-and-death nighttime patrols, dryly and technically narrated, as though extracted from the pages of a hundred strung-together after-action briefs. To wit: "He had fired twenty bullets in one excited burst, yet missed because he had used a magazine which contained no tracers. Unable to see his fire, he had failed to lead properly when the scout ducked around the corner of the house." The book is as absent of style as it is of negativity. Like any good field manual, it has no time for that. As I said, warriors are not fatalists. *The Village* deals with what works in a counterinsurgency struggle and what doesn't. It is a story meant for war colleges that the public, too, desperately needs to know. For the redeeming side of the Vietnam War it reflects was not an aberration.

The Marines of Bing West's story constituted a CAP (Combined Action Platoon), which moved into Binh Nghia in early 1966, a village terrorized by the Viet Cong, and over eighteen bloody months pacified it, taking unabashed pride in their work. "Many of the

Marines," West writes, "let months go by without writing a letter or reading a newspaper. The radius of their world was two miles." The following passage helps explain why many Vietnam veterans I meet in the course of my reporting have not altogether negative memories of that war.

> The Americans liked the village. They liked the freedom to drink beer and wear oddball clothes and joke with girls. They liked having the respect of tough PFs [Popular Forces government militia] . . . who could not bring themselves to challenge the Viet Cong alone. They were pleased that the villagers were impressed because they hunted the Viet Cong as the Viet Cong had for years hunted the PFs. . . . The Americans did not know what the villagers said of them . . . but they observed that the children, who did hear their parents, did not run or avoid them. . . . The Marines had accepted too many invitations to too many meals in too many homes to believe they were not liked by many and tolerated by most. For perhaps the only time in the lives of those . . . Americans, seven of whom had not graduated from high school, they were providing at the obvious risk of death a service of protection. This had won them open admiration . . . within the Vietnamese village society in which they were working and where ultimately most of them would die.

West, a former Marine in Vietnam who made periodic visits to the platoon, ends his story thus: "In July of 1967, Binh Nghia was no longer the scene of nightly battles . . . the enemy had accepted the persistence of the unit [the CAP], whereas his own determination to defend Binh Nghia had waned." That victory was won by Marines who never accepted that "the village" was lost, even when the platoon was surrounded by three hundred Viet Cong. The Marines had done too many nighttime stakeouts, lying immovable for too many hours in filthy puddles, with rain pouring down as though out of a shower faucet, to simply retreat.

The Village demonstrates that the military has memories that the public doesn't. To many who grew up in the 1960s, Vietnam was a cause. But to those who fought it, Vietnam was foremost a war, in all its gray shades: with its tactical successes and tactical failures, with its Marine CAPS and Green Beret infiltrations that worked, and its Big Army ones that didn't; with its Army generals who succeeded like Creighton Abrams, and its Army generals who failed like William Westmoreland; with its moments of glory like Hue, and its moments of disgrace like My Lai; and, above all, with its heroes, like the Son Tay Raiders and the Misty forward air controllers.

In 2002, Bing West returned to Binh Nghia. In a new epilogue he writes:

> Once a year, the villagers gather to pray for good crops and no floods [by] . . . a cement wall bearing a Vietnamese inscription to the Marines who built the well and the shrine in 1967. . . .
> The Village remembers.

Across the Fence: The Secret War in Vietnam (2003), by John Stryker Meyer, is even more compact, technical, and intense than *The Village*. Like Bud Day's *Duty Honor Country,* it was published by a tiny press, in this case Real War Stories Inc., and went unreviewed. It was recommended to me by a Green Beret sergeant major from rural Pennsylvania, Jack Hagen, whose friend had fought in the unit Meyer writes about. The book constitutes an intimate memory in its own right, another example of stories that warriors tell themselves.

The cheap and slightly out-of-focus jacket design suggests a term-paper-quality manuscript that will be a chore to read. Yet as combat writing goes, *Across the Fence* is pure grain alcohol. It is not replete with rich, unforgettable descriptions, but rather a work of dry realism that makes no attempt at profundity, and is thus unburdened by doubt—the warrior's great strength. There is bitching about physical discomfort, but no complaints about the purpose of the war. So little emotion is there that the author allows himself only a brief and passing broadside against Johnson's cease-fire and what he considers the antagonism of the media.

John Stryker Meyer and the men in his unit, as he writes, "were triple volunteers." They had volunteered for Army parachute jump school at Fort Benning, Georgia; then for Army Special Forces training at Fort Bragg; and finally to serve in the Command and Control element of MACV-SOG (Military Assistance Command Vietnam—Studies and Observation Group). This was a joint unit engaged in classified, unconventional warfare in Laos and Cambodia: places known respectively as the "Prairie Fire" and "Daniel Boone" AOs (areas of operations), or just plain "Indian Country" in Meyer's own words. The book's title is military lingo for across the border from Vietnam, where "the North Vietnamese Army," as the author writes, "had moved soldiers, supplies, rockets, guns, and propagandists south into the eastern provinces" of these so-called "neutral" countries, whose territories were an integral part of the Ho Chi Minh Trail Complex.

Across the Fence was published only in 2003. Meyer had "signed a government document in 1968 pledging never to write or talk publicly about SOG for 20 years." After that, he explains, "anti-Vietnam" sentiment "made it difficult to find a publisher who would buy the concept of a Vietnam book that dealt with real people striving against unbelievable odds in a politically handicapped war." Encouraged by his writing teachers at Trenton State College, Meyer eventually produced a battlefield diary of daily forays into Laos and Cambodia in 1968 and 1969.

Arriving at a SOG base in Vietnam, the author was shown into a barracks, where on "one double bunk, sweaty and naked, was a couple heavily involved in the rapture of the moment." Nearby, he "found an SF [Special Forces] trooper showering, while a naked Vietnamese woman squatted in the water, washing herself." Seeing that he was an FNG (fucking new guy), a sergeant explained to him that the prostitutes were given weekly health checkups and what the prices were. These were men away from home for many months: A significant percentage of them were soon to die. Meyer himself was momentarily to enter an existence where life was "a matter of inches":

> Three rounds slammed into the One-Zero's [recon team leader's] head, blowing off the right side of his face. . . . Nothing in the months of pulling garbage detail could prepare ST [spike team] Alabama for the grisly horror unfolding at that moment. The One-one [assistant recon leader] buried his face in the dirt and started praying. Black and the remaining ST Alabama . . . returned fire. The Green Beret stood there, firing on single shot, picking off NVA [North Vietnamese Army] soldiers on top of the rise. . . . Both the NVA and ST Alabama tended to their wounded while the living combatants slammed loaded magazines into their hot weapons. . . .

Enemy troops quickly reinforced the ambush site. It was always thus. As Meyer documents—through his own experiences, as well as through interviews he conducted for years afterward to re-create the combat sequences—whenever SOG units crossed the border into Cambodia and Laos, they uncovered a beehive of North Vietnamese Army concentrations. The border truly meant nothing. The battlefield overlapped it. Meyer spends eighteen pages describing a savage, daylong firefight in Laos that ends with many dead, as well as beer in the canteen for the survivors near midnight, before another insertion that meets another enemy troop concentration the next morning. From beginning to end, *Across the Fence* is a record of extreme heroism and technical competence that few who fought World War II surpassed.

Every time Meyer crossed the border it was with South Vietnamese "indigs" (indigenous troops) integrated into his unit. He writes about their exploits and personalities in as much detail as he does about the Americans. He identifies with them, and with the enemy whose skill he admires, more than he does with elements of the home front.

Thanksgiving is just another day "across the fence," this time in Cambodia, once again surrounded by North Vietnamese troops, once again saved by the Air Force and the five-second fuses on the claymore mines. "The gods of recon had smiled on ST [spike team] Idaho one more time," he concludes near midnight of that fourth Thursday in November 1968.

There is little sense here that the war was lost. While historians cite 1968 as a turning point because of the home front's reaction to the Tet Offensive, the My Lai Massacre, and the protests at the Democratic Party convention in Chicago, on the ground in Vietnam, 1968 marked a different trend: William Westmoreland was replaced by Creighton Abrams, population security rather than enemy body counts became the measure of merit, "clear and hold" territory replaced the dictum of "search and destroy," and building up the South Vietnamese army became the top priority. "There came a time when the war was won," even if the "fighting wasn't over," writes Lewis Sorley, a West Point graduate and career Army officer, in *A Better War: The Unexamined Victories and Final Tragedy of America's Last Years in Vietnam* (1999). By the end of 1972, Sorley goes on, one could travel almost anywhere in South Vietnam in relative security, even as American ground forces were almost gone. Retirees I know in the armed forces affirm how much more benign an environment South Vietnam was during this period than the Iraq of today. Still, as one veteran told me, everyone has different memories of Vietnam, depending upon where they served, and what time they were there.

Sorley's book was reviewed prominently by the major liberal newspapers and foreign policy journals. They gave it generally respectful write-ups, a sign of a reassessment of Vietnam based less on ideology than on paying more attention to the second half of a war: a period to which, as Sorley notes, Stanley Karnow's *Vietnam: A History* (1983) devotes only 103 out of 670 pages, and Neil Sheehan's Pulitzer Prize–winning *A Bright Shining Lie* (1988) devotes 65 out of 790 pages. Sorley told me he isn't sure what would have happened had Congress not cut off aid to South Vietnam at about the time the ground situation was at its most hopeful. He felt that a respectable case might be made that it would have survived. His book has seen a rise in sales among military officers eager to know how the ground situation in Iraq might be improved to the level it had been in Vietnam, thanks to General Abrams's change of strategy.

A similar thesis emerges in *The Battle of An Loc* (2005), by retired Army Lieutenant Colonel James H. Willbanks, who describes a sixty-day siege in mid-1972, in which heavily outnumbered South Vietnamese troops and their American advisors (including himself) rebuffed several North Vietnamese divisions. This gave Nixon the fig leaf he needed for a final withdrawal. Optimism then might not have been warranted, but it wasn't altogether blind. Lieutenant Colonel Willbanks said he wrote his book, published by Indiana University Press, for the same reason Sorley did: to give more attention to the second half of the war.

Another book that those in the combat arms community pressed me to read is *Once a Warrior King: Memories of an Officer in Vietnam* (1985), by David Donovan (a pseudonym). This is the story of a young Army civil affairs officer in a remote part of South Vietnam near Cambodia, which, as he too documents, was used as a major

staging post for the North Vietnamese Army. Herein is a series of fe-
verish accounts of horrific firefights that alternate with the struggle
to establish schools, maternity clinics, and agricultural projects. It is
as though the author were writing about today's Iraq: a corruption-
and faction-plagued central government that exists officially but
has little reality outside of the capital; a regular U.S. Army that he
despises, confined too often to big bases and which the locals hate;
and small units like his with life-and-death control over civilians.
"Terribly frustrated," he realizes that his own countrymen "would
never understand about all the small but very important things that
were needed. . . ." Take soap: Just plain old bars of soap, he informs
us, would do more to win over the villagers in his district than guns
and bullets. He ends his Vietnam saga thus: "I do not believe it was
an immoral war at all, rather a decent cause gone terribly wrong."

You cannot approach Vietnam and Iraq, or the subject of counterinsurgency in general, without reference to Jean Larteguy, a
French novelist and war correspondent who, in a very different way
than Stockdale, is an example in his own person of the civilian-
military divide. Larteguy inhabits the very soul of the modern Western warrior, alienating some civilian readers in the process. Stockdale
quotes him. Sorley told me that several editions of Larteguy's *The
Centurions* (1960) have passed through his hands in the course of a
professional lifetime dominated by Vietnam. Alistair Horne, the re-
nowned historian of the Algerian War, uses Larteguy for epigrams
in *A Savage War of Peace* (1977). Some months back, General
David Petraeus—now commander of U.S. ground forces in Iraq—
pulled *The Centurions* off a shelf at his home in Fort Leavenworth,
Kansas, and gave me a disquisition about the small-unit leadership
principles exemplified by one of the characters. For half a decade
now, Green Berets have been recommending Larteguy's *The Centurions* and *The Praetorians* (1961) to me: books about French paratroopers in Vietnam and Algeria in the 1950s.

Almost half a century ago, this Frenchman was obsessed about a home front that had no context for a hot, irregular war; about a professional warrior class alienated from its civilian compatriots as much as from its own conventional infantry battalions; about the need to engage in both combat and civil affairs in a new form of warfare to follow an age of what he called victory parades and "cinema-heroics"; about an enemy with complete freedom of action, allowed "to do what we didn't dare"; and about the danger of creating a "sect" of singularly brave iron men, whose ideals were so exalted that beyond the battlefield they had a tendency to become woolly-headed. Larteguy dedicates his book to the memory of centurions who died so that Rome might survive, but he notes in his conclusion that it was these same centurions who destroyed Rome.

Born in 1920, Jean Larteguy—a pseudonym; his real name was Jean Osty—fought with the Free French and afterward became a journalist. Because of his military experience and resistance ties, he had nearly unrivaled access to French paratroopers who fought at Dien Bien Phu and in the Battle of Algiers. His empathy for these men, some of whom were torturers, made him especially loathed by the Parisian Left, even though he broke with the paratroopers themselves, out of opposition to their political goals, which he labeled "neofascism."

Larteguy eventually found his military ideal in Israel, where he became revered by paratroopers who translated *The Centurions* into Hebrew to read at their training centers. He called these Jewish soldiers "the most remarkable of all of war's servants, superior even to the Viet, who at the same time detests war the most. . . ." By the mid-1970s, though, he became disillusioned with the Israel Defense Forces. He said it had ceased to be "a manageable grouping of commandos" and was becoming a "cumbersome machine" too dependent on American-style technology—as if foreseeing some of the problems with the 2006 Lebanon campaign.

Recently I walked into the office of the chief of staff of Army Special Forces in South Korea, Colonel David Maxwell of Springfield, Massachusetts, and noticed a plaque with Larteguy's famous "two armies" quote. (The translation is by Xan Fielding, a British Special Operations officer, who, in addition to rendering Larteguy's classics into English, was a close friend of the British travel writer Patrick Leigh Fermor, to whom Fermor addresses his introduction in his own classic, *A Time of Gifts* [1977].) In *The Centurions,* one of Larteguy's paratroopers declares:

> I'd like . . . two armies: one for display, with lovely guns, tanks, little soldiers, fanfares, staffs, distinguished and doddering generals, and dear little regimental officers . . . an army that would be shown for a modest fee on every fairground in the country.
>
> The other would be the real one, composed entirely of young enthusiasts in camouflage battledress, who would not be put on display but from whom all sorts of tricks would be taught. That's the army in which I should like to fight.

But the reply from another character in *The Centurions* to this declaration is swift: "You're heading for a lot of trouble." The exchange telescopes the philosophical dilemma about the measures that need to be taken against enemies who would erect a far worse world than you, but which, nevertheless, are impossible to carry out because of the "remorse" that afflicts soldiers when they violate their own notion of purity of arms, even in situations where such "tricks" might somehow be rationalized. They win the battle, but lose their souls.

Rather than a roughneck, Colonel Maxwell epitomizes the soft, indirect approach to unconventional war that is in contrast to "direct action." The message that Maxwell and other warriors have always taken away from Larteguy's famous quote—rooted in his Vietnam experience—is that *the mission is everything,* and conventional militaries, by virtue of being vast bureaucratic machines obsessed with rank and privilege, are insufficiently focused on the mission, regardless of whether it's direct action or humanitarian affairs. (One of the complaints of the Misty forward air controllers was that their own Air Force bureaucracy was a constant hindrance, more interested in procedure than results. The same complaint has occasionally been made against the regular Army in Iraq by Marines and Green Berets.)

The conventional officer would reply that the warrior's field of sight is so narrow that he can't see anything beyond the mission. "They're dangerous," one of Larteguy's protagonists says of the paratroopers, "because they go to any lengths . . . beyond the conventional notion of good and evil." For if the warrior's actions contradict his faith, his doubts are easily overcome by belief in the larger cause. Larteguy writes of one soldier: "He had placed the whole of his life under the sign of Christ who had preached peace, charity, brotherhood . . . and at the same time he had arranged for the delayed-action bombs at the Cat-Bi airfield. . . . 'What of it? There's a war on and we can't allow Hanoi to be captured.'"

Vietnam, like Iraq, represented a war of frustrating half measures, fought against an enemy that respected no limits. Bud Day, half-starved and broken-limbed, writes of seeing a long convoy of trucks heading out of Hanoi, safe because of our own self-imposed bombing restrictions. "I found it mind-boggling that the United States, the strongest nation in the world, would permit this flea on the buttocks of humanity to conduct a war this way." More than almost any writer I know, Larteguy communicates the intensity of such frustrations, which, in turn, create the psychological gulf that separates warriors like Bud Day from both a conscript army and a civilian home front.

The best units, according to Larteguy, while officially built on high ideals, are, in fact, products of such deep bonds of brotherhood and familiarity that the world outside requires a dose of "cynicism" merely to stomach. As one Green Beret wrote me, "There are no more cynical soldiers on the planet than the SF [Special Forces] guys I work with, they snort at the platitudes we are expected to parrot, but," he went on, "you will not find anyone who gets the job done better in tough environments like Iraq." In fact, in extreme situations like Iraq, cynics may actually serve a purpose. In the regular Army there is a tendency to report up the command chain that the mission is succeeding, even if it isn't. Cynics won't buy that, and will say so bluntly.

Larteguy writes that the warrior looks down on the rest of the military as "the profession of the sluggard," men who "get up early to do nothing." Yet as one paratrooper notes in *The Praetorians:*

> In Algeria that type of officer died out. When we came in from operations we had to deal with the police, build sports grounds, attend classes. Regulations? They hadn't provided for anything, even if one tried to make an exegesis of them with the subtlety of a rabbi.

Dirty, badly conceived wars in Vietnam and Algeria had begotten a radicalized French warrior class of noncommissioned officers, able to kill in the morning and build schools in the afternoon, which had a higher regard for its Muslim guerrilla adversaries than for regular officers in its own ranks. Such men would gladly advance toward a machine gun nest without looking back, and yet were "booed by the crowds" upon returning home, so that they saw the civilian society they were defending as "vile, corrupt, and degraded."

The estrangement of soldiers from their own citizenry is somewhat particular to counterinsurgencies, where there are no neat battle lines and thus no easy narrative for the people back home to follow. The frustrations in these wars are great precisely because they are not easily communicated. Larteguy writes: Imagine an environment where a whole garrison of two thousand troops are "held in check" by a small "band of thugs and murderers." The enemy is able to "know everything: every movement of our troops, the departure times of our convoys. . . . Meanwhile we're rushing about the bare mountains, exhausting our men; we shall never be able to find anything."

Because the enemy is not limited by Western notions of war, the temptation arises among a stymied soldiery to bend its own rules. Following an atrocity carried out by French paratroopers that calms a rural area of Algeria, one soldier rationalizes to another: " 'Fear has changed sides, tongues have been loosened. . . . We obtained more in a day than in six months fighting, and more with twenty-seven dead than with several hundreds.' " The soldiers comfort themselves further with a quotation from a fourteenth-century Catholic bishop: "When her existence is threatened, the Church is absolved of all moral commandments." It is the purest of them, according to Larteguy, who is most likely to commit torture.

Here we enter territory that is utterly unrelated to the individual Americans I've been writing about. It is important to make such distinctions. When Larteguy writes about bravery and alienation, he understands American warriors; when he writes about political insurrections and torture, some exceptions aside, he is talking about a particular caste of French paratroopers. Yet his discussion is relevant to America's past in Vietnam and present in Iraq. I don't mean My Lai and Abu Ghraib, both of which aided the enemy rather than ourselves, but the moral gray area that we increasingly inhabit concerning collateral civilian deaths.

In *The Face of War: Reflections of Men and Combat* (1976), Larteguy writes that contemporary wars are, in particular, made for the side that doesn't care about "the preservation of a good conscience." So he asks, "How do you explain that to save liberty, liberty must first be suppressed?" His answer can only be thus: "In that rests the weakness of democratic regimes, a weakness that is at the same time a credit to them, an honor."

What kind of soldier can make the most of such limitations? Larteguy found his answer in the elite Israeli units of the mid-twentieth century, which were in turn a product of Larteguy's own personal hero: Orde Wingate. Wingate is of paramount importance because of the way he confronted challenges similar to those faced by America in Vietnam, and again in Iraq.

Larteguy writes: "The Israeli army was born of . . . that mad old genius" Orde Wingate and his "midnight battalions" of Jewish warriors, which included the young Moshe Dayan and Yigael Allon. "The Israelis would say of this goy: 'If he hadn't died, he would be head of our army.'" Wingate was a Christian evangelical before the term was coined. The son of a minister in colonial India, he frequently quoted Scripture and read Hebrew. In 1936, Captain Wingate was dispatched to Palestine from Sudan. For religious reasons he developed an emotional sympathy for the Israelis, establishing himself as "the Lawrence of the Jews." He taught them "to fight in the dark with knives and grenades, to specialize in ambushes and hand-to-hand fighting."

Wingate headed to Ethiopia in 1941, leading Ethiopian irregulars in the struggle to defeat the Italians and put the *Negus Negast* ("King of Kings," Haile Selassie) back on the throne. From there it was on to Burma, where he consolidated his principles of irregular warfare with his famed "chindits," long-penetration jungle warriors, dropped by parachute behind Japanese lines.

He took the name from the legendary animal—half eagle and half lion—whose statue graces Indochinese pagodas. According to Larteguy, Wingate was openly obsessed with a dislike of conventional armies that "used parades to transform its young men into automatons." Instead, Wingate thought in terms of individuals, and believed that if he had the right young men, he could do more with ten of them than with one hundred of the conventional kind.

Wingate would teach these select few "trickery." That is, how to be assassins, how to ambush, how to get accustomed to broken sleep rhythms and brackish water for drinking, how to win over the local tribes. Larteguy's famed two-armies quote, with its reference to "tricks," was partly based on Wingate's vision, forged initially in Sudan and Palestine, and refined in the Horn of Africa and Indochina. It was in Vietnam where Larteguy first encountered the historical figure of Wingate, whose warrior ethos would ultimately merge with that of the Green Berets in the early part of the Vietnam War.

Uri Dan, a longtime Israeli journalist, a devotee of Larteguy, and an intimate of Ariel Sharon, told me that democracies of today, because of the existential threat they face from an enemy that knows no limits, "need centurions more than ever." He's right, but only up to a point. Take this story told to me by a Navy lieutenant at Annapolis who had commanded a SEAL team in Iraq:

Time after time, the lieutenant's combined American-Iraqi team would capture "bad guys with long rap sheets," who were undoubtedly terrorists. His unit would hand them over to higher authorities, but after a few weeks in prison they would be released and go back to killing civilians. "The Iraqis and my own men saw how broken the system was, and some felt it was easier just to kill these guys the moment we apprehended them. After all, it would have saved lives. But," he continued, "I told them, 'Oh no. Here is where I have to draw the line.' It was important to have an officer in charge who had studied ethics." The enlisted chief petty officers of his SEAL team—reminiscent of some of Larteguy's centurions, for all intents and purposes—were the finest men he had ever commanded. But they required supervision.

A frustrated warrior class, always kept in check by liberal-minded officers, is the sign of a healthy democracy.

7.

Iraq: The Counterfactual Game

THE ATLANTIC, OCTOBER 2008

A s an early supporter of the war in Iraq, I like others have taken refuge in counterfactuals: all the bad things that might have happened had we left Saddam Hussein in power. Counterfactuals, if you haven't noticed, have become a staple of conservative opinion pages.

Indeed, the list of what-ifs is long and compelling. Just some examples: Had we not invaded, the sanctions regime against the Iraqi dictator would soon have crumbled, without the oil-for-food scandal being exposed. The French, Russians, and Chinese would have swept in with lucrative deals for Saddam, even as he restarted his weapons program. The arms race between Iraq and Iran would have grown fierce, with many, especially the Iranians, believing Saddam already possessed weapons of mass destruction. Israel would have been the big loser in this arms race, feeling less secure and consequently more trigger-happy than ever. Saddam's grip on power would have surged with the price of oil. Drowning in oil wealth, Saddam would have, among many other nefarious deeds, increased his payments to the families of Palestinian suicide bombers. In a larger strategic sense, the success of Saddam Hussein, an implacable hater of the West, in forcing President George W. Bush to stand down his troops and beat the sanctions, too, would have had a radicalizing effect on the entire Muslim world. He would have emerged as the new Nasser of the Sunni faithful, from Morocco to Pakistan, even as he continued to murder in desultory fashion thousands of people per month in his police state. As a footnote, sooner or later an American Navy or Air Force aviator would have been shot down patrolling the no-fly zones and paraded through the streets of Baghdad, thus providing immense propaganda value. Truly, a world with Saddam still in power is awful to contemplate, as I can personally attest, having visited Iraq several times in the 1980s, the worst years of Saddam's tyranny.

Yet, there is a problem with this line of reasoning: How do all these might-have-beens, as frightfully convincing as they seem, stack up against the very real, violent deaths of more than four thousand Americans and tens, perhaps hundreds, of thousands of Iraqis, as a result of our invasion—not to mention the hundreds of billions of dollars spent on the war that could have been used to meet other threats to our national interests? To coldly state, without qualifiers, that these costs have been a price worth paying is to reduce foreign policy to the realm of inhuman abstraction. In any case, I don't believe anyone making such a claim could pass a polygraph test. And I include President Bush in this category. His attempts to compare himself with President Harry Truman—a president whose decisions were also hated at the time he made them—have the air of desperation rather than of historical thinking.

I am aware that the American death toll in Iraq is many times lower than that in Vietnam, and that aversion to casualties has become a feature of low-birth-rate, postindustrial democratic societies. But I am also aware that when I and others supported a war to liberate Iraq, we never fully or accurately contemplated the price that would have to be paid. Of course, it can be argued that the high human cost of the war was not a result of the invasion at all, but of

the negligence that characterized the subsequent military occupation. But you could well make the case that such negligence was at
least partially inherent in the hubris of the conception of regime
change in the first place.

Moreover, when you sign on to a war, you implicitly place your
confidence in those who would carry it out. Thus, a character judgment is required. And events have shown how wrong supporters of
the war were in this regard.

At a far deeper level, as with many of life's disappointments, you
are stuck with the reality that you have, not the one that might have
been. You can play the counterfactual game for all of history's great
junctures, and as enlightening as the exercise can be, it is still a game
that doesn't get you anywhere. It is where we are now that matters:
overextended in Iraq and Afghanistan, while the Russians move methodically to re-create their former Soviet near-abroad in the Caucasus and Central Asia, and the Chinese continue to use the years of
our Middle East distraction to become, in military parlance, a future peer-competitor.

We are undeniably in a far better situation in Iraq today than we
were in 2006. Credit for that must go to President Bush. He bravely,
and wisely as it turned out, ignored the advice of almost the entire
Washington establishment, surged troops into the country, changed
his strategy, his generals, and his defense secretary. In this very limited sense, he might yet be compared with Truman. Iraq could well
stumble along to greater democratic stability, leading not to a model
state, but to a viable and nonthreatening one, which can, in the fullness of time, encourage liberal movements throughout the Arab
world.

Might one then argue that the invasion was worth it? From a
purely historical perspective, perhaps. But policy is about the here
and now. It's about taking or not taking action based on a near- and
middle-term cost-benefit analysis. To subsume policy making com-

pletely to long-range historical thinking is to risk constantly getting involved in grand schemes.

Most fundamentally, does Iraq meet the parents' test? Can you look parents in the eye and tell them it was worth losing their son or daughter over? As awful as it sounds, quantity matters here, for it says much about the scope of violence that is unleashed for the sake of a higher good. If there were, say, five hundred sets of parents you had to look in the eye, the answer might well be yes, it was worth it, given where Iraq is today and what might have been had we not toppled Saddam. But at more than four thousand and counting, the answer for years to come will still be no. Counterfactuals can take you only so far.

8.

The Wounded Home Front

THE AMERICAN INTEREST, JANUARY/FEBRUARY 2011

Covering the war in Afghanistan in the 1980s, I learned that most of the land mines that the Soviets laid were designed to maim, not kill. The Soviets knew that a dead body causes no tactical inconvenience. It only removes the one dead person from the field. But a wounded person requires the assistance of people all the way down the line who could otherwise be fighting. Likewise with the home front in a war. The dead leave an awful vacancy in the lives of loved ones, but those who are seriously wounded or psychologically traumatized can disrupt families and society more. Families of the dead can move on, as difficult as it may be, and as awful as it may be to say; the families of the seriously maimed, physically or psychologically, never can.

Army Colonel Ross Brown, a squadron commander in Iraq, told me this story:

> After a suicide bomber killed four of my soldiers, my Command Sergeant-Major (CSM) and I spent a night picking up their body parts. I walked around one side of the blast area while my CSM covered the other side. An 18-year-old soldier

walked behind me towing a body bag. As I came upon a limb
or other body part, I would place it in the bag and move on to
the next body part. After six hours of walking the blast radius,
I had a full bag. Although I knew the soldier beside me was
young, and even as I tried to protect the youngest soldiers from
seeing such terrible things, I had to use him to assist me that
evening. The next day I had him see a psychologist, and had
him see one again after we returned from Iraq. However, less
than a year later, I signed paperwork releasing him from the
Army for post-traumatic stress disorder and long-term psychological damage.

To be sure, the dead and the psychologically wounded of that
terrible evening will have ripple effects upon their families and the
larger society for years to come. And this is merely one story. Nancy
Berglass, director of the Iraq-Afghanistan Deployment Impact Fund,
says "hundreds of thousands of active duty and former active duty
troops are dealing with significant mental health [and drug depen-
dence] problems that have not been adequately addressed." In each
instance of psychological disturbance, there is a story, perhaps as
bad as Colonel Brown's, behind it.

The long tail of suffering that extends from the war front to the
home front, and from dead and wounded soldiers and Marines,
sailors and airmen, to their wives and children, and to their children's children, is statistically numbing and heartrending. Of the
2.2 million American troops deployed to Iraq and Afghanistan since
2001, several hundred thousand have sustained physical and psychological wounds. The figures of 4,417 dead from Iraq and 1,368
from Afghanistan (as of November 10, 2010) are well known and
oft quoted. But the physically wounded from both wars number
more than 40,000, a staggering number, and roughly three-quarters
of them have been wounded in a serious life- and family-affecting
way. According to the Army Office of the Surgeon General, between

2001 and 2009 doctors performed 1,286 amputations, three-quarters of which were of major limbs.

Then there are the psychological wounds, to which Colonel Brown's story attests. Between 20 and 35 percent of deployed troops test positive for depression or post-traumatic stress disorder. More than 100,000 soldiers today are on prescribed anti-anxiety medication, and 40,000 are thought by the Army to be using drugs illicitly. At least one in six service members is on some form of psychiatric drug. The effect on wives and children is immense. There have been around 25,000 cases of domestic violence in military families in the past decade: 20 percent of married troops returning from deployment are planning a divorce. Problems in family relationships are reportedly four times higher following a deployment to Iraq or Afghanistan. In families where one of the spouses is deployed, instances of child abuse are 40 percent higher than the norm. In 2009 alone, 74,646 criminal offenses were committed by soldiers.

In 2009 alone there were 334 military suicides. Marine Corps suicides are now 24 per 100,000, compared to 20 in the civilian population. Eighteen veterans a day die by their own hand. As for active-duty troops, Berglass says they are taking their own lives at the rate of one every thirty-six hours. These may not seem like such high numbers, but keep in mind that in the 1990s the Army and other armed services were touted as the most disciplined and psychologically healthiest sector of the population.

Then there is homelessness. Homelessness is only partly a sign of insufficient financial means. At a deeper level it can be about the inability to cope with the complexities of modern life following a period of sustained trauma. Veterans for America estimates that 10,000 veterans of Iraq and Afghanistan are now homeless. During the Vietnam War, the number of homeless veterans exceeded the number of fatalities (58,000), and experts have told me that veterans of Iraq and Afghanistan are becoming homeless at a quicker rate than those of Vietnam. One-third of the adult homeless population are veterans, even as veterans represent only 11 percent of the population.

Furthermore, young male veterans of the Iraq War had an unemployment rate of 21.6 percent in 2009, more than double that of the general population. Foreclosure rates in military towns are running at four times the national average. Then there are the rates of underwater mortgages, in which the family owes more on the loan than the value of the house. There are no adequate statistics for this regarding the military, but experts assume the rate is much higher than for the civilian population because war means deployments, and deployments mean moving locations at a quicker rate than in a peacetime Army. That, in turn, leads to more disadvantageous house purchases. I have heard stories of returning wounded veterans with amputated limbs who have trouble finding jobs and whose mortgages are in foreclosure or underwater. Though these stories may seem apocryphal, they make unmistakable sense given the other statistics. Retired Army Major General Robert Scales indicates that such statistics are central to what "land warfare does to a ground force." Too few troops have been carrying too heavy a burden for too long, he told *Government Executive* reporter Katherine McIntire Peters. There was a debate back in the dark days of 2006, when America's land forces were suffering their highest numbers of casualties, about whether Iraq would break the Army. Such numbers indicate that it has already done so, at least partially.

Edith Wharton, in a somewhat obscure antiwar classic, *A Son at the Front* (1923), writes of war's "jaded appetite," of "the monster's daily meal," devouring all the "gifts and virtues," "brains in the bud," "imagination and poetry" of so many young men. But at least Wharton is writing about World War I in France, where there is an authentic home front to which the wounded and traumatized can return, where all of society is "swept" into the great effort, compared to which all else is trivial. So the hotels and households of the rich are "shrunken" and "understaffed." Hallways in Paris are "piled with hospital supplies." Every family has someone at the front: War is the subject of nearly every conversation. Indeed, the cruelest fate for the seriously wounded and those psychologically oppressed by awful memories is to return to a civilian society with distinctly other matters on its mind. For unlike the war Wharton wrote about, we in America famously constitute an army at war and a nation at the mall.

This is not necessarily a function of our prosperity, given that in relative terms the economy is stagnant and many people are out of work. Nor is it a matter of hostility toward the military: The post-9/11 Middle Eastern wars have not bred aversion to the soldier's profession as did Vietnam. It is a matter of the particular wages of what are termed "small wars"—that is, hot, irregular wars that are big enough to be intensely fought and are seemingly endless, but are limited in that they do not demand a state's total resources, and therefore leave the home front unscathed and unaffected, without context for the horror occurring thousands of miles away. Big wars are fought in response to a direct threat to the homeland, and by definition involve the whole society; they are wars that play to the strengths of a mass democracy. But small wars are imperial wars, even as proponents of small wars eschew the term; they are fought to preserve the balance of power and to stamp out disorder in far-flung places, motives beyond the grasp of the home front. Small wars, because they are often unconventional, lack a well-defined narrative. There is no army to follow as it marches toward its objective. Thus, the home front finds these wars confusing—that is to say, meaningless.

The wounded and other uniformed warriors who come home to such a confused and distracted society suffer a very special kind of loneliness and alienation. They might also fall prey to a dose of "cynicism," according to the French war reporter and novelist of the mid-twentieth century Jean Larteguy, who wrote of paratroopers in Vietnam and Algeria unable to adapt to the mores of civilian society after having gone through an intense and lengthy bonding experience defined by constant combat in irregular, small wars.

Because of modern communication, today's fighting men and women are arguably under greater degrees of stress regarding family issues than ever before, even as they find it difficult to talk to their families once they are back home about what is really on their minds. In the barracks every night in Iraq or Afghanistan, there is a constant stream of communication with spouses and children via email and various websites. But these troops are psychologically cut off from loved ones even as they are electronically connected to them. I can remember several instances when, as an embedded reporter, I was in a Morale, Welfare, and Recreation facility in the Middle East, overhearing American troops having heated arguments with their wives or girlfriends over a phone line, while other soldiers lined up impatiently behind them, waiting to use the same phone. Indeed, domestic disputes take on an especially intense urgency precisely because the means of contact is virtual, and yet in no way does this prepare individual soldiers for what they will encounter when they do arrive home, particularly if they are wounded or come to suffer a variant of post-traumatic stress syndrome.

The returning soldier, too, is burdened by the particular experience of small, irregular wars. Colonel Brown explains that when soldiers are killed by improvised explosive devices (IEDs), "catastrophic explosion rips them apart." Those soldiers who survive will see and hear explosions in their minds continually, which only amplifies their fear. This fear is cumulative and debilitating over the course of a deployment. In a conventional war you most fear being in the front lines; in an unconventional one you can be killed almost anywhere, at any time, so there is no time or place for fear to dissipate.

Furthermore, in an unconventional war, in which a soldier sees his comrades killed and lose limbs in explosions, there is no tangible measure of accomplishment as there is in a conventional war, where large swaths of territory are rolled up. This adds to the soldier's demoralization. And as soldiers deploy and redeploy to war zones, they and their families suffer the knowledge of what the last deployment did to them, knowing that they now have to relive it. And as the years go on, with no end in sight to at least one of these wars, Brown notes that military communities at bases in the United States become more insular, more psychologically cut off from the rest of the home front.

In *A Son at the Front,* Wharton countenances the efficacy of war in providing for historical progress: "The liberties of England had been born of the ruthless discipline of the Norman conquest," and "more freedom and a wiser order" had been born of the "hideous welter of the French Revolution and the Napoleonic wars." It is thus tempting to argue, or at least to think, that over the course of the decades, the invasions and occupations of Iraq and Afghanistan will bear fruit. After all, even a weak democracy in Iraq will be the first of its kind in a major Arab country; in addition, Iraq might become a de facto ally of the United States, with a civil society engrossed in domestic problems rather than confrontations with Israel. Moreover, the consequences of leaving Saddam Hussein in power to restart his weapons program and become the new, anti-Western "Nasser" of the Arab world were dreadful. Afghanistan, too, could yet evolve as a new Silk Road nexus of Central Asia.

But even if the United States gains strategically from these two invasions, this is mere abstract historical thinking. Policy is about the here and now. It is about taking or not taking action based on a near- and middle-term cost-benefit analysis. To subsume policy making completely to long-range historical projections is to risk constantly getting involved in grand schemes, and to ignore the concrete effects that such policies have on real people—both Americans and others. Thus, in the face of this human devastation, there is little absolution for those like myself who supported the Iraq War. Of course, the results of the Iraq War were born as much from the disastrous way in which the war and postwar phase were carried out as from the decision to invade itself. That could well be true of the war in Afghanistan as well. Still, to talk of complete absolution given these statistics is too convenient.

And yet there is a danger of taking this line of argument too far. For to focus solely on the hell to which so many families have been subjected is to blind oneself to the very real great-power responsibilities the United States has. For example, if U.S. military intervention in Bosnia and Kosovo in the 1990s had resulted in, say, 500 American dead and 5,000 seriously wounded, physically and psychologically—rather than virtually none, as was the case— would those deployments still have been worth it? I think so, because they stopped an ethnic killing machine. But where do we draw the line? When does this many or that many dead or this many wounded or that many traumatized add up to failure? The question has no good answer. But it is important that we always ask it.

For years covering the military I was told by Marines and Army Special Forces troops that they did not want anybody's pity, and that media fixation with the dead and wounded has the effect of turning all soldiers into victims. They prefer to think of themselves as warriors. That's a fine attitude for them to have, but for the home front to think similarly would dehumanize it. The home front gropes for a way to connect with the wounded and their families. The fact that this is much harder to do than we suppose it ought to be is a particular wage of small wars—wars that we should do all in our power to henceforth avoid.

9.

No Greater Honor

THE ATLANTIC, JUNE 2008

Over the decades, the Medal of Honor—the highest award for valor—has evolved into the U.S. military equivalent of sainthood. Only eight Medals of Honor have been awarded since the Vietnam War, all posthumously. "You don't have to die to win it, but it helps," says Army Colonel Thomas P. Smith. A West Point graduate from the Bronx, Smith has a unique perspective. He was a battalion commander in Iraq when one of his men performed actions that resulted in the Medal of Honor. It was then–Lieutenant Colonel Smith who pushed the paperwork for the award through the Pentagon bureaucracy, a two-year process.

On the morning of April 4, 2003, the Eleventh Engineer Battalion of the Third Infantry Division broke through to Baghdad International Airport. With sporadic fighting all around, Smith's men began to blow up captured ordnance that was blocking the runways. Nobody had slept, showered, or eaten much for weeks. In the midst of this mayhem, Smith got word that one of his platoon leaders, Sergeant First Class Paul Ray Smith (no relation), of Tampa, Florida, had been killed an hour earlier in a nearby firefight. Before he could react emotionally to the news, he was given another piece of information: The thirty-three-year-old sergeant had been hit while firing a .50-caliber heavy machine gun mounted on an armored personnel carrier. That was highly unusual, since it wasn't Sergeant Smith's job to fire the .50-cal. "That and other stray neurons of odd information about the incident started coming at me," explains Colonel Smith. But there was no time then to follow up, for within hours they were off in support of another battalion that was about to be overrun. And a few days after that, other members of the platoon, who had witnessed Sergeant Smith's last moments, were themselves killed.

Within a week the environment had changed, though. Baghdad had been secured, and the battalion enjoyed a respite that was crucial to the legacy of Sergeant First Class Paul Smith. Lieutenant Colonel Smith used the break to have one of his lieutenants get statements from everyone who was with Sergeant Smith at the time of his death. An astonishing story emerged.

Sergeant First Class Paul Ray Smith was the ultimate iron grunt, the kind of relentless, professional noncommissioned officer that the all-volunteer, expeditionary American military has been quietly producing for four decades. "The American people provide broad brand-management approval of the U.S. military," notes Colonel Smith, "about how great it is, and how much they support it, but the public truly has no idea how skilled and experienced many of these troops are."

Sergeant Smith had fought and served in Desert Storm, Bosnia, and Kosovo prior to Operation Iraqi Freedom. To his men, he was an intense, "infuriating, by-the-book taskmaster," in the words of Alex Leary of the *St. Petersburg Times,* Sergeant Smith's hometown newspaper. Long after other platoons were let off duty, Sergeant Smith would be drilling his men late into the night, checking the cleanliness of their rifle barrels with the Q-tips he carried in his pocket. During one inspection, he found a small screw missing from a soldier's helmet. He called the platoon back to drill until 10 P.M.

"He wasn't an in-your-face type," Colonel Smith told me, "just a methodical, hard-ass professional who had been in combat in Desert Storm, and took it as his personal responsibility to prepare his men for it."

Sergeant Smith's mindset epitomized the Western philosophy on war: War is not a way of life, an interminable series of hit-and-run raids for the sake of vendetta and tribal honor, in societies built on blood and discord. War is awful, to be waged only as a last resort, and with terrific intensity, to elicit a desired outcome in the shortest possible time. Because Sergeant Smith took war seriously, he never let up on his men, and never forgot about them. In a letter to his parents before deploying to Iraq, he wrote,

> There are two ways to come home, stepping off the plane and being carried off the plane. It doesn't matter how I come home because I am prepared to give all that I am to ensure that all my boys make it home.

On what would turn out to be the last night of his life, Sergeant Smith elected to go without sleep. He let others rest inside the slow-moving vehicles that he was ground-guiding on foot through dark thickets of palm trees en route to the Baghdad airport. The next morning, that unfailing regard for the soldiers under his command came together with his consummate skill as a warrior, not in a single impulsive act, like jumping on a grenade (as incredibly brave as that is), but in a series of deliberate and ultimately fatal decisions.

Sergeant Smith was directing his platoon to lay concertina wire across the corner of a courtyard near the airport, in order to create a temporary holding area for Iraqi prisoners of war. Then he noticed Iraqi troops massing, armed with AK-47s, RPGs, and mortars. Soon mortar fire had wounded three of his men—the crew of the platoon's M113A3 armored personnel carrier. A hundred well-armed Iraqis were now firing on his sixteen-man platoon.

Sergeant Smith threw grenades and fired an AT-4, a bazooka-like antitank weapon. A Bradley Fighting Vehicle from another unit managed to hold off the Iraqis for a few minutes, but then inexplicably left (out of ammunition, it would later turn out). Sergeant Smith was now in his rights to withdraw his men from the courtyard. But he rejected that option because it would have threatened American soldiers who were manning a nearby roadblock and an aid station. Instead he decided to climb atop the Vietnam-era armored personnel carrier whose crew had been wounded and man the .50-caliber machine gun himself. He asked Private Michael Seaman to go inside the vehicle, and to feed him a box of ammunition whenever the private heard the gun go silent.

Seaman, under Sergeant Smith's direction, moved the armored personnel carrier back a few feet to widen Smith's field of fire. Sergeant Smith was now completely exposed from the waist up, facing one hundred Iraqis firing at him from three directions, including from inside a well-protected sentry post. He methodically raked them, from right to left and back. Three times his gun went silent and three times the private reloaded him, while Sergeant Smith sat exposed to withering fire. He succeeded in breaking the Iraqi attack, killing perhaps dozens of the enemy while going through four hundred rounds of ammunition, before being shot in the head.

What impressed Colonel Smith about the incident was that no matter how many platoon members he solicited for statements, the story's details never varied. Even when embedded journalists like Alex Leary and Michael Corkery of the *Providence Journal-Bulletin* investigated the incident, they came away with the same narrative.

After talking with another battalion commander and his brigade commander, Colonel Smith decided to recommend his sergeant for the Medal of Honor. He was now operating in unfamiliar territory. Standards for the Medal of Honor are vague, if not undefinable. Whereas the Medal of Honor, according to the regulations, is for "gallantry and intrepidity at the risk of his or her life above and beyond the call of duty," the Distinguished Service Cross, the next-highest decoration, is for an "act or acts of heroism . . . so notable" and involving "risk of life so extraordinary as to set the individual apart" from his comrades. There is no metric to differentiate between the two awards or, for that matter, to set the Distinguished Service Cross apart from the Silver Star. It is largely a matter of a commanding officer's judgment.

Colonel Smith prepared the paperwork while surrounded by photos of Saddam Hussein in one of the Iraqi leader's palaces. The process began with Army Form DA-638, the same form used to recommend someone for an Army Achievement Medal, the lowest peacetime award. The only difference was Colonel Smith's note to "see attached."

There are nine bureaucratic levels of processing for the Medal of Honor. Smith's paperwork didn't even make it past the first. Word came down from the headquarters of the Third Infantry Division that he needed a lot more documentation. Smith prepared a Power-Point presentation, recorded the "bumper numbers" of all the vehicles involved, prodded surviving platoon members for more details, and built a whole "story book" around the incident. But at the third level, the Senior Army Decoration Board, that still wasn't enough. The bureaucratic package was returned to Colonel Smith in December 2003. "Perhaps the Board had some sort of devil's advocate, a former decorated soldier from Vietnam who was not completely convinced, either of the story or that it merited the medal."

At this point, the Third Infantry Division was going to assign another officer to follow up on the paper trail. Colonel Smith knew that if that happened, the chances of Sergeant Smith getting the medal would die, since only someone from Sergeant Smith's battalion would have the passion to battle the Army bureaucracy.

The Army was desperate for metrics. How many Iraqis exactly were killed? How many minutes exactly did the firefight last? The

Army, in its own way, was not being unreasonable. As Colonel Smith told me, "Everyone wants to award a Medal of Honor. But everyone is even more concerned with worthiness, with getting it right." There was a real fear that one unworthy medal would compromise the award, its aura, and its history. The bureaucratic part of the process is kept almost deliberately impossible, to see just how committed those recommending the award are: Insufficient passion may indicate the award is unjustified.

"Nobody up top in the Army's command is trying to find Medal of Honor winners to inspire the public with," says Colonel Smith. "It's the opposite. The whole thing is pushed up from the bottom to a skeptical higher command."

Colonel Smith's problem was that the platoon members were soldiers, not writers. To get more details from them, he drew up a list of questions and made them each write down the answers, which were then used to fill out the narrative. "Describe Sergeant Smith's state of mind and understanding of the situation. Did you see him give instructions to another soldier? What were those instructions? When the mortar round hit the M113A3, where were you? What was Sergeant Smith's reaction to it?"

"The answers came back in spades," Colonel Smith told me. Suddenly he had a much fatter storybook to put into the application. He waited another year as the application made its way up to Personnel Command, Manpower and Reserve Affairs, the chief of the Army, the secretary of the Army, the secretary of defense, and the president. The queries kept coming. Only when it hit the level of the secretary of defense did Colonel Smith feel he could breathe easier.

The ceremony in the East Room of the White House two years to the day after Sergeant Smith was killed, where President George W. Bush awarded the Medal of Honor to Sergeant Smith's eleven-year-old son, David, was fitfully covered by the media. The Paul Ray Smith story elicited 96 media mentions for the eight-week period after the medal was awarded, compared with 4,677 for the supposed abuse of the Koran at Guantánamo Bay and 5,159 for the disgraced Abu Ghraib prison guard Lynndie England, over a much longer time frame that went on for many months. In a society that obsesses over reality TV shows, gangster and war movies, and NFL quarterbacks, an authentic hero like Sergeant Smith flickers momentarily before the public consciousness.

It may be that the public, which still can't get enough of World War II heroics, even as it feels guilty about its treatment of Vietnam veterans, simply can't deliver up the requisite passion for honoring heroes from unpopular wars like Korea and Iraq. It may also be that, encouraged by the media, the public is more comfortable seeing our troops in Iraq as victims of a failed administration rather than as heroes in their own right. Such indifference to valor is another factor that separates an all-volunteer military from the public it defends. "The medal helps legitimize Iraq for them. World War II had its heroes, and now Iraq has its," Colonel Smith told me, in his office overlooking the Mississippi River, in Memphis, where he now heads the district office of the Army Corps of Engineers.

Colonel Smith believes there are other Paul Smiths out there, both in their level of professionalism and in their commitment— each a product of an all-volunteer system now in its fourth decade. How many others have performed as valiantly as Sergeant Smith and not been recommended for the Medal of Honor? After all, had it not been for that brief respite in combat in the early days of the occupation of Baghdad, the process for the sergeant's award might not have begun its slow, dogged, and ultimately successful climb up the chain of command.

THINKERS

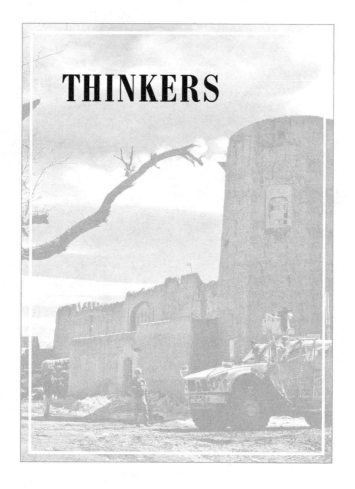

10.

In Defense of Henry Kissinger

THE ATLANTIC, MAY 2013

In the summer of 2002, during the initial buildup to the invasion of Iraq, which he supported, Henry Kissinger told me he was nevertheless concerned about the lack of critical thinking and planning for the occupation of a Middle Eastern country where, as he put it, "normal politics have not been practiced for decades, and where new power struggles would therefore have to be very violent." Thus is pessimism morally superior to misplaced optimism.

I have been a close friend of Henry Kissinger's for some time, but my relationship with him as a historical figure began decades ago. When I was growing up, the received wisdom painted him as the ogre of Vietnam. Later, as I experienced firsthand the stubborn realities of the developing world, and came to understand the task that a liberal polity like the United States faced in protecting its interests, Kissinger took his place among the other political philosophers whose books I consulted to make sense of it all. In the 1980s, when I was traveling through Central Europe and the Balkans, I encountered *A World Restored,* Kissinger's first book, published in 1957, about the diplomatic aftermath of the Napoleonic Wars. In that book, he laid out the significance of Austria as a "polyglot Em-

pire [that] could never be part of a structure legitimized by nationalism," and he offered a telling truth about Greece, where I had been
living for most of the decade: Whatever attraction the war for Greek
independence had held for the literati of the 1820s, it was not born
of "a revolution of middle-class origin to achieve political liberty,"
he cautioned, "but a national movement with a religious basis."

When policy makers disparage Kissinger in private, they tend to
do so in a manner that reveals how much they measure themselves
against him. The former secretary of state turns ninety this month.
To mark his legacy, we need to begin in the nineteenth century.

In August 1822, Britain's radical intelligentsia openly rejoiced
upon hearing the news of Robert Stewart's suicide. Lord Byron, the
Romantic poet and heroic adventurer, described Stewart, better
known as Viscount Castlereagh, as a "cold-blooded, . . . placid mis-
creant." Castlereagh, the British foreign secretary from 1812 to
1822, had helped organize the military coalition that defeated Napoleon and afterward helped negotiate a peace settlement that kept
Europe free of large-scale violence for decades. But because the
settlement restored the Bourbon dynasty in France, while providing
the forces of liberalism little reward for their efforts, Castlereagh's
accomplishment lacked any idealistic element, without which the
radicals could not be mollified. Of course, this very lack of idealism,
by safeguarding the aristocratic order, provided various sovereigns
with the only point on which they could unite against Napoleon
and establish a continent-wide peace—a peace, it should be noted,
that helped Britain emerge as the dominant world power before the
close of the nineteenth century.

One person who did not rejoice at Castlereagh's death was
Henry John Temple, the future British foreign secretary, better
known as Lord Palmerston. "There could not have been a greater
loss to the Government," Palmerston declared, "and few greater to
the country." Palmerston himself would soon join the battle against
the United Kingdom's radical intellectuals, who in the early 1820s

demanded that Britain go to war to help democracy take root in Spain, even though no vital British interest had been threatened—and even though this same intellectual class had at times shown only limited enthusiasm for the war against Napoleon, during which Britain's very survival seemed at stake.

In a career spanning more than two decades in the Foreign Office, Palmerston was fated on occasion to be just as hated as Castlereagh. Like Castlereagh, Palmerston had only one immutable principle in foreign policy: British self-interest, synonymous with the preservation of the worldwide balance of power. But Palmerston also had clear liberal instincts. Because Britain's was a constitutional government, he knew that the country's self-interest lay in promoting constitutional governments abroad. He showed sympathy for the 1848 revolutions on the Continent, and consequently was beloved by the liberals. Still, Palmerston understood that his liberal internationalism, if one could call it that, was only a general principle—a principle that, given the variety of situations around the world, required constant bending. Thus Palmerston encouraged liberalism in Germany in the 1830s but thwarted it there in the 1840s. He supported constitutionalism in Portugal but opposed it in Serbia and Mexico. He supported any tribal chieftain who extended British India's sphere of influence northwest into Afghanistan, toward Russia, and opposed any who extended Russia's sphere of influence southeast, toward India—even as he cooperated with Russia in Persia.

Realizing that many people—and radicals in particular—tended to confuse foreign policy with their own private theology, Palmerston may have considered the moral condemnation that greeted him in some quarters as natural. (John Bright, the Liberal statesman, would later describe Palmerston's tenure as "one long crime.")

Yet without his flexible approach to the world, Palmerston could never have navigated the shoals of one foreign policy crisis after another, helping Britain—despite the catastrophe of the Indian Mutiny in 1857—manage the transition from its ad hoc imperialism of the first half of the nineteenth century to the formal, steam-driven empire built on science and trade of the second half.

Decades passed before Palmerston's accomplishments as arguably Britain's greatest diplomat became fully apparent. In his own day, Palmerston labored hard to preserve the status quo, even as he sincerely desired a better world. "He wanted to prevent any power from becoming so strong that it might threaten Britain," one of his biographers, Jasper Ridley, wrote. "To prevent the outbreak of major wars in which Britain might be involved and weakened," Palmerston's foreign policy "was therefore a series of tactical improvisations, which he carried out with great skill."

Like Palmerston, Henry Kissinger believes that in difficult, uncertain times—times like the 1960s and '70s in America, when the nation's vulnerabilities appeared to outweigh its opportunities—the preservation of the status quo should constitute the highest morality. Other, luckier political leaders might later discover opportunities to encourage liberalism where before there had been none. The trick is to maintain one's power undiminished until that moment.

Ensuring a nation's survival sometimes leaves tragically little room for private morality. Discovering the inapplicability of Judeo-Christian morality in certain circumstances involving affairs of state can be searing. The rare individuals who have recognized the necessity of violating such morality, acted accordingly, and taken responsibility for their actions are among the most necessary leaders for their countries, even as they have caused great unease among generations of well-meaning intellectuals who, free of the burden of real-world bureaucratic responsibility, make choices in the abstract and treat morality as an inflexible absolute.

Fernando Pessoa, the early-twentieth-century Portuguese poet and existentialist writer, observed that if the strategist "thought of the darkness he cast on a thousand homes and the pain he caused in three thousand hearts," he would be "unable to act," and then there would be no one to save civilization from its enemies. Because many artists and intellectuals cannot accept this horrible but necessary truth, their work, Pessoa said, "serves as an outlet for the sensitivity [that] action had to leave behind." That is ultimately why Henry Kissinger is despised in some quarters, much as Castlereagh and Palmerston were.

To be uncomfortable with Kissinger is, as Palmerston might say, only natural. But to condemn him outright verges on sanctimony, if not delusion. Kissinger has, in fact, been quite moral—provided, of course, that you accept the Cold War assumptions of the age in which he operated.

Because of the triumphalist manner in which the Cold War suddenly and unexpectedly ended, many have since viewed the West's victory as a foregone conclusion, and therefore have tended to see the tough measures that Kissinger and others occasionally took as unwarranted. But for those in the midst of fighting the Cold War— who worked in the national security apparatus during the long, dreary decades when nuclear confrontation seemed abundantly possible—its end was hardly foreseeable.

People forget what Eastern Europe was like during the Cold War, especially prior to the 1980s: the combination of secret-police terror and regime-induced poverty gave the impression of a vast, dimly lit prison yard. What kept that prison yard from expanding was mainly the projection of American power, in the form of military divisions armed with nuclear weapons. That such weapons were never used did not mean they were unnecessary. Quite the opposite, in fact: The men who planned Armageddon, far from being the Dr. Strangeloves satirized by Hollywood, were precisely the people who kept the peace. Many Baby Boomers, who lived through the Cold War but who have no personal memory of World War II, artificially separate these two conflicts. But for Kissinger, a Holocaust refugee and U.S. Army intelligence officer in occupied Germany; for General Creighton Abrams, a tank commander under George Patton in World War II and the commander of American forces in Vietnam from 1968 onward; and for General Maxwell Taylor, who parachuted into Nazi-occupied France and was later the U.S. ambassador to South Vietnam, the Cold War was a continuation of the Second World War.

Beyond Eastern Europe, revolutionary nihilists were attempting to make more Cubas in Latin America, while a communist regime in China killed at least 20 million of its own citizens through the collectivization program known as the Great Leap Forward. Meanwhile, the North Vietnamese communists—as ruthless a group of people as the twentieth century produced—murdered perhaps tens of thousands of their own citizens before the first American troops arrived in Vietnam. People forget that it was, in part, an idealistic sense of mission that helped draw us into that conflict—the same well of idealism that helped us fight World War II and that motivated our interventions in the Balkans in the 1990s. Those who fervently supported intervention in Rwanda and the former Yugoslavia yet fail to comprehend the similar logic that led us into Vietnam are bereft of historical memory.

In Vietnam, America's idealism collided head-on with the military limitations imposed by a difficult geography. This destroyed the political consensus in the United States about how the Cold War should be waged. Reviewing Kissinger's book *Ending the Vietnam War* (2003), the historian and journalist Evan Thomas implied that the essence of Kissinger's tragedy was that he was perennially trying to gain membership in a club that no longer existed. That club was "the Establishment," a term that began to go out of fashion during the nation's Vietnam trauma. The Establishment comprised all the great and prestigious personages of business and foreign policy—all male, all Protestant, men like John J. McCloy and Charles Bohlen—whose influence and pragmatism bridged the gap between the Republican and Democratic parties at a time when communism was the enemy, just as fascism had recently been. Kissinger, a Jew who had escaped the Holocaust, was perhaps the club's most brilliant protégé. His fate was to step into the vortex of foreign policy just as the Establishment was breaking up over how to extricate the country from a war that the Establishment itself had helped lead the country into.

Kissinger became President Richard Nixon's national security advisor in January 1969 and his secretary of state in 1973. As a Harvard professor and "Rockefeller Republican," Kissinger was distrusted by the anti-intellectual Republican right wing. (Meanwhile, the Democratic Party was slipping into the de facto quasi-isolationism that would soon be associated with George McGovern's "Come Home, America" slogan.) Nixon and Kissinger inherited from President Lyndon Johnson a situation in which almost 550,000 American troops, as well as their South Vietnamese allies (at least 1 million soldiers all told), were fighting a similar number of North Vietnamese troops and guerrillas. On the home front, demonstrators—drawn in large part from the nation's economic and educational elite—were demanding that the United States withdraw all its troops virtually immediately.

Some prominent American protesters even visited North Vietnam to publicly express solidarity with the enemy. The communists in turn seduced foreign supporters with soothing assurances of Hanoi's willingness to compromise. When Charles de Gaulle was negotiating a withdrawal of French troops from Algeria in the late 1950s and early 1960s (as Kissinger records in *Ending the Vietnam War*), the Algerians knew that if they did not strike a deal with him, his replacement would certainly be more hard-line. But the North Vietnamese probably figured the opposite—that because of the rise of McGovernism in the Democratic Party, Nixon and Kissinger were all that stood in the way of American surrender. Thus Nixon and Kissinger's negotiating position was infinitely more difficult than De Gaulle's had been.

Kissinger found himself caught between liberals who essentially wanted to capitulate rather than negotiate, and conservatives ambivalent about the war who believed that serious negotiations with China and the Soviet Union were tantamount to selling out. Both positions were fantasies that only those out of power could indulge.

Further complicating Kissinger's problem was the paramount assumption of the age—that the Cold War would have no end, and that therefore regimes like those in China and the Soviet Union would have to be dealt with indefinitely. Hitler, a fiery revolutionary, had expended himself after twelve bloody years. But Mao Zedong and Leonid Brezhnev oversaw dull, plodding machines of repression that were in power for decades—a quarter century in Mao's case, and more than half a century in Brezhnev's. Neither regime showed any sign of collapse. Treating Communist China and the Soviet Union as legitimate states, even while Kissinger played China off against the Soviet Union and negotiated nuclear arms agreements with the latter, did not constitute a sellout, as some conservatives alleged. It was, rather, a recognition of America's "eternal and perpetual interests," to quote Palmerston, refitted to an age threatened by thermonuclear war.

In the face of liberal capitulation, a conservative flight from reality, and North Vietnam's relentlessness, Kissinger's task was to withdraw from the region in a way that did not betray America's South Vietnamese allies. In doing so, he sought to preserve America's powerful reputation, which was crucial for dealing with China and the Soviet Union, as well as the nations of the Middle East and Latin America. Sir Michael Howard, the eminent British war historian, notes that the balance-of-power ethos to which Kissinger subscribes represents the middle ground between "optimistic American ecumenicism" (the basis for many global disarmament movements) and the "war culture" of the American Wild West (in recent times associated with President George W. Bush). This ethos was never cynical or amoral, as the Post Cold War generation has tended to assert. Rather, it evinced a timeless and enlightened principle of statesmanship.

Within two years, Nixon and Kissinger reduced the number of American troops in Vietnam to 156,800; the last ground combat forces left three and a half years after Nixon took office. It had taken Charles de Gaulle longer than that to end France's involvement in Algeria. (Frustration over the failure to withdraw even more quickly rests on two difficult assumptions: that the impossibility of preserving South Vietnam in any form was accepted in 1969, and that the North Vietnamese had always been negotiating in good faith. Still, the continuation of the war past 1969 will forever be Nixon's and Kissinger's original sin.)

That successful troop withdrawal was facilitated by a bombing incursion into Cambodia—primarily into areas replete with North Vietnamese military redoubts and small civilian populations, over which the Cambodian government had little control. The bombing, called "secret" by the media, was public knowledge during 90 percent of the time it was carried out, wrote Samuel Huntington, the late Harvard professor who served on President Jimmy Carter's National Security Council. The early secrecy, he noted, was to avoid embarrassing Cambodia's Prince Norodom Sihanouk and complicating peace talks with the North Vietnamese.

The troop withdrawals were also facilitated by aerial bombardments of North Vietnam. Victor Davis Hanson, the neoconservative historian, writes that, "far from being ineffective and indiscriminate," as many critics of the Nixon-Kissinger war effort later claimed, the Christmas bombings of December 1972 in particular "brought the communists back to the peace table through its destruction of just a few key installations." Hanson may be a neoconservative, but his view is hardly a radical reinterpretation of history; in fact, he is simply reading the news accounts of the era. Soon after the Christmas bombings, Malcolm W. Browne of *The New York Times* found the damage to have been "grossly overstated by North

Vietnamese propaganda." Peter Ward, a reporter for *The Baltimore Sun,* wrote, "Evidence on the ground disproves charges of indiscriminate bombing. Several bomb loads obviously went astray into civilian residential areas, but damage there is minor, compared to the total destruction of selected targets."

The ritualistic vehemence with which many have condemned the bombings of North Vietnam, the incursion into Cambodia, and other events betrays, in certain cases, an ignorance of the facts and of the context that informed America's difficult decisions during Vietnam.

The troop withdrawals that Nixon and Kissinger engineered, while faster than De Gaulle's had been from Algeria, were gradual enough to prevent complete American humiliation. This preservation of America's global standing enabled the president and the secretary of state to manage a historic reconciliation with China, which helped provide the requisite leverage for a landmark strategic arms pact with the Soviet Union—even as, in 1970, Nixon and Kissinger's threats to Moscow helped stop Syrian tanks from crossing farther into Jordan and toppling King Hussein. At a time when defeatism reigned, Kissinger improvised in a way that would have impressed Palmerston.

Yes, Kissinger's record is marked by nasty tactical miscalculations—mistakes that have spawned whole libraries of books. But the notion that the Nixon administration might have withdrawn more than five hundred thousand American troops from Vietnam within a few months in 1969 is problematic, especially when one considers the complexities that smaller and more gradual withdrawals in Bosnia, Iraq, and Afghanistan later imposed on military planners. (And that's leaving aside the diplomatic and strategic fallout beyond Southeast Asia that America's sudden and complete betrayal of a longtime ally would have generated.)

Despite the North Vietnamese invasion of eastern Cambodia in

1970, the U.S. Congress substantially cut aid between 1971 and 1974 to the Lon Nol regime, which had replaced Prince Sihanouk's, and also barred the U.S. Air Force from helping Lon Nol fight against the Khmer Rouge. Future historians will consider those actions more instrumental in the 1975 Khmer Rouge takeover of Cambodia than Nixon's bombing of sparsely populated regions of Cambodia six years earlier.

When Saigon fell to the communists, in April 1975, it was after a heavily Democratic Congress drastically cut aid to the South Vietnamese. The regime might not have survived even if Congress had not cut aid so severely. But that cutoff, one should recall, was not merely a statement about South Vietnam's hopelessness; it was a consequence of Watergate, in which Nixon eviscerated his own influence in the capital and seriously undermined Gerald Ford's incoming administration. Kissinger's own words in *Ending the Vietnam War* deserve to echo through the ages:

> None of us could imagine that a collapse of presidential authority would follow the expected sweeping electoral victory [of Nixon in 1972]. We were convinced that we were working on an agreement that could be sustained by our South Vietnamese allies with American help against an all-out invasion. Protesters could speak of Vietnam in terms of the excesses of an aberrant society, but when my colleagues and I thought of Vietnam, it was in terms of dedicated men and women— soldiers and Foreign Service officers—who had struggled and suffered there and of our Vietnamese associates now condemned to face an uncertain but surely painful fate. These Americans had honestly believed that they were defending the cause of freedom against a brutal enemy in treacherous jungles and distant rice paddies. Vilified by the media, assailed in Congress, and ridiculed by the protest movement, they had sus-

tained America's idealistic tradition, risking their lives and expending their youth on a struggle that American leadership groups had initiated, then abandoned, and finally disdained.

Kissinger's diplomatic achievements reached far beyond Southeast Asia. Between 1973 and 1975, Kissinger, serving Nixon and then Gerald Ford, steered the Yom Kippur War toward a stalemate that was convenient for American interests, and then brokered agreements between Israel and its Arab adversaries for a separation of forces. Those deals allowed Washington to reestablish diplomatic relations with Egypt and Syria for the first time since their rupture following the Six-Day War in 1967. The agreements also established the context for the Egyptian-Israeli peace treaty of 1979 and helped stabilize a modus vivendi between Israel and Syria that has lasted well past the turn of the twenty-first century.

In the fall of 1973, with Chile dissolving into chaos and open to the Soviet bloc's infiltration as a result of Salvador Allende's anarchic and incompetent rule, Nixon and Kissinger encouraged a military coup led by General Augusto Pinochet, during which thousands of innocent people were killed. Their cold moral logic was that a right-wing regime of any kind would ultimately be better for Chile and for Latin America than a leftist regime of any kind—and would also be in the best interests of the United States. They were right—though at a perhaps intolerable cost.

While much of the rest of Latin America dithered with socialist experiments, in the first seven years of Pinochet's regime the number of state companies in Chile went from 500 to 25—a shift that helped lead to the creation of more than 1 million jobs and the reduction of the poverty rate from roughly one-third of the population to as low as one-tenth. The infant mortality rate also shrank, from 78 deaths per 1,000 births to 18. The Chilean social and economic miracle has become a paradigm throughout the developing world, and in the ex-communist world in particular. Still, no amount of economic and social gain justifies almost two decades of systematic torture perpetrated against tens of thousands of victims, in more than one thousand detention centers.

But real history is not the trumpeting of ugly facts untempered by historical and philosophical context—the stuff of much investigative journalism. Real history is built on constant comparison with other epochs and other parts of the world. It is particularly useful, therefore, to compare the records of the Ford and Carter administrations in the Horn of Africa, and especially in Ethiopia—a country that in the 1970s was more than three times as populous as Pinochet's Chile.

In his later years, Kissinger has not been able to travel to a number of countries where legal threats regarding his actions in the 1970s in Latin America hang over his head. Yet in those same countries, Jimmy Carter is regarded almost as a saint. Let's consider how Carter's morality stacks up against Kissinger's in the case of Ethiopia, which, like Angola, Nicaragua, and Afghanistan, was among the dominoes that became increasingly unstable and then fell in the months and years following Saigon's collapse, partly disproving another myth of the Vietnam antiwar protest movement—that the domino theory was wrong.

As I've written elsewhere, including in my 1988 book, *Surrender or Starve,* the left-leaning Ethiopian Dergue and its ascetic, pitiless new leader, Mengistu Haile Mariam, had risen to power while the United States was preoccupied with Watergate and the fall of South Vietnam. Kissinger, now President Ford's secretary of state, tried to retain influence in Ethiopia by continuing to provide some military assistance to Addis Ababa. Had the United States given up all its leverage in Ethiopia, the country might have moved to the next stage and become a Soviet satellite, with disastrous human rights consequences for its entire population.

Ford and Kissinger were replaced in January 1977 by Jimmy Carter and his secretary of state, Cyrus Vance, who wanted a policy that was both more attuned to and less heavy-handed toward sub-Saharan Africa. In the Horn of Africa, this translated immediately into a Cold War disadvantage for America, because the Soviets—spurred on by the fall of South Vietnam—were becoming more belligerent, and more willing to expend resources, than ever.

With Ethiopia torn apart by revolutionary turmoil, the Soviets used their Somali clients as a lever against Addis Ababa. Somalia then was a country of only 3 million nomads, but Ethiopia had an urbanized population ten times that size: excellent provender for the mechanized African satellite that became Leonid Brezhnev's supreme objective. The Soviets, while threatening Ethiopia by supplying its rival with weapons, were also offering it military aid—the classic carrot-and-stick strategy. Yet partly because of the M-60 tanks and F-5 warplanes that Mengistu was still—largely thanks to Kissinger—receiving from the United States, the Ethiopian leader was hesitant about undertaking the disruptive task of switching munitions suppliers for an entire army.

In the spring of 1977, Carter cut off arms deliveries to Ethiopia because of its human rights record. The Soviets dispatched East German security police to Addis Ababa to help Mengistu consolidate his regime, and invited the Ethiopian ruler to Moscow for a weeklong state visit. Then Cuban advisors visited Ethiopia, even while tanks and other equipment arrived from pro-Soviet South Yemen. In the following months, with the help of the East Germans, the Dergue gunned down hundreds of Ethiopian teenagers in the streets in what came to be known as the "Red Terror."

Still, all was not lost—at least not yet. The Ethiopian Revolution, leftist as it was, showed relatively few overt signs of anti-Americanism. Israel's new prime minister, Menachem Begin, in an attempt to save Ethiopian Jews, beseeched Carter not to close the door completely on Ethiopia and to give Mengistu some military assistance against the Somali advance.

But Begin's plea went unheeded. The partial result of Carter's inaction was that Ethiopia went from being yet another left-leaning regime to a full-fledged Marxist state, in which hundreds of thousands of people died in collectivization and "villagization" schemes—to say nothing of the hundreds of thousands who died in famines that were as much a consequence of made-in-Moscow agricultural policies as they were of drought.

Ethiopians should have been so lucky as to have had a Pinochet.

The link between Carter's decision not to play Kissingerian power politics in the Horn of Africa and the mass deaths that followed in Ethiopia is more direct than the link between Nixon's incursion into a rural area of Cambodia and the Khmer Rouge takeover six years later.

In the late nineteenth century, Lord Palmerston was still a controversial figure. By the twentieth he was considered by many to have been one of Britain's greatest foreign ministers. Kissinger's reputation will follow a similar path. Of all the memoirs written by former American secretaries of state and national security advisors during the past few decades, his are certainly the most vast and the most intellectually stimulating, revealing the elaborate historical and philosophical milieus that surround difficult foreign policy decisions. Kissinger will have the final say precisely because he writes so much better for a general audience than do most of his critics. Mere exposé often has a shorter shelf life than the work of a statesman aware of his own tragic circumstances and able to connect them to a larger pattern of events. A colleague of mine with experience in government once noted that, as a European-style realist, Kissinger has thought more about morality and ethics than most self-styled moralists. Realism is about the ultimate moral ambition in foreign policy: the avoidance of war through a favorable balance of power.

Aside from the successful interventions in the Balkans, the greatest humanitarian gesture in my own lifetime was President Richard Nixon's trip to the People's Republic of China in 1972, engineered by Kissinger. By dropping the notion that Taiwan was the real China, by giving China protection against the Soviet Union, and by providing assurances against an economically resurgent Japan, the two men helped place China in a position to devote itself to peaceful economic development; China's economic rise, facilitated by Deng Xiaoping, would lift much of Asia out of poverty. And as more than one billion people in the Far East saw a dramatic improvement in living standards, personal freedom effloresced.

Pundits chastised Kissinger for saying, in 1973, that Jewish emigration from the Soviet Union was "not an American concern." But as J. J. Goldberg of *The Jewish Daily Forward* was careful to note (even while being very critical of Kissinger's cynicism on the subject), "Emigration rose dramatically under Kissinger's detente policy"—but "plummeted" after the 1974 passage of the Jackson-Vanik amendment, which made an open emigration policy a precondition for normal U.S.-Soviet trade relations; aggrieved that the Americans would presume to dictate their emigration policies, the Soviets began authorizing fewer exit visas. In other words, Kissinger's realism was more effective than the humanitarianism of Jewish groups in addressing a human rights concern.

Kissinger is a Jewish intellectual who recognizes a singular unappealing truth: that the Republican Party, its strains of anti-Semitism in certain periods notwithstanding, was better able to protect America than the Democratic Party of his era, because the Republicans better understood and in fact relished the projection of American power at a juncture in the Cold War when the Democrats were undermined by defeatism and quasi-isolationism. (That Kissinger-style realism is now more popular in Barack Obama's White House than among the GOP indicates how far today's Republicans have drifted from their core values.)

But unlike his fellow Republicans of the Cold War era—dull and practical men of business, blissfully unaware of what the prestigious intellectual journals of opinion had to say about them—Kissinger has always been painfully conscious of the degree to which he is loathed. He made life-and-death decisions that affected millions, entailing many messy moral compromises. Had it not been for the tough decisions Nixon, Ford, and Kissinger made, the United States might not have withstood the damage caused by Carter's bouts of moralistic ineptitude; nor would Ronald Reagan have had the luxury of his successfully executed Wilsonianism. Henry Kissinger's classical realism—as expressed in both his books and his statecraft—is emotionally unsatisfying but analytically timeless. The degree to which Republicans can recover his sensibility in foreign policy will help determine their own prospects for regaining power.

11.

Samuel Huntington: Looking the World in the Eye

THE ATLANTIC, DECEMBER 2001

I.

The most memorable review that Samuel Phillips Huntington, the Albert J. Weatherhead III University Professor at Harvard, ever got was a bad one. "Imagine," Huntington recalled recently, sitting in his home on Boston's Beacon Hill. "The first review of my first book, and the reviewer compares me unfavorably to Mussolini." He blinked and squinted shyly through his eyeglasses. Huntington, seventy-four, speaks in a serene and nasal voice, the East Bronx modified by high Boston. He described how the reviewer, Matthew Josephson, writing in the left-wing opinion magazine *The Nation,* had ridiculed the militarism and "brutal sophistries" of *The Soldier and the State* and had sneered that Mussolini's sentiments had been similar though his words had more panache: "Believe, obey, fight!"

The review was published on April 6, 1957. The Cold War was scarcely a decade old. *The Soldier and the State* constituted a warning: America's liberal society, Huntington argued, required the protection of a professional military establishment steeped in conservative realism. In order to keep the peace, military leaders had to take for granted—and anticipate—the "irrationality, weakness, and evil in human nature." Liberals were good at reform, not at national security. "Magnificently varied and creative when limited to domestic issues," Huntington wrote, "liberalism faltered when applied to foreign policy and defense." Foreign policy, he explained, is not about the relationship among individuals living under the rule of law but about the relationship among states and other groups operating in a largely lawless realm. *The Soldier and the State* concluded with a rousing defense of West Point, which, Huntington wrote, "embodies the military ideal at its best . . . a bit of Sparta in the midst of Babylon."

The book enraged many of Huntington's colleagues in Harvard's Department of Government, and the following year the department denied him tenure. With his close friend Zbigniew Brzezinski (whom Harvard also did not promote), Huntington went off to teach at Columbia University.

Four years later, in 1962, Harvard invited both Huntington and Brzezinski back, as tenured professors. Carl J. Friedrich, the German-born professor who had led the opposition to Huntington, met with him at Columbia. Friedrich talked of his admiration for the younger professor, until Huntington gently reminded him of his earlier hostility. It had become obvious to Friedrich and others that both Huntington and Brzezinski were rising stars in political science, and Harvard prided itself on its domination of the field. Brzezinski chose to stay at Columbia, but Huntington returned to Harvard, where he joined another rising star in the Department of Government, Henry A. Kissinger.

The Soldier and the State, now in its fourteenth printing, went on to become an academic classic. Telford Taylor, the chief American prosecutor at the Nuremberg trials, had this to say about the book when it was first published:

"Civilian control" [of the military] has become a piece of cant that politicians mouth worshipfully but with little understanding. This is an area where iconoclasm is badly needed; Professor Huntington's store of this commodity seems virtually inexhaustible, and it is refreshing to follow his trail of destructive exposure.

In recent decades scholarly commentary has focused less on one aspect of Huntington's book and more on another—less on the need for the military's sense of realism and more on the threat a military may pose to civilian authority. Because democracies lack the disciplined political cadres that dictatorships produce, they are especially prone to subtle manipulation by powerful militaries. The Founding Fathers, Huntington observed, while providing for a separation of powers within civilian government, did not foresee the potential encroachment on civilian government of a gigantic defense establishment over time.

The Soldier and the State initiated what has become a familiar pattern in Huntington's long career: His work has not immediately earned brilliant reviews and academic awards but, rather, has garnered mixed reviews and harsh denunciations that ultimately yield to widespread if grudging acceptance. Even Huntington's enemies unwittingly define and worry about the world in ways and in phrases that originated with Huntington. Roger Hilsman, a specialist on Southeast Asia and a Huntington critic, complained in 1957 that many parts of *The Soldier and the State* "are noisy with the sounds of sawing and stretching as the facts are forced into the bed that has been prepared for them." Well, maybe. Nonetheless, *The Soldier and the State* put the issue of civil-military relations on the map.

The subject that Huntington has more recently put on the map is the "clash of civilizations" that is occurring as Western, Islamic, and Asian systems of thought and government collide. His argument is more subtle than it is usually given credit for, but some of the main points can be summarized.

- The fact that the world is modernizing does not mean that it is Westernizing. The impact of urbanization and mass communications, coupled with poverty and ethnic divisions, will not lead to peoples' everywhere thinking as we do.
- Asia, despite its ups and downs, is expanding militarily and economically. Islam is exploding demographically. The West may be declining in relative influence.
- Culture-consciousness is getting stronger, not weaker, and states or peoples may band together because of cultural similarities rather than because of ideological ones, as in the past.
- The Western belief that parliamentary democracy and free markets are suitable for everyone will bring the West into conflict with civilizations—notably, Islam and the Chinese—that think differently.
- In a multipolar world based loosely on civilizations rather than on ideologies, Americans must reaffirm their Western identity.

The 2001 terrorist attacks on the World Trade Center and the Pentagon highlight the tragic relevance not just of Huntington's ideas about a clash of civilizations but of his entire life's work. Since the 1950s he has argued that American society requires military and intelligence services that think in the most tragic, pessimistic terms. He has worried for decades about how American security has mostly been the result of sheer luck—the luck of geography—and may one day have to be truly earned. He has written that liberalism thrives only when security can be taken for granted—and that in the future we may not have that luxury. And he has warned that the West may one day have to fight for its most cherished values and, indeed, for physical survival against extremists from other cultures who despise our country and who will embroil us in a civilizational war that is real, even if political leaders and polite punditry must call it by another name. While others who hold such views have

found both happiness and favor working among like-minded thinkers in the worlds of the corporation, the military, and the intelligence services, Huntington has deliberately remained in the liberal
bastion of Ivy League academia, to fight for his ideas on that lonely
but vital front.

II.

The history of the intellectual battles surrounding American foreign
policy since the early Cold War can be told, to an impressive degree,
through Huntington's seventeen books and scores of articles. Kissinger and Brzezinski have also produced distinguished works of
scholarship, but these men will be remembered principally for their
service in government—Kissinger as national security advisor under
Richard Nixon and secretary of state under Nixon and Gerald Ford,
and Brzezinski as national security advisor under Jimmy Carter.
Huntington, though he served briefly in the administrations of Lyndon Johnson and Carter, is a man of the academy to a far greater
extent than his two friends. His ideas emerge from seminars and
lectures, not from sudden epiphanies. If he couldn't teach, he probably couldn't write. And unlike many professors, he values his un-
dergraduate students more than he does his graduate students.
Graduate students, he told me, "are more reluctant to challenge this
or that professor" and have often been "captured by the jargon and
orthodoxy of the discipline."

One of his former undergraduates observes, "Other academics want to ram down your throat what they know, and then go
on to the next victim. Huntington never dominates classroom discussions, and he listens intensely." Huntington disdains "rational-
choice theory," the reigning fad in political science, which assumes
that human behavior is predictable but which fails to take account
of fear, envy, hatred, self-sacrifice, and other human passions that
are essential to an understanding of politics. In an age of academic

operators he is an old-fashioned teacher who speculates historically and philosophically on the human condition. His former students include Francis Fukuyama, the author of the famous Post Cold War anthem *The End of History and the Last Man* (1992), and Fareed Zakaria, the former managing editor of *Foreign Affairs* and the current editor of *Newsweek International*.

You aren't likely to see Huntington on C-SPAN, let alone on *The McLaughlin Group*. He is a worse than indifferent public speaker: hunched over, reading laboriously from a text. His status and reputation have come the hard way: through writing books that, though often publicly denounced, have had a pervasive influence among people who count. Although he is the classic insider (a former president of the American Political Science Association and a cofounder of *Foreign Policy* magazine), he writes as an outsider, someone willing to enrage the very experts who will ultimately judge him. "If a scholar has nothing new to say he should keep quiet," Huntington wrote in 1959. "The quest for truths is synonymous with intellectual controversy."

In many ways Samuel Huntington represents a dying breed: someone who combines liberal ideals with a deeply conservative understanding of history and foreign policy. Huntington is a life-long Democrat. He was a speechwriter for Adlai Stevenson in the 1950s (and met his wife, Nancy, during the 1956 campaign), a foreign policy advisor to Hubert Humphrey in the 1960s, and one of the authors of Jimmy Carter's speeches on human rights in the 1970s. This same Huntington, though, is the founder of Harvard's John M. Olin Institute for Strategic Studies, a redoubt of foreign policy realism that has been financed by a triad of conservative philanthropies: the John M. Olin Foundation, the Smith Richardson Foundation, and the Bradley Foundation.

When I suggested to Huntington that he is "an old-fashioned Democrat, the kind that no longer exists," he indulged in a rare display of emotional animation. He snapped in reply, "That's it—

that's what I am. As Arthur Schlesinger would say, I am a child of Niebuhr." Reinhold Niebuhr was the leading Protestant theologian of twentieth-century America—a devout Christian who believed that men are sufficiently wicked to require tough methods for the preservation of order. Huntington, an Episcopalian, was attracted to what he describes as Niebuhr's "compelling combination of morality and practical realism." Though an ardent Cold Warrior, Niebuhr never succumbed to moral triumphalism, believing that history was more profoundly characterized by irony than by progress. Even if the United States were to win the Cold War, Niebuhr wrote in 1952, this outcome might only cause the nation to overextend itself, dissipating its power in an excess of righteousness. Niebuhr's tragic sensibility constitutes a thread connecting all of Huntington's major works. It is the key to Huntington's definition of conservatism.

In the June 1957 edition of *The American Political Science Review,* Huntington published a monograph titled "Conservatism as an Ideology." Liberalism, he wrote, is an ideology of individualism, free markets, liberty, and the rule of law. "Classic conservatism," in contrast, has no particular vision: It is a rationale, "high and necessary," for ensuring the survival of liberal institutions. Conservatism, Huntington observed, is the "rational defense of being against mind, of order against chaos." In England, he explained, Edmund Burke mounted a conservative defense of a "commercial society and a moderate, liberal constitution." Real conservatism is about conserving what is, rather than crusading abroad for what is not or proposing radical changes at home. In the United States, Federalists like John Adams and Alexander Hamilton expounded conservative principles to defend a liberal constitution. "The American political genius," Huntington wrote, "is manifest not in our ideas but in our institutions." And in his view, "The greatest need is not so much the creation of more liberal institutions as the successful defense of those which already exist."

III.

Samuel Huntington was born in 1927 in New York City and grew up in middle-class housing projects in the Astoria section of Queens and in the East Bronx. He was the only child of Richard Thomas Huntington, a publisher of hotel trade journals, and Dorothy Sanborn Phillips, a short-story writer, and he was the grandson of John Sanborn Phillips, the co-editor of the muckraking magazine *McClure's*. Huntington was a prodigy. He went to Yale from Peter Stuyvesant High School at age sixteen and graduated with "exceptional distinction" after two and a half years. He served in the U.S. Army and then earned a master's degree in political science from the University of Chicago and a Ph.D. from Harvard. He believes that the strain of writing his Ph.D. dissertation over the course of four grueling months in 1950 is what precipitated the diabetes he suffers, which has necessitated six daily blood tests and three daily insulin injections ever since. (He interrupted our conversation to test his blood sugar level and to jab himself with a syringe. After looking at the blood sugar number, he said, "Good, I can have a salad and a glass of wine for lunch.") His doctoral dissertation, "Clientalism," carried on in the muckraking tradition of his grandfather. It described how federal agencies, notably the Interstate Commerce Commission, get taken over by the very industries that they are supposed to regulate. "We were all liberals, and Franklin Roosevelt was God," Huntington told me. "I couldn't imagine that anyone thought differently." Psychologically, Huntington's world at this time bore the imprint of the New Deal. Still, Harvard manifested an occasional irregularity. "There was one student who vigorously opposed collective bargaining, the minimum wage—all the conventional wisdom, in fact. It was quite a shock for all of us." This student, William Rehnquist, eventually left for Stanford Law School.

Two towering intellectual figures then ruled Harvard's Department of Government: Carl Friedrich and William Yandell Elliott.

Friedrich, the more liberal of the two, had helped to write the constitution for the Federal Republic of Germany (that is, the old West Germany). Huntington gravitated toward Elliott, an Oxford-educated southerner and a conservative philosopher with much experience in Washington. Elliott believed in a vigorous stance against the Soviet Union and loathed moral relativism. "Elliott would travel to Cambridge once a week from Washington to meet with his graduate students," Huntington recalled. Among those profoundly influenced by Elliott was Huntington's contemporary Henry Kissinger. "We would wait in [Elliott's] outer office as the minutes went by, incensed that he was running late because of the time he took mentoring this one student, whom Elliott had identified as showing particular promise. Then the door would open and this chubby student would walk out." Kissinger dedicated his first book to Elliott: *A World Restored* (1957), which described Metternich's creation of a stable, post-Napoleonic world order. "Elliott was no great theorist," Kissinger told me, "but a good teacher is someone who sees talents in you that you didn't know you had. After I had written a paper on Kant, Elliott told me, 'You have a fine mind, but now you have to read novelists, like Dostoyevsky.' And so I read Dostoyevsky. This is how he helped his students grow."

Sweeping and icy statements dominate Huntington's books. These blunt judgments contrast sharply with Huntington's unimposing physical presence and unaffected demeanor. He looks like a character from a John Cheever story, someone you might forget that you had ever met. He blinks. He plays nervously with keys. He is balding, and stares intently at his palms as he talks. The fragile exterior conceals a flinty core. "Sam is very shy," Brzezinski says. "He's not one of those guys who can shoot the breeze at a bar. But get him into a debate and he is confident and tenacious." A former student says, "Sam is a geek with a backbone of steel." Another of his students demurs: "Sam isn't a geek. He's a quintessential Victorian man of honor—very quiet and contained, yet extraordinarily tough when the occasion demands."

In the early 1980s, walking home one night from a Cambridge dinner party with his wife and Francis Keppel, the retired dean of the Harvard Graduate School of Education, Huntington was approached by three young men who demanded his money. "What?" Huntington asked. "We're not fucking around, we want your cash," one of the young men said before attacking him. Huntington repulsed him and wrestled him to the ground, calling for help. Then he took on a second, who was on top of Keppel. Ultimately the three men ran off. Huntington did not volunteer this story: I learned about it from one of his former students, and then had to get the details from Nancy. When I asked Huntington himself about it, he said, "A week before there had been an article in one of the newsmagazines recommending that you shouldn't fight with a mugger. But my immediate impulse was to fight back."

IV.

From the outset Huntington's thinking has been focused on the big issues of the modern world; he was always interested in applying intellectual rigor to real-life concerns. Henry Kissinger's first book was largely inspired by early-nineteenth-century European history. Huntington's first book was inspired by what was going on in America when he was a graduate student. As Robert D. Putnam, of Harvard, has written in an essay on Huntington, *The Soldier and the State* was inspired by President Harry Truman's firing of General Douglas MacArthur for insubordination, in 1951. MacArthur's political generalship had disturbed Huntington, in part because it undermined the idea of a professional military. The military—and the U.S. Senate, another conservative institution—would later prove to be the most effective bulwarks against Senator Joseph McCarthy's assault on America's liberal values. *The Soldier and the State* was no apologia for militarism, as some simplistic critiques have claimed, but, rather, a penetrating analysis of the relationship between the military and society.

The most telling passage in *The Soldier and the State* is in the preface, where the twenty-nine-year-old Huntington came to a conclusion that formed the template of an entire career. On the one hand, he conceded that "actual personalities, institutions, and beliefs do not fit into neat logical categories." But on the other, he argued passionately that "neat logical categories are necessary if man is to think profitably about the real world in which he lives and to derive from it lessons for broader application and use." A scholar, in order to say anything significant, is "forced to generalize." The true measure of a theory is not that it accounts for all the relevant facts but that it accounts for those facts "better than any other theory." Without abstraction and simplification there can be no understanding, Huntington maintained. Those who concentrate on the imperfections of a theory, without coming up with a better alternative, are helping no one. Thus begins a book of relentless, empirical generalizations.

From the end of the War of 1812 through the attack on Pearl Harbor, Huntington wrote, Americans had little reason to worry about foreign threats. National security was taken for granted—an inheritance of geographical circumstance, rather than a creation of wise policy. With neither security nor economic expansion on a resource-rich continent in doubt, the liberal ideology that Americans acquired from their English forebears could be firmly established without contradiction. In the absence of any threat to the nation's liberal institutions, there was little need to defend them, and thus little need for real conservatism. Conservatives like Hamilton and Adams could thrive only because during the first years of the Republic it was surrounded by French, English, and Spanish territory, and was hampered by the British fleet. But for many decades thereafter no foreign threats existed on any significant scale, and the "low view of man" cultivated by conservatives entered a state of dormancy. Indeed, when President Woodrow Wilson read in *The Baltimore Sun* in 1915 that his general staff was preparing pragmatically for the possibility of war with Germany, he was "trembling and white with passion," and insisted to his aides that if the story was true, the staff officers should be fired. "Liberalism," Huntington observed, "does not understand and is hostile to military institutions and the military function."

Of course, the early twentieth century did witness a brief rebirth of Hamiltonian realism and interventionism, identified with the aggressive foreign policy of President Theodore Roosevelt. But the aversion to power politics was so deeply ingrained in the American psyche that Wilson's foreign policy failures in the aftermath of World War I led to "abandoning intervention altogether and returning to liberal isolationism." With no one left to carry the torch of Hamilton, whose realist philosophy could reconcile the military to the rest of society, the American military in the interwar period withdrew into itself. It did so just as it was undergoing intensive professionalization and specialization, near the climax of the Industrial Revolution.

Huntington reminded us that the modern officer is a professional, whose job is the management of violence and whose client is the state. Although war is as old as humankind, a professional military essentially began with the Napoleonic Wars. The Founding Fathers put their uniforms on and off as the occasion demanded, and saw little distinction between soldiers and civilians. The Constitution does not provide for "objective civilian control" of government, which came about, again, because of the accident of geography: Without a foreign threat, our standing army long remained small and politically weak, and could be reduced in size after every war. But the advance of technology that culminated in World War II, with Pearl Harbor and the atomic bomb, meant that geography was no longer a barrier. Security might at times have to take precedence over liberal values.

The liberal values that a democracy holds dear, Huntington explained, are also the values that can undermine a professional officer corps. "The heart of liberalism is individualism," he wrote. "It emphasizes the reason and moral dignity of the individual." But the military man, because of the nature of his job, has to assume irrationality and the permanence of violent conflict in human relations. "The liberal glorifies self-expression" because the liberal takes national security for granted; the military man glorifies "obedience" because he does not take that security for granted. A democracy may fight better than a dictatorship, because its middle-level officers are more inclined to make risky decisions; that is one reason for our success on the beaches of Normandy, and for the success of the Israelis over Arab armies. Nevertheless, a truly liberal military would lack the lethal effectiveness required to defend a liberal society threatened by technologically empowered illiberal adversaries.

Only conservatism, Huntington argued, proves properly conducive to military professionalism. Indeed, conservatism grows organically out of the military ethic that dominated society in ancient times. Conservatism recognizes the primacy of power in international affairs; it accepts existing institutions; and its goals are limited. It eschews grand designs, because it has no universal value system that it seeks to impose on others. The conservative mind, like the military one, believes that human beings learn only from human experience, which leads to an accent on the study of history. History forms the centerpiece of war college curricula.

But don't assume, Huntington said, that the conservatism of the military is inherently reactionary, in an ideological sense. In nineteenth-century Europe the professionalization of militaries allowed men of all backgrounds to advance in the ranks; militaries challenged the aristocratic basis of society. In egalitarian America the dynamic between the military and society was bound to be dif-

ferent. The United States was already democratic, and under no
threat. The military was more isolated, and over time it developed
an ethos that was markedly more aristocratic than that of society.
The more a liberal society isolates and reproaches the military, Huntington implied, the more conservative the military may become in
response.

Now here is where the young Huntington really got interesting.
Our very greatness, he said, is what makes it difficult for the American liberal mind to deal with the outside world. "American nationalism," he wrote, "has been an idealistic nationalism, justified, not
by the assertion of the superiority of the American people over other
peoples, but by the assertion of the superiority of American ideals
over other ideals." French foreign policy can be whatever the French
decide it is, provided it is in their momentary self-interest. But
American foreign policy is judged by the criteria of universal principles. According to Huntington, this leads to a pacifist strain in
American liberalism when it comes to defending our hardcore national interests, and an aggressive strain when it comes to defending
human rights. Although the professional soldier accepts the reality
of never-ending and limited conflict, "the liberal tendency," Huntington explained, is "to absolutize and dichotomize war and
peace." Liberals will most readily support a war if they can turn it
into a crusade for advancing humanistic ideals. That is why, he
wrote, liberals seek to reduce the defense budget even as they periodically demand an adventurous foreign policy. It came as no surprise to readers of *The Soldier and the State* that the same
intellectuals and opinion-makers who consistently underappreci-
ated NATO in the 1970s and 1980s, when the outcome of the Cold
War remained in doubt, demanded aggressive NATO involvement
in the 1990s, in Bosnia and Kosovo, when the stakes for our national security were much lower, but the assault on liberal principles
was vivid and clear-cut.

The only way to preserve a liberal society, Huntington wrote, is to define the limits of military control. And the only way to do that across the uncertain decades and centuries ahead is to keep the military and the advice it offers strictly professional. Therefore, a soldier should recommend battle only in the case of national interest. If he is to fight for other reasons, even humanitarian ones, the pressure to do so must come from his civilian superiors.

In 1993, General Colin Powell, then the chairman of the Joint Chiefs of Staff, expressed opposition to U.S. military involvement in Bosnia and was branded a "political general" by some. But a reader of Huntington might think a little differently about Powell. If his client's territory is under no direct danger, the professional officer cannot recommend "the involvement of the state in war except when victory is certain," as Huntington wrote. Powell's opposition to war in a case where the impact on our national interest was inconclusive and where victory appeared unsure was not so much a "Powell doctrine" as it was the age-old dictum of the military professional, who seeks to avoid becoming "political" and refuses to promote moral crusades, however justified they may be. (Of course, the military's ability to intimidate our civilian leadership into inaction in Bosnia points up Huntington's other realization: about how democracies are encroached on by overbearing defense establishments.)

The first decade of the Cold War indicated to Huntington that although tension would persist between a liberal society and a vast new defense establishment, the two would find ways to coexist. He saw Truman as a harbinger of this emerging order: liberal at home, but profoundly conservative in foreign affairs. It was the civilian business community, Huntington observed, that was now providing a bridge between the military and the rest of society. For many of us, big business embodies conservative pragmatism and what is known as the military-industrial complex. But Huntington exposed this image as a Cold War artifact. "Business pacifism" is how he describes the capitalist's view of the world through most of our earlier history. Religious moralism and economic liberalism combined to make most American businessmen see international trade and multilateral treaties as more important than power politics. The end of the Cold War has revived that view of the world. Liberals and neoconservatives who now worry about the American business community's growing economic involvement with an authoritarian China are revisiting an old Huntington argument.

V.

By the mid-1960s Samuel Huntington had settled into the life of a Harvard professor, quietly raising a family in the Boston area. This life was briefly interrupted by an assignment for the Johnson administration in 1967: as a State Department consultant, he prepared a one-hundred-page report on the Vietnam War that was later declassified and used as the basis for an article in the July 1968 issue of *Foreign Affairs*. The article caused a tremendous furor. It embraced the administration's objective of defeating the North Vietnamese, but explained why the administration's methods for achieving that objective were all wrong.

Huntington rejected the significance of the Johnson administration's claim that the proportion of the South Vietnamese population under government control (rather than under Viet Cong control) had risen from 40 percent to 60 percent. "This change," he wrote, is "the result of the movement of the population into the cities rather than the extension of the Government's control into the countryside"—where the Viet Cong were as strong as ever. But although the Johnson administration was guilty of "unwarranted optimism," its critics, he asserted, were guilty of "misplaced moralism." Huntington pointed out that the question *Whom does the majority of the population really support?* was relevant only in a stable constitutional democracy like America's, not amid the mounting chaos and violence of a country like Vietnam. Further, winning popular support by promoting rural development would achieve nothing; it wasn't rural poverty that drove people into the arms of the Viet Cong but rather "the absence of an effective structure of authority." And where such a strong authority existed, Huntington wrote, "even though it be quite hierarchical and undemocratic, the Viet Cong make little progress." The one-third of the rural population that had withstood Viet Cong infiltration had done so because of tough ethnic and religious communal organizations that were often as inimical to Western values as the Viet Cong were. "Even back then we were nation-building," Huntington told me, with disapproval. "We rejected religious and ethnic loyalties as counterweights to the Viet Cong because we wanted a modern, democratic nation-state with a national army. One problem with Vietnam was our idealism."

Such idealism, he says, now characterizes other American involvements overseas: "The media appeal to our national egotism, which assumes our values and political structures are those the rest of the world wants; and if it doesn't want them, it ought to." Huntington believes that we should proclaim our values abroad in ways that allow us to take advantage of our adversaries but do not force us to remake societies from within. Thus in the late 1970s he helped Zbigniew Brzezinski and Jimmy Carter to implement a human rights policy designed to embarrass the Soviet Union, but he has remained skeptical about putting troops on the ground to build Western-style democracy in places with no tradition of it.

Huntington's analysis of Vietnam derived from his newly emerging worldview. In the 1950s and 1960s the big issue in social science was political modernization. The conventional academic wisdom was that new countries in Africa and elsewhere would develop democracies and legal systems similar to ours. Huntington would have none of this. His insight about Vietnam—that the kind of authority that worked there was not at all like ours—fit into the larger theme elaborated in his book *Political Order in Changing Societies*

(1968). *Political Order* is a study of how states are formed, and is perhaps Huntington's most important book. In the fourteenth century the Arab historian Ibn Khaldun described in his *Muqaddimah* how desert nomads, in aspiring to the comforts of a sedentary life, created the dynamic for urbanization that was then captured by powerful dynasties. Huntington continued the story. He described how development leads to new patterns of instability, including upheavals and revolutions, which result in the building of more-complex institutions. *Political Order in Changing Societies,* though written three and a half decades ago, is still the clearest road map to what developing countries face in their attempts to establish stable and responsive governments in an era of globalization. The book opens with a bold assertion.

> The most important political distinction among countries concerns not their form of government but their degree of government. The differences between democracy and dictatorship are less than the differences between those countries whose politics embodies consensus, community, legitimacy, organization, effectiveness, [and] stability, and those countries whose politics is deficient in these qualities.

The statement that the distinction between democracies and dictatorships is less important than it seems will come as no surprise to those who have experienced the social chaos in, say, Nigeria and Ghana, despite the elections that those countries hold, and have also experienced the relative openness and civil stability of more autocratic societies, such as Jordan, Tunisia, and Singapore. More than other academics, Huntington pays attention to ground-level realities. Throughout his career he has displayed an academically atypical fondness for quoting on-the-scene observers (as well as academics) in his footnotes. "There are no academic sources for recent events," he told me. "There is only academic opinion."

The central argument in *Political Order* is that despite what we may instinctively believe, the American historical experience is inappropriate for understanding the challenges that developing countries face. "Americans believe in the unity of goodness," Huntington wrote. They "assume that all good things go together"—social progress, economic growth, political stability, and so on. But consider India, he suggested. India had one-tenth the per capita income of Argentina and Venezuela in the 1950s, yet it was politically more stable. Why? Part of the answer is something "bad": India's illiteracy. Illiteracy in India fostered democratic stability, because rural illiterates make fewer demands on government than a newly literate urban proletariat. Illiterates or semiliterates merely vote; literate people organize, and challenge the existing system. India, Huntington contended, was stable and democratic for decades despite its poverty because of an unusual combination of factors: a poorly educated electorate and a highly educated elite large enough to administer modern governmental institutions. Now that a newly literate lower middle class is emerging in India, the nation's politics have become far nastier.

Another problem for American thinking, Huntington continued, is that our history has taught us how to limit government, not how to build it from scratch. Just as our security, a product of geography, was largely unearned, so were our governing institutions and practices, an inheritance from seventeenth-century England. The Constitution is about controlling authority; throughout Asia, Africa, Latin America, and the formerly communist world the difficulty is to establish authority. "The problem," Huntington wrote, "is not to hold elections but to create organizations."

In politically advanced states loyalty is to institutions, not to groups. States like ours are the result of a long process of urbanization and enlightenment, but this process can be destabilizing in its own right. "The faster the enlightenment of the population, the more frequent the overthrow of the government," he observed. The

French and Mexican revolutions were preceded not by poverty but by sustained social and economic development. The economic growth that the global elite now champions around the world will lead to instability and upheaval before it leads to politically advanced societies.

At international conferences experts frequently wring their hands about corruption. *Political Order* demonstrates that the very modernization they champion causes corruption in the first place. The eighteenth century saw unprecedented levels of corruption in England, owing to the onset of the Industrial Revolution; the same can be said of nineteenth-century America. But corruption at this stage of development can be useful, Huntington wrote, and should not be high-mindedly disparaged. Corruption provides the means for assimilating new groups into the system. The selling of parliamentary seats, for example, is typical of an emerging democracy, and preferable to armed attacks against Parliament itself. Corruption, Huntington pointed out, is a less extreme form of alienation than violence: "He who corrupts a system's police officers is more likely to identify with the system than he who storms the system's police stations." In late-nineteenth-century America, legislatures and city councils were corrupted by utilities, railway companies, and new industrial corporations—the same forces that were spurring economic growth and helping to make the United States a world power. In India many economic activities would be paralyzed without baksheesh. Corruption in moderate doses can overcome unresponsive bureaucracy and be an instrument of progress.

At the same time, Huntington explained, the hurly-burly of modernization and corruption invites a puritanical reaction. The seamy trade-offs necessary for growth and stability are denounced by zealots, delegitimizing the political process. This happened in Iran a decade after *Political Order* was published.

The United States, Huntington said, has trouble understanding revolutionary ferment in the rest of the world because it never experienced a real revolution. Instead it went through a war of independence—and not even one "of natives against alien conquerors," like that of the Algerians against the French, but one of settlers against the home country. Real revolutions are different—bad—Huntington made clear. Fortunately, they are rare. Even as the proletariat in third-world slums continues to radicalize, the middle classes become increasingly conservative and more willing to fight for the existing order. Writing in the late 1960s, Huntington was describing the world of the early twenty-first century. When a revolution does occur, continued economic deprivation "may well be essential to its success." The idea that food shortages and other hardships caused by economic sanctions will lead to the overthrow of a revolutionary regime like Saddam Hussein's or Fidel Castro's is nonsense, in Huntington's view. Material sacrifices, although intolerable in a normal situation, are proof of ideological commitment in a revolutionary one: "Revolutionary governments may be undermined by affluence; but they are never overthrown by poverty." The Spanish and Canadian developers now building hotels in Havana may know better than the American government does how to undermine a revolutionary regime.

Huntington portrayed the problem of revolutions, monarchies, praetorian regimes, and feudal states by drawing on a wealth of examples from all over the world. He offered a panorama of the messiness, intractability, and complexity of our times, even as he efficiently distilled and summarized. In one sentence (in *Political Order*) he laid out the different roles played by militaries throughout the twentieth century: "In the world of oligarchy, the soldier is a radical; in the middle class world, he is a participant and arbiter; as the mass society looms . . . he becomes the conservative guardian of the existing order." A better description of the changing role of the Turkish army over the decades, or of the evolving status of the Egyptian army, has never been written. Indeed, the more backward the society, the more progressive the role of the military may be—

and the more cautious the West should be about wanting to replace it with civilian politicians.

America's confidence in "democratic" reform for its own sake is misplaced. "Reform can be a catalyst of revolution," Huntington wrote, "rather than a substitute for it . . . great revolutions have followed periods of reform, not periods of stagnation and repression." In any case, reform in underdeveloped societies is effected not by transparency and greater public participation but, as Mustafa Kemal Atatürk showed in Turkey, by "celerity and surprise—those two ancient principles of war." If a reform program is revealed gradually, a free press will dissect it and create opposition to it. Because one sector of society will support one reform but not another, a reformer must work by stealth, isolating one set of issues from the next, and often relying not on the media but on the gaps in communication that exist within a society.

But mass communications work their own magic, as Huntington admitted in a long coda to *Political Order* that he published later, *The Third Wave* (1991). This book, subtitled "Democratization in the Late 20th Century," has been called "universalist and militantly pro-democracy" by the French scholar and otherwise harsh Huntington critic Pierre Hassner. Huntington has always been a liberal, but one who refuses to retreat into easy platitudes for the sake of a carefully constructed reputation. His books illustrate what academic tenure is supposed to be about but often isn't: the freedom, provided by occupational security, to express views that are (at least in the academy) unpopular, unconventional, unwelcome, and bold.

VI.

The 1960s presented Huntington with some trying moments. He was followed through Harvard Yard by chanting demonstrators, who had read in the *Harvard Crimson* about his association with the Johnson administration. The Center for International Affairs, where Huntington worked, was occupied and then firebombed. Huntington's young son awoke one morning to find the words "War Criminal Lives Here" painted on the front door.

Huntington was not deterred from further government service. As noted, he joined the Carter administration, and helped President Carter to craft a foreign policy that was an expression of our human rights ideals. This was not a matter of soft sanctimony but a hard-edged tool that posed severe political problems for the Soviets. As the coordinator for security planning, a job created for him by Brzezinski, Carter's national security advisor, Huntington also wrote "Presidential Directive 18," a comprehensive overview of U.S.-Soviet relations that helped to galvanize the National Security Council against accommodation with Moscow. At a time when pessimism was widespread, after Soviet advances in Angola and Ethiopia, and with leftist third-world majorities dominating the United Nations, Huntington created a battalion of task forces to evaluate where the Soviets and the Americans stood with regard to weapons production, intelligence gathering, economics, diplomacy, and other areas. He and his team concluded that the Soviet advantage was temporary, and that the West would eventually move out ahead. They strongly recommended that the United States commence a military buildup and create a Persian Gulf rapid-reaction force. The last two years of Carter's presidency and the eight years of Ronald Reagan's presidency would see those recommendations become reality.

Only in 1981 did Huntington get around to publishing a book about the 1960s, *American Politics: The Promise of Disharmony*. Most generations in history have been organizational ones, preferring to motor along in their daily grooves, directed by others. Why, Huntington asked, are some generations different? His answer was that the 1960s constituted a "creedal passion period," something that erupts every few generations in Anglo-Saxon culture and has its roots in England's seventeenth-century Civil War; the New World experienced something similar in the Protestant Great Awakening of the 1740s. Despite all the drugs and sex, Huntington viewed the 1960s demonstrators as essentially Puritans, upset that our institutions were not living up to our ideals. It is the very promise of those ideals—which cannot possibly be fulfilled in any age—that accounts for the "central agony" in American politics.

Like America in the 1950s and 1960s, early-seventeenth-century England was in the throes of rapid economic development and social change—even as the peers and the gentry became frustrated with an increasingly impersonal government. The result was a Puritan uprising against the Crown in the hopes of erecting a morality-based society. It culminated in the conservative Restoration. The Great Awakening, a century later, was another Puritan revival, as American evangelicals, imbued with pioneer optimism and impatient with the status quo, fanned out over New England in a contest for souls.

The Great Awakening, Huntington wrote, "bequeathed to the American people the belief that they were engaged in a righteous effort to insure the triumph of good over evil"—which resulted in what Huntington and others called the American Creed. The creed became the touchstone of our national identity, because for the first few decades of our country's history there was little else to separate us from our English cousins. Allegiance to the creed would allow one generation of immigrants after another to Americanize rapidly while retaining elements of their ethnic cultures. Unlike other national creeds, ours is universalistic, democratic, egalitarian, and individualistic. The Jacksonian age of the 1820s and 1830s was a creedal-passion period, and so were the Populist-Progressive years at the turn of the twentieth century.

"Opposition to power, and suspicion of government as the most dangerous embodiment of power, are the central themes of American political thought," Huntington wrote. And it is true: Just look at our extremist groups. Whereas both the right and the left in Europe have traditionally favored a strong state, both right-wing and left-wing radicals in America have always demanded more "popular control." Indeed, the very institutions required to deal with foreign enemies were excoriated by the 1960s militants. "The arrogance of power was superseded by the arrogance of morality," Huntington wrote. The Old Left was identified with the working class and the labor unions, but the New Left "eschewed the working class and stressed moralism rather than ideology." The New Left, explained a leader of Students for a Democratic Society whom Huntington quoted, "begins from moral values, which are held as absolute"—Puritanism in its most unadulterated form.

The aftermath of creedal passion is cynical indifference followed by the return of conservatism; creedal passion holds government and society to standards that they simply cannot meet. Nevertheless, Huntington believes, creedal passion is at the core of America's greatness. By holding officials and institutions to impossible standards in a way no other country does, the United States has periodically reinvented itself through evolution rather than revolution. What will the next creedal-passion period be about? "Power is now seen as corporate. So the next outburst of creedal passion may be against hegemonic corporate capitalism."

VII.

The early 1990s were a time of optimism and even triumphalism in the West. The Cold War had just been won. Neoconservatives assumed that democratic elections and the unleashing of market forces would improve life everywhere. Liberals assumed that power politics and huge defense budgets were relics of the past. News stories heralded the growing clout and effectiveness of the United Nations. A new transnational elite was emerging, composed of prominent academics and business leaders who believed that the world was on the verge of creating a truly global culture.

Then Samuel Huntington published an article titled "The Clash of Civilizations?" The article, which appeared in *Foreign Affairs* in 1993, was partly conceived in one of Huntington's seminars, where the paradigm of a world unified by globalization was challenged in classroom discussion. There was little evidence that any sort of universal civilization existed outside the confines of a small, highly educated elite. The fact that the United States and China, for example, could communicate with each other more easily did not mean that they were any more likely to agree with each other. Indeed, the global media spotlight in places like the West Bank and Northern Ireland often magnified misunderstandings. Considering the contrarian nature of Huntington's previous ideas—corruption can sometimes be good; the difference between democracy and dictatorship is less than we think; the sixties radicals were puritanical— "The Clash of Civilizations?" should not have caused much of a stir. In light of subsequent events Huntington's thesis may even seem unremarkable—the ironic fate of true prescience.

> It is my hypothesis that the fundamental source of conflict in this new world will not be primarily ideological or primarily economic. The great divisions among humankind and the dominating source of conflict will be cultural. Nation states will remain the most powerful actors in world affairs, but the principal conflicts of global politics will occur between nations and groups of different civilizations. . . . Conflict between civilizations will be the latest phase of the evolution of conflict in the modern world.

But these words did indeed stir passions. An angry response was instantaneous. So was the sheer interest in what Huntington had to say. "The Clash of Civilizations?" was translated into twenty-six languages; scholarly conferences were organized around the world to debate the article. "Unlike Sam's previous works," Brzezinski told me, "the title of this one said it all. So people reacted to a captivating title without reading the interesting nuances in the text itself." Huntington's statement that beyond the universities, luxury hotels, and spanking new suburbs the world was being coarsened with new social and cultural tensions—feeding new political conflicts—was immensely threatening to an elite whose cosmopolitan lifestyle was insulated from the realities that Huntington was describing. For elites in the third world especially, to acknowledge the truth of Huntington's points would have been to acknowledge the fragility of their own status in their respective societies.

Huntington did not merely say that parts of the world were anarchic, and that catastrophe loomed in Africa and Asia; many analysts were willing to admit that, even if they refused to accord it the proper significance. He also said that the demise of communism in no way meant the demise of the atavistic territorial battles that had been the stuff of power politics since time immemorial. The liberal project to unite the world through universal values was destined to be stillborn. For those who thought that the end of the Cold War meant a less dangerous world, this sort of thinking was an insult. Many of the criticisms of "The Clash" amounted to mere value judgments—"morally dangerous," "a self-fulfilling prophecy"—rather than substantive disputation.

But there was an attack on grounds of substance, too. The central charge: Huntington was being simplistic. The Islamic world, for example, wasn't uniform. Individual Muslim states often fought or denounced one another. Huntington answered his critics in a second *Foreign Affairs* article, later in 1993, maintaining that simplicity was the very point: "When people think seriously, they think abstractly; they conjure up simplified pictures of reality called concepts, theories, models, paradigms. Without such intellectual constructs, there is, William James said, only 'a bloomin' buzzin' confusion.'" The paradigm of the Cold War, Huntington pointed out, did not account for many of the conflicts and other developments from 1945 to 1989; nevertheless, it summed up reality better than other paradigms did. In an age when so many academics and intellectuals, fearful of attacks from other academics and intellectuals, prefer the safety of mutually canceling subtleties, Huntington was asserting—and defending—the scholar's duty to say what he actually thinks in stark and general terms.

In the book that emerged from his article, *The Clash of Civilizations and the Remaking of World Order* (1996), Huntington offered a wealth of other insights. He showed that whereas the West has generated ideologies, the East has generated religions—and explained that religion is now the more menacing force on the international scene. He pointed out, counterintuitively, that because communism was a Central European ideology, the Soviet Union was philosophically closer to the West than is the Eastern Orthodox Russia that has succeeded it. He reminded us that the Cold War was a fleeting event compared with the age-old struggle between the West and Islam. In the Middle Ages, Muslim armies advanced through Iberia as far as France, and through the Balkans as far as the gates of Vienna. A similar process of advance, demographically rather than militarily, is now under way in Europe. "The dangerous clashes of the future," Huntington wrote, "are likely to arise from the interaction of Western arrogance, Islamic intolerance, and Sinic [Chinese] assertiveness."

In the years since his article and book were published, NATO has expanded into three Protestant-Catholic countries while leaving out several Eastern Orthodox countries, so that the map of NATO, with some exceptions, resembles that of medieval Western Christendom. Meanwhile, Christians continue to flee the Middle East as the specter of Islamic oppression rises in Lebanon, Syria, and the Palestinian territories. American church groups, liberal and conservative alike, have united to support Christians fighting for human rights in China, and against Muslims slaughtering Christians in Sudan. Huntington's ability to account for these and so many other phenomena within a general theory points up the lasting importance of his work. Meanwhile, where are the Kremlinologists who during the Cold War told us that the Soviet system was basically stable; or the Africanists who in the 1960s and 1970s predicted growth and development in places that have since been torn apart by war?

How do Huntington's ideas apply to the current crisis stemming from the terrorist attacks in New York and Washington? He speaks with reluctance about specific policies the United States ought to pursue. Huntington has warned in the past that it is pointless to expect people who are not at all like us to become significantly more like us; this well-meaning instinct only causes harm. "In the emerging world of ethnic conflict and civilizational clash, Western belief in the universality of Western culture suffers three problems: it is false, it is immoral, and it is dangerous." In the incipient war being led by the United States, the utmost caution is required to keep the focus on the brute fact of terrorism. He observes that Osama bin Laden, for his part, clearly hopes to incite civilizational conflict between Islam and the West. The United States must prevent this from happening, chiefly by assembling a coalition against terrorism that crosses civilizational lines. Beyond that, the United States must take this opportunity to accomplish two things: first, to draw the nations of the West more tightly together; and second, to try to understand more realistically how the world looks through the eyes of other people. This is a time for a kind of tough-minded humility in our objectives and for an implacable but measured approach in our methods.

And he adds this coda, about the world in which we live: "It is a dangerous place, in which large numbers of people resent our wealth, power, and culture, and vigorously oppose our efforts to persuade or coerce them to accept our values of human rights, democracy, and capitalism. In this world America must learn to distinguish among our true friends who will be with us and we with them through thick and thin; opportunistic allies with whom we have some but not all interests in common; strategic partner-competitors with whom we have a mixed relationship; antagonists who are rivals but with whom negotiation is possible; and unrelenting enemies who will try to destroy us unless we destroy them first."

VIII.

Huntington has never confused good intentions with clarity of analysis. He knows that the job of a political scientist is not necessarily to improve the world but to say what he thinks is going on in it— and then to prescribe a course of action that serves the interests of his government. In an article for *Foreign Affairs* in 1997, "The Erosion of American National Interests," he wrote, "At some point in the future, the combination of security threat and moral challenge will require Americans once again to commit major resources to the defense of national interests." Such a renewed mobilization, he continued, is easier to accomplish when it proceeds from "a low base" than when it is redirected from entrenched foreign policy enterprises that are less vital to our security. Thus, a restrained approach to the world might allow us in case of emergency to mobilize more quickly than if we were involved too deeply in too many places, in the service of either "particularistic" lobbies or some grand conception of human rights or how to organize the world.

Real conservatism cannot aspire to lofty principles, because its task is to defend what already exists. The conservative dilemma is that conservatism's legitimacy can come only from being proved right by events, whereas liberals, whenever they are proved wrong, have universal principles to fall back on. Samuel Huntington has always held liberal ideals. But he knows that such ideals cannot survive without power, and that power requires careful upkeep.

If American political science leaves any lasting intellectual monument, the work of Samuel Huntington will be one of its pillars. A passage in the conclusion of *American Politics* has always seemed to me to capture the essence of Huntington's enduring judgment and political sensibility: "Critics say that America is a lie because its reality falls so far short of its ideals. They are wrong. America is not a lie; it is a disappointment. But it can be a disappointment only because it is also a hope."

12.

Why John Mearsheimer Is Right (About Some Things)

THE ATLANTIC, JANUARY/FEBRUARY 2012

"I—China—want to be the Godzilla of Asia, because that's the only way for me—China—to survive! I don't want the Japanese violating my sovereignty the way they did in the twentieth century. I can't trust the United States, since states can never be certain about other states' intentions. And as good realists, we—the Chinese— want to dominate Asia the way the Americans have dominated the Western Hemisphere." John J. Mearsheimer, the R. Wendell Harrison Distinguished Service Professor of Political Science at the University of Chicago, races on in a mild Brooklyn accent, banging his chalk against the blackboard and erasing with his bare hand, before two dozen graduate students in a three-hour seminar titled "Foundations of Realism."

Mearsheimer writes "ANARCHY" on the board, explaining that the word does not refer to chaos or disorder. "It simply means that there is no centralized authority, no night watchman or ultimate arbiter, that stands above states and protects them." (The opposite of anarchy, he notes, borrowing from Columbia University's Kenneth Waltz, is hierarchy, which is the ordering principle of domestic politics.) Then he writes "THE UNCERTAINTY OF INTENTIONS" and explains: The leaders of one great power in this anarchic jungle of a world can never know what the leaders of a rival great power are thinking. Fear is dominant. "This is the tragic essence of international politics," he thunders. "It provides the basis for realism, and people hate people like me, who point this out!" Not finished, he adds: "*The uncertainty of intentions* is my Sunday punch in defense of realism, whenever realism is attacked."

After class, Mearsheimer leads me down grim, cement-gray hallways to his office in Albert Pick Hall, whose brutalist Gothic architecture he describes as "East Germany circa the 1960s." At sixty-four years of age, with round wire-framed glasses, and gray hair fringing his balding head, he is genial, voluble, animated: the opposite of the dry, heartless, muscular prose that he is known for and that has enraged so many people. His office, littered with books and file boxes, is graced with pictures of America's two preeminent realists: Hans Morgenthau from the first half of the twentieth century, and Samuel Huntington from the second half. Morgenthau, a German Jewish refugee who, like Mearsheimer, taught at the University of Chicago, once wrote that realism "appeals to historic precedent rather than to abstract principles [of justice] and aims at the realization of the lesser evil rather than of the absolute good." Huntington, the late Harvard professor who died in 2008, challenged the policy elite with his famous idea of a "clash of civilizations," and with his earlier notion, perhaps more provocative, that how people are governed—democratically or not—matters less than the degree to which they are governed: In other words, the United States always had more in common with the Soviet Union than with any weakly governed state in Africa.

Mearsheimer reveres both men for their bravery in pointing out unpopular truths, and throughout his career he has tried to emulate them. Indeed, in a country that has always been hostile to what realism signifies, he wears his "realist" label as a badge of honor. "To realism!" he says as he raises his wineglass to me in a toast at a local restaurant. As Ashley J. Tellis, Mearsheimer's former student and now, after a stint in the Bush administration, a senior associate at the Carnegie Endowment, later tells me: "Realism is alien to the American tradition. It is consciously amoral, focused as it is on interests rather than on values in a debased world. But realism never dies, because it accurately reflects how states actually behave, behind the façade of their values-based rhetoric."

Mearsheimer's intellectually combative nature first disturbed the policy elite in 1988, with the publication of his critical biography, *Liddell Hart and the Weight of History*. In it he asserts that the revered British military theorist Sir Basil H. Liddell Hart was wrong on basic strategic questions of the period between the first and second world wars, especially in his opposition to the use of military force against the Third Reich, and was a de facto appeaser even after evidence had surfaced about the systematic murder of Jews. Mearsheimer expected that his perspective would draw fire from British reviewers who had been close to Liddell Hart, which it did. "Other political scientists work on capillaries. John goes for the jugular," notes Richard Rosecrance, a retired professor at the University of California, Los Angeles, who mentored Mearsheimer in the 1970s.

Mearsheimer certainly triggered a bloodbath with a 2006 article that became a 2007 book written with the Harvard professor Stephen M. Walt and dedicated to Huntington, *The Israel Lobby and U.S. Foreign Policy*, which alleges that groups supportive of Israel have pivotally undermined American foreign policy interests, especially in the run-up to the Iraq War. Some critics, like the Johns Hopkins University professor Eliot Cohen, accused Mearsheimer and Walt outright of anti-Semitism, noting that their opinions had won the endorsement of the white supremacist David Duke. Many others accused them of providing potent ammunition for anti-Semites. A former Chicago colleague of Mearsheimer labeled the book "piss-poor, monocausal social science."

Last fall, Mearsheimer reenergized his critics by favorably blurbing a book on Jewish identity that many commentators denounced as grotesquely anti-Semitic. The blurb became a blot on Mearsheimer's judgment, given the book's author's revolting commentary elsewhere, and was considered evidence of an unhealthy obsession with Israel and Jewishness on Mearsheimer's part.

The real tragedy of such controversies, as lamentable as they are, is that they threaten to obscure the urgent and enduring message of Mearsheimer's life's work, which topples conventional foreign policy shibboleths and provides an unblinking guide to the course the United States should follow in the coming decades. Indeed, with the most critical part of the world, East Asia, in the midst of an unprecedented arms race fed by acquisitions of missiles and submarines (especially in the South China Sea region, where states are motivated by old-fashioned nationalism rather than universal values), and with the Middle East undergoing less a democratic revolution than a crisis in central authority, we ignore Mearsheimer's larger message at our peril.

In fact, Mearsheimer is best known in the academy for his equally controversial views on China, and particularly for his 2001 magnum opus, *The Tragedy of Great Power Politics*. Writing in *Foreign Affairs* in 2010, the Columbia University professor Richard K. Betts called *Tragedy* one of the three great works of the Post Cold War era, along with Francis Fukuyama's *The End of History and the Last Man* (1992) and Huntington's *The Clash of Civilizations and the Remaking of World Order* (1996). And, Betts suggested, "once China's power is full grown," Mearsheimer's book may pull ahead of the other two in terms of influence. *The Tragedy of Great Power Politics* truly defines Mearsheimer, as it does realism. Mearsheimer sat me down in his office, overlooking the somber Collegiate Gothic structures of the University of Chicago, and talked for hours, over the course of several days, about *Tragedy* and his life.

One of five children in a family of German and Irish ancestry, and one of the three who went to service academies, Mearsheimer graduated from West Point in the bottom third of his class, even after he fell in love with political science in his junior year. He got his master's degree at the University of Southern California while stationed nearby in the Air Force, and went to Cornell for his doctorate. "I disagreed with almost everything I read, I venerated nobody. I found out what I thought by what I was against." After stints at the Brookings Institution and Harvard, he went to the University of Chicago in 1982, and has never left.

Whereas Harvard, at least in Mearsheimer's telling, is inclined to be a "government-policy shop" with close ties to Washington, the University of Chicago comes closer to a "pure intellectual environment." At Harvard, many students and faculty members alike are on the make, networking for that first, or next, position in government or the think tank world. The environment is vaguely unfriendly to theories or bold ideas, Huntington being the grand exception that proves the rule. After all, social science theories are gross simplifications of reality; even the most brilliant theories can be right, say, only 75 percent of the time. Critics unfailingly seize on any theory's shortcomings, damaging reputations. So the truly ambitious tend to avoid constructing one.

The University of Chicago, set off the beaten path in a society dominated by bicoastal elites, explains Mearsheimer, has always attracted "oddballs" with theories: political scientists who, while deeply respected, are at the same time not truly embraced by the American academic power structure. These iconoclasts have included Hans Morgenthau, as well as Leo Strauss, another German Jewish refugee, whom some link with neoconservatism. Realists especially have been outsiders in a profession dominated by liberal internationalists and others to the left.

For Mearsheimer, academia's hostility to realism is evident in the fact that Harvard, which aims to recruit the top scholars in every field, never tried to hire the two most important realist thinkers of the twentieth century, Morgenthau and Kenneth Waltz. But at Chicago, a realist like Mearsheimer, who loves teaching and never had ambitions for government service, can propound theories and unpopular ideas, and revel in the uproar they cause. Whatever the latest groupthink happens to be, Mearsheimer almost always instinctively wants to oppose it—especially if it emanates from Washington.

The best grand theories tend to be written no earlier than middle age, when the writer has life experience and mistakes behind him to draw upon. Morgenthau's 1948 classic, *Politics Among Nations,* was published when he was forty-four, Fukuyama's *The End of History* was published as a book when he was forty, and Huntington's *Clash of Civilizations* as a book when he was sixty-nine. Mearsheimer began writing *The Tragedy of Great Power Politics* when he was in his mid-forties, after working on it for a decade. Published just before 9/11, the book intimates the need for America to avoid strategic distractions and concentrate on confronting China. A decade later, with the growth of China's military might vastly more apparent than it was in 2001, and following the debacles of the Iraq and Afghanistan wars, its clairvoyance is breathtaking.

Tragedy begins with a forceful denial of perpetual peace in favor of perpetual struggle, with great powers primed for offense, because they can never be sure how much military capacity they will need in order to survive over the long run. Because every state is forever insecure, Mearsheimer counsels, the internal nature of a state is less important as a factor in its international behavior than we think. "Great powers are like billiard balls that vary only in size," he intones. In other words, Mearsheimer is not one to be especially impressed by a state simply because it is a democracy. As he asserts early on, "Whether China is democratic and deeply enmeshed in the global economy or autocratic and autarkic will have little effect on its behavior, because democracies care about security as much as non-democracies do." Indeed, a democratic China could be more technologically innovative and economically robust, with consequently more talent and money to lavish on its military. (A democratic Egypt, for that matter, could create greater security challenges for the United States than an autocratic Egypt. Mearsheimer is not making moral judgments. He is merely describing how states interact in an anarchic world.)

Face it, Mearsheimer says in his book, quoting the historian James Hutson: the world is a "brutal, amoral cockpit." To make sure readers get the point, he taps the British scholar E. H. Carr's 1939 book, *The Twenty Years' Crisis, 1919–1939,* which takes a wrecking ball to liberal internationalism. One of its main points: "Whatever moral issues may be involved, there is an issue of power which cannot be expressed in terms of morality." To wit, in the 1990s we were able to intervene to save lives in the Balkans only because the Serbian regime was weak and had no nuclear weapons; against a Russian regime that was at the same time committing incalculable human rights violations in Chechnya, we did nothing, just as we did nothing to halt ethnic cleansing in the Caucasus. States take up human rights only if doing so does not contradict the pursuit of power.

But being a realist is not enough for Mearsheimer; he needs to be an "offensive realist," as he calls himself. "Offensive realism," he writes in *Tragedy,* "is like a powerful flashlight in a dark room": It cannot explain every action throughout hundreds of years of history, but he exhaustively goes through that history to demonstrate just how much it does explain. Whereas Hans Morgenthau's realism is rooted in man's imperfect nature, Mearsheimer's is structural, and therefore that much more inexorable. Mearsheimer cares relatively little about what individual statesmen can achieve, for the state of anarchy in the international system simply guarantees insecurity. Compared with Mearsheimer, Henry Kissinger and the late American diplomat Richard Holbrooke—two men usually contrasted with each other—are one and the same: romantic figures who believe they can pivotally affect history through negotiation. Kissinger, in fact, has written lush histories of statesmen in *A World Restored: Metternich, Castlereagh and the Problems of Peace 1812–1822* (1957) and *Diplomacy* (1994), embracing his subjects with charm and warmth, whereas Mearsheimer's *Tragedy* is cold and clinical. Kissinger and Holbrooke care deeply about the contingencies of each situation, and the personalities involved; Mearsheimer, who was always good at math and science in school, sees only schemata, even as his own historical analyses have helped to rescue political science from the purely quantitative studies favored by others in his field.

Just as Mearsheimer's theory of realism is opposed to Morgenthau's in being structural, it is also opposed to the structural realism of Columbia's Waltz in being offensive. Offensive realism posits that status quo powers don't exist: All great powers are perpetually on the offensive, even if obstacles may arise to prevent them from expanding their territory or influence.

What was Manifest Destiny, Mearsheimer asks the reader, except offensive realism? "Indeed, the United States was bent on establishing regional hegemony, and it was an expansionist power of the first order in the Americas": acquiring territory from European powers, massacring the native inhabitants, and instigating war with Mexico, in good part for the sake of security. Mearsheimer details Japan's record of aggression in Korea, China, Russia, Manchuria, and the Pacific Islands after its consolidation as a nation-state following the nineteenth-century Meiji Restoration. To demonstrate that the anarchic structure of the international system, not the internal characteristics of states, determines behavior, he shows how Italy, during the eight decades that it was a great power, was equally aggressive under both liberal and fascist regimes: going after North Africa, the Horn of Africa, the southern Balkans, southwestern Turkey, and southern Austria-Hungary. He characterizes Germany's

Otto von Bismarck as an offensive realist who engaged in conquest during his first nine years in office, and then restrained himself for the next nineteen. "In fact, [that restraint] was because Bismarck and his successors correctly understood that the German army had conquered about as much territory as it could without provoking a great-power war, which Germany was likely to lose." But when Mearsheimer picks up the story at the start of the twentieth century, Germany is again aggressive, because by now it controls a larger percentage of the world's industrial might than any other European state. Behind every assertion in this book is a wealth of historical data that helps explain why *Tragedy* continues, as Richard Betts predicted, to grow in influence.

"To argue that expansion is inherently misguided," Mearsheimer writes, "implies that all great powers over the past 350 years have failed to comprehend how the international system works. This is an implausible argument on its face." The problem with the "moderation is good" thesis is that "it mistakenly equates [so-called] irrational expansion with military defeat." But hegemony has succeeded many times. The Roman Empire in Europe, the Mughal Dynasty in the Indian subcontinent, and the Qing Dynasty in China are some of his examples, even as he mentions how Napoleon, Kaiser Wilhelm II, and Adolf Hitler all came close to success. "Thus, the pursuit of regional hegemony is not a quixotic ambition," though no state has yet achieved regional hegemony in the Eastern Hemisphere the way the United States achieved it in the Western Hemisphere.

The edgiest parts of *Tragedy* are when Mearsheimer presents full-bore rationales for the aggression of Wilhelmine Germany, Nazi Germany, and imperial Japan.

> The German decision to push for war in 1914 was not a case of wacky strategic ideas pushing a state to start a war it was sure to lose. It was . . . a calculated risk motivated in large part

by Germany's desire to break its encirclement by the Triple Entente, prevent the growth of Russian power, and become Europe's hegemon.

As for Hitler, he "did indeed learn from World War I." Hitler learned that Germany could not fight on two fronts at the same time, and he would have to win quick, successive victories, which, in fact, he achieved early in World War II. Japan's attack on Pearl Harbor was a calculated risk to avoid abandoning the Japanese empire in China and Southeast Asia in the face of a U.S. embargo on imported energy and machine tools.

Mearsheimer is no warmonger or militarist. His job as a political scientist is not to improve the world, but to say what he thinks is going on in it. And he thinks that while states rightly yearn for a values-based foreign policy, the reality of the anarchic international system forces them to behave according to their own interests. In his view, either liberal internationalism or neoconservatism is more likely than offensive realism to lead to the spilling of American blood. Indeed, because, as some argue, realism in the classical sense seeks the avoidance of war through the maintenance of a balance of power, it is the most humanitarian approach possible. (In this vein, fighting Nazi Germany was essential because the Nazis were attempting to overthrow the European balance-of-power system altogether.)

In the course of his five-hundred-plus-page defense of his own brand of realism, Mearsheimer popularizes two other concepts: "buck-passing" and the "stopping power of water." The latter concept leads Mearsheimer to propose—in 2001, mind you—an American foreign policy of restraint. But first, consider buck-passing. Whenever a new great power comes on the scene, one or more states will end up checking it. But every state will initially try to get someone else to do the checking: buck-passing "is essentially about who does the balancing, not whether it gets done." The United Kingdom, France, and the Soviet Union all buck-passed prior to World War II, each trying to get the other to be the one to bear the brunt of Hitler's onslaught. In Asia today, the United States quietly encourages Japan and India to build up their militaries in order to check China, but in the end, it has no country to whom it can pass the buck. Hence Mearsheimer's plea from a decade ago that we need to focus on China.

The "stopping power of water" is where *Tragedy,* in an analytical sense, builds toward its powerful conclusion. "Large bodies of water are formidable obstacles that cause significant power-projection problems," Mearsheimer writes. Great navies and air forces can be built, and soldiers transported to beachheads and airstrips, but conquering great land powers across the seas is difficult. This is why the United States and the United Kingdom have rarely been invaded by other great powers. It is also why the United States has almost never tried to permanently conquer territory in Europe or Asia, and why the United Kingdom has never tried to dominate continental Europe. Therefore, the "central aim of American foreign policy" is "to be the hegemon in the Western Hemisphere" only, and to prevent the rise of a similar hegemon in the Eastern Hemisphere. In turn, the proper role for the United States is as an "offshore balancer," balancing against the rise of a Eurasian hegemon and going to war only as a last resort to thwart it. But better to try buck-passing first, Mearsheimer advises, and come into a war only at the last moment, when absolutely necessary.

Mearsheimer tells me that the United States was right to enter World War II very late; that way it paid a smaller "blood price" than the Soviet Union. "Before D-Day, ninety-three percent of all German casualties had occurred on the eastern front," he says, adding that the devastation of the Soviet Union helped the United States in the Cold War to follow.

"How is offshore balancing different from neo-isolationism?" I ask him. "Isolationists," he responds, "believe that there is no place outside of the Western Hemisphere to which it is worth deploying our troops. But offshore balancers believe there are three critical areas that no other hegemon should be allowed to dominate: Europe, the Persian Gulf, and Northeast Asia. Thus," he goes on, "it was important to fight Nazi Germany and Japan in World War II. American history suits us to be offshore balancers—not isolationists, not the world's sheriff." Later, when I ask Mearsheimer about the Obama administration's slightly standoffish policies toward Libya and whether they are a good example of buck-passing, he says the problem with leading from behind in this case was that America's European allies lacked the military capacity to do the job efficiently. "If mass murder was truly in the offing, as it was in Rwanda," he tells me, "then I would have been willing to intervene in Libya. But it is unclear that was the case."

Such thinking is prologue to Mearsheimer's admonition that a struggle with China awaits us. "The Chinese are good offensive realists, so they will seek hegemony in Asia," he tells me, paraphrasing the conclusion to *Tragedy*. China is not a status quo power. It will seek to dominate the South China Sea as the United States has dominated the Greater Caribbean Basin. He continues: "An increasingly powerful China is likely to try to push the U.S. out of Asia, much the way the U.S. pushed European powers out of the Western Hemisphere. Why should we expect China to act any differently than the United States did? Are they more principled than we are? More ethical? Less nationalistic?" On the penultimate page of *Tragedy,* he warns:

> Neither Wilhelmine Germany, nor imperial Japan, nor Nazi Germany, nor the Soviet Union had nearly as much latent power as the United States had during their confrontations. . . . But if China were to become a giant Hong Kong, it would probably have somewhere on the order of four times as

much latent power as the United States does, allowing China
to gain a decisive military advantage over the United States.

Ten years after those lines were written, China's economy has
passed Japan's as the world's second largest. Its total defense spend-
ing in 2009 was $150 billion, compared with only $17 billion in
2001. But even more revealing is the pattern of China's military
modernization. "Force planning—the product of long-term com-
mitments and resource allocation decisions—is the heart of strategy," the military expert Thomas Donnelly, of the American
Enterprise Institute, wrote last year. And for more than a decade
now, China's military

> has shifted its focus from repelling a Soviet invasion and con-
> trolling domestic unrest to the sole problem of defeating U.S.
> forces in East Asia. This has been a strategic surprise to which
> no American administration has appropriately responded.

China is increasing its submarine fleet from 62 to 77 and has
tested a stealth fighter jet as part of a buildup also featuring surface
warships, missiles, and cyberwarfare. Andrew F. Krepinevich, the
president of the Center for Strategic and Budgetary Assessments,
believes that nations of the Western Pacific are slowly being "Fin-
landized" by China: They will maintain nominal independence but
in the end may abide by foreign policy rules set by Beijing. And the
more the United States is distracted by the Middle East, the more it
hastens this impending reality in East Asia, which is the geographical heart of the global economy and of the world's navies and air
forces.

Mearsheimer's critics say that offensive realism ignores ideology
and domestic politics altogether. They argue that he takes no account of China's society and economy and where they might be

headed. Indeed, simple theories like offensive realism are inherently superficial, and wrong in instances. Mearsheimer, for example, is still waiting for NATO to collapse, as he predicted it would in a 1990 *Atlantic* article. The fact that it hasn't owes as much to the domestic politics of Western states as it does to the objective security situation. And the stopping power of water did not prevent Japan from acquiring a great maritime empire in the early and middle part of the twentieth century; nor did it prevent the Allied invasion of Normandy. More generally, Mearsheimer's very cold, mathematical, states-as-billiard-balls approach ignores messy details—like the personalities of Adolf Hitler, Mao Zedong, Franklin Delano Roosevelt, and Slobodan Milošević—that have had a monumental impact in deciding how wars and crises turn out. International relations is as much about understanding Shakespeare—and the human passions and intrigues that Shakespeare exposes—as it is about understanding political science theories. It matters greatly that Deng Xiaoping was both utterly ruthless and historically perceptive, so that he could set China in motion to become such an economic and military juggernaut in the first place. Manifest Destiny owes as much to the canniness of President James K. Polk as it does to Mearsheimer's laws of historical determinism.

But given the limits of social science theories, even as we rely on them to help us make some sense of the Bruegelesque jumble of history, *The Tragedy of Great Power Politics* is a signal triumph. As Huntington once told his protégé Fareed Zakaria: "If you tell people the world is complicated, you're not doing your job as a social scientist. They already know it's complicated. Your job is to distill it, simplify it, and give them a sense of what is the single [cause], or what are the couple of powerful causes that explain this powerful phenomenon."

Truly, Mearsheimer's theory of international relations allowed him to get both Gulf wars exactly right—and he's one of the few people to do so. As a good offshore balancer, Mearsheimer supported the First Gulf War against Saddam Hussein, in 1991. By occupying Kuwait, Iraq had positioned itself as a potential hegemon in the Persian Gulf, justifying U.S. military action. Moreover, as Mearsheimer asserted in several newspaper columns, the United States could easily defeat the Iraqi military. This assertion made him something of a lone wolf in academic circles, where many were predicting a military quagmire or calamity. The Democratic Party, to which most scholars subscribed, overwhelmingly opposed the war. Mearsheimer's confidence that fighting Saddam would be a "cakewalk" was based in part on his trips to Israel in the 1970s and '80s, when he was studying conventional military deterrence. The Israelis had told him that the Iraqi army, mired as it was in Soviet doctrine, was one of the Arab world's worst militaries.

But Mearsheimer's finest hour was the run-up to the Second Gulf War against Saddam, in 2003. This time, offshore balancing did not justify a war. Iraq was already contained and was not on the brink of becoming the hegemon of the Persian Gulf. And Mearsheimer felt strongly that a new war was a bad idea. He joined with Harvard's Stephen Walt and the University of Maryland's Shibley Telhami to lead a group of thirty-three scholars, many of them card-carrying academic realists, to sign a declaration opposing the war. On September 26, 2002, they published an advertisement on the *New York Times* op-ed page that cost $38,000, and they paid for it themselves. The top of the ad ran, WAR WITH IRAQ IS *NOT* IN AMERICA'S NATIONAL INTEREST. Among the bullet points was this: "Even if we win easily, we have no plausible exit strategy. Iraq is a deeply divided society that the United States would have to occupy and police for many years to create a viable state."

Mearsheimer opposed not only the Iraq War, but also the neo-conservative vision of regional transformation, which, as he tells me, was the "polar opposite" of offshore balancing. He was not against democratization in the Arab world per se, but felt that it should not be attempted—and could not be accomplished—by an extended deployment of U.S. troops in Iraq and Afghanistan. And as he explains to me, he now sees an attack on Iran as yet another distraction from dealing with the challenge of China in East Asia. A war with Iran, he adds, would drive Iran further into the arms of Beijing.

During the buildup to the Iraq War, Mearsheimer and Walt began work on what would become a *London Review of Books* article and later *The Israel Lobby and U.S. Foreign Policy*. (*The Atlantic* had originally commissioned the piece, only to reject it owing to a profound disagreement between the editors and the authors over its objectivity.) In some respects, *The Israel Lobby* reads as an appendix to *The Tragedy of Great Power Politics*—almost a case study of how great powers should not act. Many of those loosely associated with the lobby supported the Iraq War, which Mearsheimer saw as a diversion from the contest with China. The so-called special relationship between the United States and Israel, by further entangling the United States in the problems of the Middle East, contradicted the tenets of offshore balancing. And proponents of the special relationship have routinely justified it by citing Israel's status as a stable democracy in the midst of unstable authoritarian states—but that internal attribute, in Mearsheimer's view, is largely irrelevant.

Mearsheimer denies that he cowrote the book to explain away the contradictions that the U.S.-Israel relationship poses to his larger theory. He wrote it, he says, because the special relationship is a major feature of U.S. foreign policy in its own right. He might also have said that the Israel lobby is an example of how domestic politics do intrude in foreign policy; thus his theory of offensive realism is less an explanation of events than an aspiration for how states should behave. He has said elsewhere that the lobby is an "anomaly" in American history. An anomaly is certainly what his book about it is.

Whereas *Tragedy* is a theory, *The Israel Lobby* is a polemic, a tightly organized marshaling of fact and argument that does not necessarily delegitimize Israel, but does delegitimize the American-Israeli special relationship. *Lobby* lacks the commanding, albeit cruel, objectivity that Mearsheimer evinces in *Tragedy*. It negatively distorts key episodes in Israel's history—beginning with its founding—and in effect denies Israel the license that Mearsheimer grants other countries, including China, to act as good offensive realists. He and Walt equate U.S. support for Israel with Soviet support for Cuba, thereby equating a pulsating democracy with a semi-failed authoritarian state. And while *Tragedy* is rich in explication, *Lobby* is merely tedious, pummeling the reader with lists of names of people and organizations whom the authors group together as advancing the American-Israeli special relationship and the Iraq War, but who in fact often have had profound disagreements among themselves. Meanwhile, the motivations of America's political leaders at the time—the putative targets of the lobby's pressure, and thus the ones best able to assess the lobby's strength—go largely unexplored. This failure to establish a link between the lobby and White House decision making undermines the book. As the Middle East expert Dennis Ross has suggested, had Al Gore been elected president in 2000, he probably would not have invaded Iraq, even though he had much closer ties to prominent Jews and others in the lobby than did Bush.

Nevertheless, *The Israel Lobby* contains a fundamental analytic truth that is undeniable: The United States and Israel, like most states, have some different interests that inevitably push up against any enduring special relationship, especially because their security situations are so vastly different. To start with, the United States is a continent-size country protected by oceans, while Israel is a small country half a world away, surrounded by enemy states. Because the geographical situations of the United States and Israel are so dissimilar, their geopolitical interests can never completely overlap in the way that Israel's most fervent supporters contend. (Iran's nuclear program is a far more acute threat to Israel than it is to the United States.) "The fact that Israel is a democracy is important," Mearsheimer tells me. "But it is not sufficient to justify the terms of the special relationship. We should treat Israel as a normal country, like we treat Britain or Japan."

What particularly exasperates Mearsheimer and Walt is the lack of conditionality in the special relationship. They admit that making American support for Israel "more conditional would not remove all sources of friction" between Arab countries and the United States; nor do they deny "the presence of genuine anti-Semitism in various Arab countries." But they cannot condone a situation in which the United States has, over the decades, given Israel more than $180 billion in economic and military assistance, "the bulk of it comprising direct grants rather than loans," and yet can barely achieve modest negotiating goals such as getting Israel to stop expanding West Bank settlements for ninety days, let alone dismantle them, even though the Palestinians have been willing at times to make major concessions. (And the United States has been willing to throw in major sweeteners in the form of advanced military hardware.) Mearsheimer and Walt repeatedly say in their book that they believe the United States should militarily defend Israel if it is in mortal danger, but that the Israelis must be much more cooperative in light of all the aid they get. But, as they also argue, the reason the Israelis are not more cooperative is that in the final analysis, they don't have to be—which, in turn, is because of the pro-Israel lobby. Thus, in the spirit of Huntington, the authors distill a complicated situation down to a single, powerful cause.

I see nothing wrong or illegitimate about this core argument. And no amount of nitpicking by their critics of *The Israel Lobby*'s hundred pages of endnotes can detract from it. I say this as someone who is a veteran of the Israel Defense Forces and who supported the Iraq War (a position I have come to deeply regret). Say what you will about *The Israel Lobby*, but as Justine Rosenthal—who is a former editor of *The National Interest,* a leading foreign policy journal, and is now with *Newsweek*—told me, "It changed the debate on Israel, even if it did not change the policy." She added: "John is one of the clearest logical thinkers I know, who hammers his points home well." Indeed, if you put *Lobby* together with *Tragedy,* you have the beginnings of a prudent grand strategy for America: Invest less in one part of the world and more in another, events permitting. Secretary of State Hillary Clinton recently proposed that the United States should attempt to pivot away from the Middle East toward the Asia-Pacific region, a realization that Mearsheimer came to years ago.

On several occasions, Mearsheimer and Walt approvingly bring up the Middle East policy of President Dwight D. Eisenhower, which was more evenhanded vis-à-vis Israel and the Arab states: Without being hostile, it lacked the effusive warmth that more-recent American presidents have demonstrated toward the Jewish state. When I say to Mearsheimer, "That's the kind of American policy you and Walt really want in the Middle East, isn't it?" he responds: "That's exactly right. Eisenhower came down like a ton of bricks on Britain, France, and Israel—U.S. allies, all three—to force them to withdraw from Sinai in 1956. Imagine," he goes on, "if we had Eisenhower in the post-'67 period, or now." Mearsheimer's argument is that Eisenhower would have quickly forced Israel out of the occupied territories, and all parties concerned—Israel especially—would have benefited over the long run. No doubt decades of occupation have fueled hatred of Israel among Egyptians, Jordanians, and others. Given that Israel's electoral system helps assure weak governments—which are beholden in varying degrees to small right-wing parties opposed to substantial territorial withdrawal—perhaps the only chance Israel has of not becoming an apartheid society is if an American president finds the gumption to adopt an Eisenhower-esque approach and force Israel to withdraw from significant portions of the West Bank, wrangling Palestinian concessions in the process. "You don't have to trust me, Steve Walt, or Jimmy Carter, just listen to former Israeli prime minister Ehud Olmert," whose November 28, 2007, statement Mearsheimer quotes to me:

> If the day comes when the two-state solution collapses, and we face a South African–style struggle for equal voting rights . . . then, as soon as that happens, the State of Israel is finished.

Moreover, the revolt against calcified central authority in the Middle East, while in the long run beneficial to the emergence of more-liberal regimes, may in the short and middle term yield more-chaotic and more-populist ones, which will create more rather than fewer security problems for Israel. The cost to Israel of its unwillingness to make territorial concessions will grow rather than diminish.

Even as Mearsheimer is attacked, whenever he publishes something—a recent book on why diplomats are forced to lie, or a recent essay decrying both liberal and neoconservative imperialism—he breaks new ground. A collection of his critics' academic essays published in 2010, *History and Neorealism,* takes aim at Mearsheimer's theories in *Tragedy.* Some of the criticism is scathing, proving that Mearsheimer is the political science world's enfant terrible much more because of *Tragedy* than because of *The Israel Lobby.* (The essayists attack his theory for its lack of historical subtlety, but here, too, like Huntington, Mearsheimer is setting the terms of the debate.) Despite the media controversy that surrounded *The Israel Lobby,* his latest book, *Why Leaders Lie* (2011), attracted generous jacket blurbs from academic eminences such as the Princeton professor Robert O. Keohane and former editors of both *Foreign Affairs* and *Foreign Policy.* Within media ranks, *The Israel Lobby* has delegitimized Mearsheimer. Inside the service academy where I taught for two years, in the think tank world where I work, and in various government circles with which I am acquainted, Mearsheimer is quietly held in higher regard because of familiarity with his other books, but the controversy (and its echoes last fall) has surely hurt him.

Mearsheimer, who is not modest, believes it is a reliance on theory that invigorates his thinking. Returning to his principal passion, China, he tells me: "I have people all the time telling me that they've just returned from China and met with all these Chinese who want a peaceful relationship. I tell them that these Chinese will not be in power in twenty or thirty years, when circumstances may be very different. Because we cannot know the future, all we have to rely upon is theory. If a theory can explain the past in many instances, as my theory of offensive realism can, it might be able to say something useful about the future." And it is likely to be China's future, rather than Israel's, that will ultimately determine Mearsheimer's reputation. If China implodes from a socioeconomic crisis, or evolves in some other way that eliminates its potential as a threat, Mearsheimer's theory will be in serious trouble because of its dismissal of domestic politics. But if China goes on to become a great military power, reshaping the balance of forces in Asia, then Mearsheimer's *Tragedy* will live on as a classic.

REFLECTIONS

13.

On Foreign Policy, Donald Trump Is No Realist

THE WASHINGTON POST, NOVEMBER 13, 2016

President-elect Donald Trump is being called a "realist" in for-eign policy. Don't believe it. He may have some crude realist instincts, but that only makes him a terrible messenger for realism. Realists like myself should be very nervous about his election.

Realism is a sensibility, not a specific guide to what to do in each crisis. And it is a sensibility rooted in a mature sense of the tragic—of all the things that can go wrong in foreign policy, so that caution and a knowledge of history are embedded in the realist mindset. Realism has been with us at least since Thucydides wrote *The Pelo-ponnesian War* in the fifth century B.C., in which he defined human nature as driven by fear (*phobos*), self-interest (*kerdos*), and honor (*doxa*). Because the realist knows that he must work with such ele-mental forces rather than against them, he also knows, for example, that order comes before freedom and interests come before values. After all, without order there is no freedom for anybody, and with-out interests a state has no incentive to project its values.

Trump has given no indication that he has thought about any of this. He appears to have no sense of history and therefore no mature sense of the tragic. A sense of history comes mainly from reading.

That's how we know in the first place about such things as our obligations to allies and our role as the defender of the West. All previous presidents in modern times, without being intellectuals, have been readers to some extent. But Trump seems post-literate, a man who has made an end run around books directly to the digital age, where nothing is vetted, context is absent, and lies proliferate.

Realists worship truth—for the ultimate lesson of history is that the truth of situations is often unpleasant. But Trump's statements throughout the campaign have repeatedly revealed a basic disregard of facts.

Realists know that while the balance of power is not a panacea, maintaining an advantageous balance of power with rivals is generally in a nation's interest. Russian president Vladimir Putin has upset the balance of power from Central Europe to the Middle East, something that we need urgently to rectify, at the very least for the sake of a stronger negotiating position with Russia. Trump appears to have no understanding of this. Indeed, rather than being realistic, his benign statements about Putin are dangerously naïve.

Realists know that because values follow interests and not the other way around, a free-trading regime in Asia gives us a greater stake in the region so that we have more incentive to project our values there. A free-trading regime among our allies also counters China's overbearing influence, which Trump claims he wants to curtail but—because he is not a realist—has no responsible idea about how to do it.

Realism is about moderation. It sees the value in the status quo while idealists only see the drawbacks in it. It is, therefore, wary of change. Trump, by contrast, wants an upheaval in the international system: from sparking trade wars, to increasing tensions with Mexico, to undermining NATO. Admitting the Baltic states into NATO may not have been altogether prudent from a realist point of view. But now that they are in the alliance, the credibility of NATO (and of the West) depends on defending them. Trump and his supporters clearly do not grasp this.

Realism, again, because it is a sensibility, and not a strategy, must be merged with a historically accurate vision of America's place in the world. That place is no better defined than by the location of the Holocaust Memorial Museum adjacent to the Mall, showing that the Holocaust, which happened to Jews in Europe, has been by consensus granted entry into our national consciousness. This does not mean that the United States must intervene every time there is a major human rights violation somewhere—for that would be unrealistic. But it does mean that it must always take notice and, when practical, participate in a response, because America's duty emerging out of the crucible of World War II and the Cold War has been to try—wherever possible—to expand the boundaries of civil society worldwide. Idealists are obsessed with this; realists are not. Realists know that national interest comes before any global interest. But realists, too, at least the respectable kind, harbor an internationalist vision.

History moves on. World War II and the Cold War recede. But the United States is the most well-endowed and advantageously located major state on Earth. That good fortune comes with responsibilities that extend beyond our own borders. Just look at the size of our three-hundred-warship Navy and the location of our aircraft carriers on any given week. Realism is about utilizing such power to protect allies without precipitating conflict. It is not about abandoning them and precipitating conflict as a consequence. Hopefully, Trump will become a realist, but he has a long way to go.

14.

The Post-Imperial Moment

THE NATIONAL INTEREST, MAY 2016

In 1935, the anti-Nazi writer and Austrian-Jewish intellectual Joseph Roth published a story, "The Bust of the Emperor," about an elderly count at the chaotic fringe of the former Habsburg Empire, who refused to think of himself as a Pole or an Italian, even though his ancestry encompassed both. In his mind, the only mark of "true nobility" was to be "a man above nationality," in the Habsburg tradition. "My old home, the Monarchy, alone," the count says, "was a great mansion with many doors and many chambers, for every condition of men." Indeed, the horrors of twentieth-century Europe, Roth wrote presciently, had as their backdrop the collapse of empires and the rise of uni-ethnic states, with fascist and communist leaders replacing the power of traditional monarchs.

Empire clearly had its evils, but one cannot deny its historical function—to provide stability and order to vast tracts of land occupied by different peoples. *If not empire, what then?* In fact, though very few will admit it, a rules-based international system and the raft of supranational and multinational groupings such as the North Atlantic Treaty Organization, European Union, International Monetary Fund, International Court of Justice, World Economic Forum, and so on are all attempts to replace—to greater and lesser extents—the function of empire. Silently undergirding this process since World War II has been the undeniable fact of American power—military, diplomatic, and economic—protecting the sea-lanes, the maritime choke points, and access to hydrocarbons, and in general providing some measure of security to the world. These tasks are amoral to the extent that they do not involve lofty principles, but without them there is no possibility for moral action anywhere. This is not traditional imperialism, which is no longer an option, but it is the best available replacement for it.

However, while the United States still remains the single strongest power on the globe, it is less and less an overwhelming one. The diffusion of central authority in new democracies everywhere, the spread of chaos in the Middle East and North Africa, and the rise of Russia, China, and Iran as regional hegemons all work to constrain the projection of American power. This is part of a process that has been going on for a century. At the end of World War I, formal multi-ethnic empires in Europe—those of the Habsburgs and Ottomans—crumbled. At the end of World War II, the overseas empires of the British and French began to do the same. The end of the Cold War heralded the collapse of the Soviet Empire in Eastern Europe and parts of Eurasia. The early twenty-first century witnessed the collapse or erosion of post-imperial strongmen in Iraq, Syria, Libya, and elsewhere: men who ruled absolutely within artificial borders erected by European imperialists. The American empire-of-sorts—that is, the last power standing whose troops and diplomats have found themselves in an imperial-like situation—is now giving way, too.

This partial retreat of American power has international and domestic causes. On the international front, vast urbanization, absolute rises in population, and natural-resource scarcities—as well as the rise of individual consciousness thanks to the communications revolution—have subtly eroded the power of central authority everywhere. The United States just cannot influence the decisions of individual countries the way it used to. Meanwhile, the maturation of both violent millennial movements and regional hegemons are direct threats to U.S. power projection. On the domestic front, the Obama administration, wishing to transform American society, has deliberately avoided major entanglements overseas and has sought to ameliorate relations with adversaries, principally Iran. This is a sign of imperial fatigue—a good thing, arguably, but something that nevertheless works to constrain U.S. power rather than to project it. The United States is signaling that it will less and less be providing world order, in other words. Rather than exclusively the philosophical work of one president, I suspect that this development is the beginning of a new phase in American foreign policy, following the hyperactivity of World War II and the Cold War—and their long aftershocks in the Balkans and the Middle East. Driving this relative retrenchment in Washington are social and economic turmoil at home and intractable complexity and upheaval abroad. Again, I am not saying that this is a wise course for the United States, but I am saying that it is real—and it is happening.

Because it is happening, and because of the economic, environmental, and social disruptions I have alluded to above, world disorder will only grow. The weakening and dissolution of small and medium-size states in Africa and the Middle East will advance to quasi-anarchy in larger states on which the geographic organization of Eurasia hinges: namely Russia and China. For the external aggression of these new regional hegemons is, in part, motivated by internal weakness, as they employ nationalism to assuage unraveling domestic economies upon which the stability of their societies rests. Then there is the European Union, which, if not crumbling, is surely weakening. Rather than a unified and coherent superstate, Europe will increasingly be a less than coherent confection of states and regions, as it dissolves internally—and also externally into the fluid geography of Eurasia, the Levant, and North Africa: demonstrated by Russian revanchism and the demographic assault of Muslim refugees. Of course, on a longer time horizon there is technology itself. As the strategist T. X. Hammes points out, the convergence of cheap drones, cyberwarfare, 3-D printing, and so on will encourage the diffusion of power among many states and stateless groups, rather than the concentration of it into a few imperial-like hands.

We are entering an age of what I call *comparative anarchy*, that is, a much higher level of anarchy compared to that of the Cold War and Post Cold War periods.

After all, globalization and the communications revolution have reinforced, rather than negated, geopolitics. The world map is now smaller and more claustrophobic, so that territory is more ferociously contested, and every regional conflict interacts with every other as never before. A war in Syria is inextricable from a terrorist outrage in France, even as Russia's intervention in Syria affects Europe's and America's policies toward Ukraine. This happens at a moment when, as I've said, multinational empires are gone, as are most totalitarian regimes in artificially drawn states where official borders do not configure with ethnic and sectarian ones. The upshot is a maelstrom of national and subnational groups in violent competition. And so, geopolitics—the battle for space and power—now occurs within states as well as between them. Cultural and religious differences are particularly exacerbated: for as group differences melt down in the crucible of globalization, they have to be artificially reinvented in more blunt and ideological form by, as it turns out, the communications revolution. It isn't the clash of civilizations so much as the clash of artificially reconstructed civilizations that is taking place. Witness the Islamic State, which does not represent Islam per se, but Islam igniting with the tyrannical conformity and mass hysteria inspired by the Internet and social media. The postmodern reinvention of identities only hardens geopolitical divides.

In the course of all this, technology is not erasing geography—it is sharpening it. Just look at China and India. For most of history, with exceptions like the spread of Buddhism in antiquity and the nineteenth-century Opium Wars, China and India had relatively little to do with each other, emerging as two civilizations separated by the Himalayas. But technological advances have collapsed distance. Indian intercontinental ballistic missiles can reach Chinese cities and Chinese fighter jets can include the Indian subcontinent in their arc of operations, even as Indian warships have visited the South China Sea and Chinese warships have sailed throughout the Indian Ocean. A new strategic geography of rivalry now exists between China and India. Geopolitics, rather than a vestige of previous centuries, is a more tightly woven feature of the globe than ever, as India seeks new allies in Vietnam and Japan, and China seeks closer links with Russia and Iran.

In fact, there are no purely regional problems anymore, since local hegemons like Russia, China, and Iran have been over the decades engaged in cyberattacks and terrorism worldwide. Thus crises are both regional and global at the same time. And as wars and state collapses persist, the fear we should harbor should be less that of appeasement and more that of hard landings for the troubled regimes in question. We know that soft landings for totalitarian regimes in Iraq and Syria have been impossible to achieve: The United States invaded Iraq yet stood aside in Syria, the result being virtually the same, with hundreds of thousands of people killed in each country and a radical, millenarian group like ISIS filling the void.

Another thing: Remember that globalization is not necessarily associated with growth or stability, but only with vast economic and cultural linkages, which can amplify geopolitical disorder in the event of an economic slowdown—which is what we are seeing now. Take Africa, which has had years of steady economic growth thanks less to the development of a manufacturing sector and more to a rise in commodity prices. Commodity prices are now falling, along with Chinese infrastructure investment in Africa, as China itself experiences a dramatic decrease in GDP growth. Thus African stability, to the degree that it exists, is imperiled because of economic changes in Asia. Then there are the various radical Islamic movements rampaging across Sahelian Africa. This is actually the latest phase of African anarchy—in which the communications revolution brings millenarian Islam to weak and failed states. Obviously, the United States has little power over any of this.

In sum, everything is interlinked as never before, even as there is less and less of a Night Watchman to keep the peace worldwide and hierarchies everywhere break down. Just look at the presidential primaries in the United States, which demonstrate an upheaval from below for which the political establishment has no answer. Meanwhile, like "the brassiness of marches" and "the heavy stomp of peasant dances" that composer Gustav Mahler employed, as he invaded "the well-ordered house of classical music" in the waning decades of the Habsburg Empire (to quote the late Princeton professor Carl E. Schorske), the twenty-first century will be defined by vulgar, populist anarchy that elites at places like Aspen and Davos will have less and less influence upon, and will less and less be able to comprehend. Imperialism, then, will be viewed as much with nostalgia as with disdain.

15.

Fated to Lead

THE NATIONAL INTEREST, JANUARY 2015

The sleep of any president, prime minister, or statesman is haunted by what-ifs.

What if I had only fired that defense secretary sooner, or replaced that general in Iraq with the other one before it was too late? What if I had not wholly believed the air force when they told me that the war in southern Lebanon could be won from the skies? What if I had more troops on the ground in Iraq from the start? What if I had called off those fruitless negotiations between the Israelis and Palestinians a few months—or even a few weeks—earlier than I did? What if I had asked more questions at that meeting, and listened sooner to the pleas of my assistant secretary or whoever it was that said something could be done about Rwanda? The whole world, and my reputation, would be different.

Counterfactuals haunt us all in the policy community. We all want to be right, and to assign failure to someone else. We all want to deny fate, even as we recognize that it exists. For example, we know that despite Isaiah Berlin's admonition against the very idea of *vast impersonal forces,* such as geography and culture, these forces really do matter, and they affect the tasks ahead: Whatever the intervention strategy, Iraqis will never behave like Swedes, and Afghans or Libyans will never behave like Canadians. And sometimes it is that simple. While individuals are more real and concrete than the national groups to which they belong, group characteristics actually do exist and must play a role in the foresight of any analyst. For group characteristics are merely the sum total of a people's experience on a given landscape throughout hundreds or thousands of years of history.

But that is only the half of it. We also know that grand historical events can turn on a hair's breadth, on this or that contingency. While the destiny of Afghanistan or Libya might never be that of Canada, better or worse outcomes in such places are possible depending upon the choices of individual policy makers, so that all of us, as Berlin rightly suggests, must take moral responsibility for our actions. And because wrong choices and unfortunate opinions are part and parcel of weighing in on foreign policy, we go on torturing ourselves with counterfactuals.

What is fate—what the Greeks called *moira,* "the dealer-out of portions"? Does it exist? If it does, Herodotus best captures its complexities: From his geographical determinism regarding the landmasses of Greece and Asia Minor and the cultures they raise up to his receptivity to the salience of human intrigues, he skillfully conveys how self-interest is often calculated within a disfiguring whirlwind of passion, so that the most epic events emerge from the oddest of incidents and personal dramas. With such a plethora of factors, fate is inscrutable. In Jorge Luis Borges's short tale "The Lottery in Babylon," fate means utter randomness: A person can get rich, be executed or tortured, provided with a beautiful woman, or be thrown into prison solely because of a roll of the dice. Nothing appears to be predetermined, but neither is there moral responsibility. I find this both unsatisfying and unacceptable, despite the story's allegorical power.

How can a great episode in history be determined in advance? It seems impossible. The older I get, with the experience of three decades as a foreign correspondent behind me, the more I realize that outside of a class of brilliantly intuitive minds—including the late Samuel Huntington, Zbigniew Brzezinski, and Henry Kissinger—political *science* is still mainly an aspiration, and that Shakespeare's tragedies and histories offer a much better guide to the bizarre palace maneuverings of the last Romanov czar and czarina of Russia, of Nicolae and Elena Ceaușescu of Romania, of Slobodan Milošević and Mirjana Marković of Yugoslavia, or of Zviad and Manana Gamsakhurdia of Georgia. In short, there is no scientific formula to understanding international relations. There is primarily insight, which by definition is Shakespearean.

Yes, geography and culture matter. Tropical abundance produces disease, just as temperate climates with good natural harbors produce wealth. But these are merely the backdrops to the immense and humming beehive of human calculation, the details of which can never be known in advance. And yet, over the course of my life I have known people who are abrasive and confrontational, and generate one crisis after another to the detriment of themselves and their relations, even as I have known others who are unfailingly considerate and modest, who go from one seemingly easy success to another. Character, which itself is partly physiological, can indeed be destiny, and *that* is fate.

It is this very contradiction concerning fate that produces our finest historians: men and women who discern grand determinative patterns, but only within an impossible-to-predict chaos of human interactions, themselves driven by the force of vivid personalities acting according to their own agency, for better and for worse. A classic work that comes to mind is University of London historian Orlando Figes's *A People's Tragedy: The Russian Revolution, 1891–1924.* "It was by no means inevitable that the [Russian] revolution should have ended in the Bolshevik dictatorship," he writes. "There were a number of decisive moments, both before and during 1917, when Russia might have followed a more democratic course." Nevertheless, Figes adds,

> Russia's democratic failure was deeply rooted in its political culture and social history . . . [for example, in] the absence of a state-based counterbalance to the despotism of the Tsar; the isolation and fragility of liberal civil society; the backwardness and violence of the Russian village that drove so many peasants to go and seek a better life in the industrial towns; and the strange fanaticism of the Russian radical intelligentsia.

Figes gives us the determinative forces, but then, like a good novelist, he provides in capacious detail the other factors, without any one of which such seemingly determinative forces might have been stayed. Had only Czar Alexander III not died of kidney disease at the age of forty-nine, long before his son Nicholas II was temperamentally ready to rule. Had only Nicholas truly supported Prime Minister Pyotr Stolypin and recognized the talent of another bureaucrat, Prince Lvov, early on. Had only the Czarevitch Alexei not had hemophilia, forcing the royal family to rely for treatment on the mystic Grigory Rasputin, whose baleful influence fatally weakened the regime. Had only Alexander Kerensky been better grounded emotionally and less in love with his own rhetoric, and had only his provisional government not bet its fortunes so completely on the spring 1917 offensive against the Germans. Had only Lenin's past as a member of the nobility not awarded him such a "dogmatic" and "domineering manner," and had Lenin only been arrested or even temporarily detained by a nighttime patrol while he walked in disguise to the Smolny Institute in Petrograd, to take control of the squabbling Bolsheviks and declare an insurrection in October 1917. And so on. Again, we are in the realm of geography and culture, until we are in the realm of Shakespeare, and finally in the realm of sheer chance. Although Figes says that "historians should not really concern themselves with hypothetical questions," his textured rendition of history allows the reader to ponder other outcomes.

Human events, because they involve human beings, will not be reduced to formulas. That is ultimately why historians are more valuable than political scientists. Of course, the Holocaust had its roots in centuries of anti-Semitism in Europe that were, in turn, the partial result of determinative social and cultural patterns. But would the Holocaust—or World War II in Europe, for that matter—have happened without the singular character of Hitler, who combined an obsession with killing Jews with a talent for operatic, megalomaniacal leadership in the teeth of a massive depression?

So, are we back to the so-called great-man theory of history (or dreadful man, in Hitler's case)? That would be far too simplistic. For the most forceful personalities always operate inside geopolitical contexts that are mechanistic and deterministic. Liberal internationalists credit Richard Holbrooke as the great man who stopped the slaughter in Bosnia in 1995, and whose behind-the-scenes spirit drove the murderous Serbs out of Kosovo in 1999. But there was a fatalistic geopolitical context to this, without which Holbrooke could not have succeeded quite as he did. That context was Russia's weakness, brought about by the end of the Cold War and the collapse of the Soviet Union. The 1990s saw Russia in the enfeebled chaos that was Boris Yeltsin's rule. Had Russia been able to exert its usual historical influence in the Slavic Balkans, Holbrooke and the West would not have been able to act with such impunity. The discussions the Clinton administration held with the Russian government over the former Yugoslavia in the 1990s were about saving Russia's face—not about fundamentally compromising with it. Were Russia in the 1990s like the Russia of Vladimir Putin's aggressive and centralizing rule, that certainly would not have been possible.

That is a counterfactual, obviously. It is interesting because, like all counterfactuals, it shows how complex and even metaphysical such a thing as fate can be. But we are still left with history as it has actually turned out. Great character, after all, is character that deals heroically with the situation at hand, not with a theoretical situation that can only be imagined.

Both supporters and opponents of the Iraq War can agree that the leading figures in the George W. Bush administration did not have outstanding characters. Their mistakes were serial. It wasn't only that the Iraqi army was disbanded and the Baath Party outlawed. To give the administration the benefit of the doubt, the Iraqi army did, in fact, disintegrate on its own and the Baath Party at the upper levels had to be removed, if only to win the support of the Shia in the early phase of the occupation. But so many other things were done wrong. The occupation simply wasn't planned and staffed out in advance. The Coalition Provisional Authority competed with rather than complemented the military occupation forces. Too much faith was put in the hands of returning exiles. The critical first phase of the occupation was handed over to an inexperienced three-star general, Ricardo Sanchez. Then came George W. Casey, Jr., a stolid peacetime general if ever there was one, who utterly lacked the intuitive and cultural skills to deal with Iraqis or the larger situation at hand. Given the quickened pace of modern war, President George W. Bush and Secretary of Defense Donald Rumsfeld did not fire and replace generals with sufficient speed. The list goes on and on.

I supported the Iraq War. I mention this whenever publicly discussing the issue. I was not in favor of exporting democracy. Anyone who knows my work knows that I have seen the benefits of enlightened dictatorship in many instances, and still do. But Saddam Hussein's regime was not a dictatorship: It constituted a suffocating totalitarianism somewhere south of Stalin and north of the Assads in Syria. I knew it intimately from several reporting trips to Iraq in the 1980s, and thus I was a journalist who had gotten too close to his story. In short, I became committed. Yet, no matter how Iraq turns out in the future, even if there is a sharp improvement and the Islamic State is defeated, the price America paid there will still have been far too steep. The war as it turned out—not how it might have turned out according to some counterfactual—was a disaster.

But that is where my certainty ends. The *what-ifs,* because there are so many, are indeed tantalizing, even as the sheer amount of mistakes in prosecuting the war leads one inexorably to the conclusion that the decision to invade in the first place was just that, another mistake. But grand themes, because they are teased out of a plethora of intricate little details, must remain an interpretation, not a fate. Maybe the Iraq invasion, precisely *because* of the many mistakes involved with it, was not even given a chance to succeed. I desperately want to believe this, given my previous support of the war, but at the end of a sleepless night I can't. I sense instead that the legions of mistakes were inherent in the hubris of the conception.

Here is a counterfactual: Bush, in the summer of 2002, decides not to invade Iraq. Saddam's regime soldiers on. The sanctions against him are gradually lifted. And so the fact that he has no weapons of mass destruction does not become known. The Arab Spring arrives in 2011. The Shia and Kurds in Iraq immediately revolt. Saddam—in his trademark sanguinary fashion—kills proportionately more or as many people as Bashar al-Assad kills in Syria. The Bushes, father and son, are then blamed for not dealing with Saddam when they had the chance (remember that the elder Bush's wisdom of not pushing on to Baghdad only became apparent after his son had gotten bogged down in Iraq).

In other words, there may never have been even the possibility of a soft landing for the Baathist regimes in the Levant, given how much these regimes pulverized society, eviscerating all forms of intermediary social organizations except for the state at the top and the tribe and extended family at the bottom. Whether we acted militarily or not, in Iraq or in Syria, the result in any event was going to be anarchy. This is fatalism, I know. It denies human agency—and, therefore, moral responsibility on our part. But while that might be reprehensible, it does not necessarily make my assertion false.

Libya and Syria are the current poster children of this conundrum. We intervened in Libya with airpower, special-operations forces, and logistical assets in order to prevent dictator Muammar Qaddafi from killing masses of civilians in the Benghazi area. We then aided and abetted the toppling of his regime. The result has been sheer chaos in Libya, the undermining of Mali, and the spread of weaponry throughout the Sahara. Tripoli is no longer the capital of a country, but a mere dispatch point for negotiations among tribes, gangs, and militias. Chaos in Benghazi led to the murder of U.S. ambassador J. Christopher Stevens. Thus, was the decision to help topple Qaddafi a mistake—not only in geopolitical terms, but in moral terms as well? Proponents of the intervention claim that had we put more effort into stabilizing Libya after Qaddafi was killed, much of this would not have happened. But I seriously doubt—especially given the experiences in Vietnam and Iraq—that we have ever been capable of engineering reality on the ground in complex, alien societies. Germany and Japan were destroyed, defeated, and occupied countries—and thus exceptions to the rule. And they had the tradition of being modern, industrialized societies and economies, unlike the countries of the Greater Middle East. At some point, at some level, we must respect the workings of fate, if only to restrain our vanity. It is for the same reason that we believe in God.

The question of Syria is harder. We did not try in earnest to help politically moderate fighters amid the Grand Guignol of forces battling to topple the Baathist Assad regime. Had we done so, the chances of being drawn into an intractable and infernally complex conflict, with dozens upon dozens of different militias arrayed, would have been substantial. But had we done so, there was also a chance of both toppling Assad and undermining both the birth and spread of the Islamic State. And yet there was also a chance of toppling Assad, even as we would have been unable to micromanage events on the ground, therefore helping to midwife a Sunni jihadist regime to power in Damascus. Take your pick. The truth is unknowable. And because it is unknowable, we cannot assume what fate has held in store for Syria since 2011.

What is the answer to all of this?

Determinism, as Berlin writes, may have been argued about since the Greek Stoics identified two seemingly contradictory notions: individual moral responsibility and "causation"—the belief that our acts are the unavoidable result of a chain of prior events. The French philosopher Raymond Aron wrote of what Daniel J. Mahoney described in these pages in 1999 as a "sober ethic rooted in the truth of 'probabilistic determinism,'" because "human choice always operates within certain contours or restraints such as the inheritance of the past." That is, Aron believed in a soft determinism that accepts obvious differences between groups and regions but, nevertheless, does not oversimplify, and leaves many possibilities open. That may be the best answer available.

Whether we admit it or not, we are all soft determinists. That is the only way we could survive in the world and at the same time, for example, be good parents: by assuming that if we or our children behave in a certain way, some outcomes are more likely than others. And we adjust our actions accordingly. Therefore, the other term for soft determinism is common sense. To take a dull and ordinary illustration, if our son or daughter gets into the best college to which they applied, we generally encourage them to go there, since the likelihood of him or her going on to a good career and earning more money increases. We make such decisions every hour of every day—decisions based on the assumption that the record of the past indicates a certain result in the present or future. This is all to some degree fatalism. And we're all guilty of it. Why should this commonsensical fatalism, which is reasonable and hesitant, rarely dogmatic, not apply to foreign policy?

Just consider the case of promoting democracy abroad: It took England nearly half a century to hold the first meeting of a parliament after the signing of the Magna Carta, and more than seven hundred years to achieve women's suffrage. What we in the West define as a healthy democracy took England the better part of a millennium to achieve. A functioning democracy is not a tool kit that can be easily exported, but an expression of culture and historical development. Great Britain's democracy did not come from civil-society programs taught by aid workers: It was the offshoot of bloody dynastic politics and uprisings in the medieval and early modern eras. In a similar spirit, whatever indigenous cultural elements India possessed for the establishment of democracy, the experience of almost two hundred years of British imperial rule under the colonial civil service was crucial. Certain other countries in Asia had many years of economic and social development under enlightened authoritarians to prepare them for democracy. In Latin America, the record of democracy remains spotty, with virtual one-man rule in some places, and near chaos and social and economic upheaval in others. African democracies are often that in name only, with few or no governing authorities outside of the capital cities. Holding elections is easy; it is building institutions that counts. Given this evidence, and with the Arab world having suffered the most benighted forms of despotism anywhere in the world, how can one expect to export democracy overnight to the Middle East?

Yes, all this is determinism of a sort. It is also common sense.

In sum, foreign policy cannot function properly without a reasonable level of determinism. Determinism constitutes an awareness of limits: limits to what the United States can and cannot do in the world. This is a searing reality. And because it is so, whether we know it or not, we define great statesmen as those who work near the edges of those limits, near the edges of what is possible. Great statesmen rebel against limits, they rebel against determinism, even as their very skillful diplomacy constitutes an implicit acceptance that such limits exist.

Of course, many will try to break through these limits, in statesmanship and in other pursuits. President Theodore Roosevelt's famous "man in the arena" speech was in a larger sense a tribute to all those who have fought the good fight, even if they failed. But not many take heed of that worthy sentiment. For example, one of Bill Clinton's secretaries of state, Warren Christopher, made more than twenty trips to the Middle East in search of a deal between Israel and Syria that proved just out of reach. His efforts have been completely forgotten, as Secretary of State John Kerry's failed attempt to make peace between Israel and the Palestinians will be. In those cases, determinism appears to have ruled.

Henry Kissinger, on the other hand, demonstrated that what was first seen as merely a vague possibility could actually be done. Kissinger became legendary because he succeeded against fate. Strategy, ground down to its essentials, is merely a road map for overcoming fate. Kissinger saw the opportunity created by the Sino-Soviet split and negotiated an understanding with China that balanced against the Soviet Union, even as he used détente with the Soviets to keep both the Chinese and America's Western European allies honest. By granting China implicit protection against both the Soviet Union and an economically rising Japan, and by conceding that there was only one China (and it wasn't Taiwan), the actions of the Nixon administration provided the basis for China, in this new and more secure environment, to focus internally rather than externally. That would enable Deng Xiaoping to introduce a form of capitalism to the most populous country on earth, something that would lift a billion or so people out of poverty throughout Asia. For the Asian economic miracle of the late twentieth and early twenty-first centuries is impossible to even imagine without President Richard Nixon's 1972 trip to China. Thus does an amoral strategy, in the service of a naked national interest, have a moral result.

Because what drove Kissinger was the amoral pursuit of the national interest, he is respected without being loved. Holbrooke, on the other hand, is beloved by those who put moral humanitarian goals above amoral national interest. Kissinger was interested in the survival of his country in an anarchic world that lacks a night watchman to keep the peace; Holbrooke took such survival for granted and, by doing so, was able to pursue universalism. And because intellectuals and liberal journalists are generally universalist rather than nationalist in spirit, Holbrooke became their romantic avatar. Kissinger rearranged the chess pieces on a global scale; Holbrooke brought peace and ended genocide in one country of some—but not overwhelming—importance to the United States. But that was more than enough in the eyes of his followers.

Kissinger, a Holocaust refugee, knew that American foreign policy could not simply be a branch of Holocaust studies, while Holbrooke, also the descendant of Jewish refugees, demonstrated that Holocaust studies were indeed central to American foreign policy.

But where both men are alike is that neither was a fatalist. And unlike Christopher and Kerry, Kissinger and Holbrooke, as they say, *got things done,* which very few people in Washington (or in the foreign policy community at large) are capable of.

So, is President Barack Obama a fatalist? Or, rather, since strategy is the principal means to conquer fate, does he have a strategy? Let me answer this in a provocative way, by outlining what I think fate holds in store for the United States in the early twenty-first century. Let me be a soft determinist, in other words.

While geography is not where analysis ends, it is where all serious analysis begins. For geopolitics is the struggle of states against the backdrop of geography. America's geography is the most favored in the world. The United States is not only protected by two

oceans and the Canadian Arctic, but it also, as the geopolitical fore-
casting firm Stratfor notes, has the advantage of more miles of navigable inland waterways than much of the rest of the world
combined. The Mississippi, Missouri, Ohio, Arkansas, and Tennes-
see river systems flow diagonally across the continent, thereby uniting the temperate zone of North America, which happens to be
overwhelmingly occupied by the United States. Further enhancing
the economic power of these river systems is the abundance of barrier islands and deepwater ports along the Atlantic and Gulf coasts.
The commerce that feeds down to the mouth of the great Mississippi is what originally made the Gulf of Mexico and Caribbean Sea
central to American power and prosperity. The result has been both
a country and a continental empire.

It is also a hemispheric empire. The great Dutch American strategist Nicholas Spykman explained that by gaining effective control
of the Greater Caribbean at the turn of the twentieth century, the
United States came to dominate the Western Hemisphere, and with
that had resources to spare to affect the balance of power in the
Eastern Hemisphere. That proved to be the essential geopolitical
dynamic of the twentieth century, as the United States tipped the
balance of forces in its favor in two world wars and the Cold War
that followed. This all had to do with many factors, obviously, but
without geography they would have been inoperable.

Of course, history did not stop with the end of the Cold War.
The Soviet Union may have collapsed, and China may have ad-
opted a form of capitalism, but both Russia and China are vast, illiberal, and multi-ethnic empires that have the capacity to together
dominate the Eastern Hemisphere. This means the United States
has equities of some value in such far-flung places as Ukraine and
Afghanistan. Furthermore, because technology has mitigated the
protective wall of two oceans—as 9/11 demonstrated—Islamic extremism must also (to say the least) be balanced against, if not con-

tained or defeated outright. What all of this amounts to is something stark: America is *fated* to lead. That is the judgment of geography.

And there is something else. In the course of being fated to lead for many unceasing decades, the United States has incurred, like it or not, other obligations. For example, there is the delicate point of the United States Holocaust Memorial Museum. The fact that this museum constitutes both a monument and a historical repository is actually less significant than (as others have noted) the undeniable reality of its location, adjacent to the National Mall in Washington, within sight of the Jefferson Memorial. In short, the Holocaust—which happened in Europe—has, nevertheless, been officially granted entry into the American historical experience, so that whenever large-scale atrocities happen anywhere, America must at the very least take notice, if not lead some sort of a response. No, America is not a normal country, as the late conservative luminary Jeane J. Kirkpatrick recommended that it become at the end of the Cold War. A normal country would not have such a museum as part of its pantheon. America, rather, has empire-like obligations: Just look at the size of its navy and air force, and how they are dispersed around the globe!

This is the material at hand. Faced with such objective truths, the debate between realists and idealists is at once unnecessarily Manichaean and a mere row over tactics. Realism wasn't the evil invention of Henry Kissinger, but an American tradition going back to George Washington, John Quincy Adams, and wise men like George F. Kennan and Dean Acheson. Idealism, for its part, is so deeply rooted in the American tradition that Wilsonianism lives on long after the passing of America's twenty-eighth president, no matter how often it is shown to be flawed. Neither unremitting humanitarianism (because it is unsustainable) nor neo-isolationism (because it fails to accept America's *fate* as a world leader) can be the basis of any responsible foreign policy.

Here I must bring in my personal hero, a once-celebrated literary figure now forgotten, Bernard DeVoto. An environmentalist and fierce defender of civil liberties, DeVoto spent a lifetime as a *continentalist* dedicated to one subject: that of the American West, so much so that he never once set foot outside North American soil. Yet this intellectual, who wrote so obsessively and sensuously about the Great Plains and the Rocky Mountains, the way that Patrick Leigh Fermor wrote about the Balkans and Central Europe, and whom you would expect to have been an isolationist in the years prior to World War II, traveled throughout the interior of the United States in 1940, passionately arguing in local community gatherings for America to enter the war against Nazi Germany. DeVoto loved the continent that he called both a republic and an empire. There was just so much going on inside it that the world beyond was never quite real. Thus he saw the good in Manifest Destiny before generations of academics would see nothing but evil in it. Yet he also understood—perhaps at a more profound level than anyone else, before or since—that the blessings of geographical fate had freighted America with global responsibilities.

Has Obama measured up to these responsibilities? He has backed into a strategy of sorts rather than proactively crafted one. So he is a reluctant strategist at best. Arguably, he has shown some good tactical instincts—stay out of Syria (at least until recently), don't get involved on the ground in Libya, and don't get into an air or ground war in a place that matters more to Russia than it does to the United States or even to Western Europe. In all this he might be compared to the president he not so secretly admires, George H. W. Bush. The elder Bush backed into a strategy to end the Cold War after the Cold War had begun to end on its own in Europe. He also showed good tactical instincts in not breaking relations with China after Tiananmen, and in limiting the First Gulf War to the liberation of Kuwait only. But there the similarities end.

The elder Bush had elite New England schools, the Texas oil fields, and the naval war in the Pacific as his rite-of-passage points of reference. The elder Bush was no intellectual, but he intuitively grasped what the bookish DeVoto knew by travel, study in the Harvard library, and his own Utah upbringing: that America was a continent of such dimensions that to lead was not a choice but a fate. But Obama's sensibility seems not to be continental. Continentalism, in Kennan's estimation, is opposed to universalism. But I disagree. I believe that without one there is not the other. If you haven't internalized moments like the California gold rush and westward expansion, you can't fully grasp why America *deserves* to lead. Only by conquering the Great Plains and Rocky Mountains first could America defeat Hitler and Tojo second. Whereas the elder Bush made incessant phone calls to many world leaders from the start of his presidency—long before such crises as the collapse of the Soviet Empire and Iraq's invasion of Kuwait—Obama waits until he is buried in a crisis, and even then he often delegates such responsibilities. Obama does not relish the projection of American power, without which you cannot challenge fate.

Obama has tried until recently to get America's allies in different theaters to do the balancing for it. Get Japan to balance against China, get Saudi Arabia and Israel to balance against Iran, and get Germany to balance against Russia. This is laudable. Why not at least try to lessen the imperial burden? The problem has been that a resurgent and nationalistic Japan, which has not fully come to terms with its own World War II–era crimes, frightens others in Asia. Israel's air force, as good as it is, is a small, tactical air force and not a big, strategic one, and thus of imperfect use against Iran. Saudi Arabia is a benighted despotism more fragile than it looks, increasingly undermined by a weaker and more decentralized monarchy, chaos in neighboring Yemen, and the deterministic forces of a rising population and a diminishing underground water table. Germany is fundamentally compromised by its addiction to Russian energy and its inherent pacifism, stemming from the legacy of Nazi crimes. Delegating power to allies thus has limits, and they are severe.

Still, it is true that while Russia is bad and the Islamic State is evil and both are dangerous, the Soviet Union was also quite dangerous and "evil," in Ronald Reagan's memorable estimation. And we did not go to war with the Soviet Union, but, rather, patiently contained it for decades, until it collapsed from its own contradictions. Likewise, Russia's exalted position in world energy markets as well as the size of its population will decline as the years go by, and the Islamic State may be weakened by tribalism and competing groups and caliphates. Containment is, therefore, in both cases a defensible strategy, if not an appealing one. Obama's deliberative instinct is therefore apt for the circumstances.

Cries of appeasement will continue to be heard, though.

The problem with the charge of appeasement is that the situation only became clear-cut after the fact. When Neville Chamberlain went to Munich, the deaths of 16 million troops and civilians during World War I had happened only twenty years before. Anyone in middle age or older knows that twenty years is merely the blink of an eye. And Chamberlain was sixty-nine years old at Munich. Such mass suffering, all for a war born of miscalculation, that yielded no constructive result! By this logic, one world war was quite enough. And who—perhaps not even Winston Churchill—could have imagined the Holocaust in 1938? The industrialized extermination of an entire people as the central, organizing principle of a modern state was simply unimaginable until it was actually happening. So even getting Hitler right was not quite as simple as it now seems. And no adversary we face now or in the future will reach the Hitler standard, in terms of possessing both an ideology of death and the ability to implement it on a mass scale. Thus appeasement will be a mundane part of any president's future. Using it as a *gotcha* phrase will not work. Fate is not that knowable in advance.

Still, it must be said: A student of Shakespeare would have grasped Vladimir Putin's character long before an international relations wonk, just as a philosopher would most profoundly grasp the danger of people who behead innocent journalists in order to make slick videos to spread a barbaric message. The dangers that lurk now are numerous, even as overreach on our part also lies in wait. Thus, in this age of comparative anarchy to follow the age of imperialism and that of the Cold War, getting it right will be harder than ever. For many decisions are by their very nature close calls. We require leaders who will stretch the limits of what is achievable, while at the same time respecting such limits. Fate is like the gods of ancient Greece: fickle and morally imperfect, but pliable for those who are brave.

16.

The Great Danger of a New Utopianism

THE AMERICAN INTEREST,
NOVEMBER/DECEMBER 2015

What is our worst existential fear, worse than any cyber, bio-logical, environmental, or even nuclear threat? It is the threat of a utopian ideology in the hands of a formidable power. Because Utopia is, in and of itself, the perfect political and spiritual arrangement, this means that any measures to bring it about are morally justified: including totalitarianism and mass murder. But what, on the individual level, has always been the attraction of utopian ideology, despite what it wrought in the twentieth century? Its primary attraction lies in what it does to the soul.

Aleksander Wat, the great Polish poet and intellectual of the early and mid-twentieth century, explains that communism, and Stalinism specifically, was the "global answer to negation. . . . The entire illness stemmed from that need, that hunger for something all-embracing." The problem was "too much of everything. Too many people, too many ideas, too many books, too many systems." Who could cope? So a "simple catechism" was required, especially for the intellectuals, which explains their initial attraction to communism and, yes, to Stalinism. For once converted, the intellectuals could then unload this all-embracing catechism on the masses, who would accept it as a replacement for the normal catechism of religion. Whereas traditional religions fill a void in the inner life of the individual, thereby enriching it, Stalinism turned that inner life immediately, in Wat's words, "to dust." Stalinism represented "the killing of the inner man": it stood for the "exteriorization" of everything. That was its appeal. For without an interior life, there would be less for a person to think and worry about.

Wat's clinical insights come in the midst of one of the most urgent memoirs of the modern era, *My Century: The Odyssey of a Polish Intellectual,* published posthumously in 1977. This is not a memoir in the traditional sense: Rather, it is a transcribed series of interviews with the author conducted in the mid-1960s by the Nobel Laureate Czeslaw Milosz. Wat was ill at the time, both physically and mentally, and was simply unable to write. We place him in the highest category of intellectuals: those who do not necessarily have to write. It is enough to listen to their voice.

My Century as a title is neither exaggerated nor self-referential. For Wat did indeed live the life of the twentieth century in all its horror. His older brother perished at Treblinka, his younger brother at Auschwitz. Wat himself spent seven years during and after World War II in Soviet prisons, including the Lubyanka, and in exile in the deserts of Central Asia. He returned to public life in the East Bloc in 1957, in the wake of de-Stalinization, and committed suicide in France a decade later. The pages of his conversations with Milosz ache with recollections of the ghastly deportations—where people froze to death in train cars even as women were giving birth. He remembers the icy cold prison cells that were steaming hot in summer; the constant dread, day after day, year after year, of being tortured; the gnawing anxiety in prison about the fate of his family; the deranged cell mates; the filth and chaos of the railway stations: the life of millions in the twentieth century, in other words, all the wages of ideology. Wat was a Central European whose family and personal history was "at the borderline of Judaism, Catholicism, and atheism," and anti-Semitism in his telling is part of the permanent tapestry of Soviet prison life.

Oh, you might say, the twentieth century was unique. Tyrants of the scale of Hitler and Stalin come along only once in a thousand years. Wat's story is an overpowering classic, but it is about the last century: What does it have to do with this one?

Clearly, the Final Solution was unique, and has no equivalents—none. Stalin's machine of terror was singular in its industrialized and ideological horror. And because these things exist only one lifetime removed from our own, a virtual nanosecond in history, intellectual and policy debates are still rightly obsessed with them. But at the same time there is a belief, a certainty, very true up to a point, that the twenty-first century is radically different than the previous one, and will therefore have radically different pathologies. Thus we study Hitler and Stalin as past, not as prologue. Like scary dinosaurs they are extinct, so they are no longer threatening, at least according to the conventional wisdom.

For the twentieth century was about *bigness:* big industrialized states with big military machines that monopolized the use of force, and thus were capable of great evil; whereas the twenty-first century is about *smallness:* the erosion of state power by postindustrial cyber and informational tools, tools that put power into the hands of stateless groups and lessen the domination of states. Thus, the horror of totalitarianism has been replaced by the horror of chaos. Saddam Hussein, the Arab Stalin, was brutal beyond description, but the anarchy that followed in Iraq was even worse. Yes, Wat *bears witness,* and so his memoir is a work of literature. But it is about his time, not ours.

Yet what if that's not the whole story? What if in describing the psychological attraction of Stalinist ideology, Wat is also providing a warning about now? What if the response to sustained chaos will lead back, inversely, to the ideological intensities of the twentieth century? I am not talking about new Hitlers and Stalins, so much as about disease-variants of them.

Our time on earth, in fact, may be ripe for utopian ideologies. Far more than the early twentieth century even, we are bombarded by stimuli: If there were too many books and ideas, too many people and systems, back in Wat's time, they were only a fraction of what people must cope with now. The soul itself, explains the contemporary Romanian philosopher Horia-Roman Patapievici, is being hollowed out because of the substitution of the inner imagination by technology: smartphones, intelligent toys, the array of electronics at malls. Technology, as Martin Heidegger saw, is in many respects devoid of purpose, with mental anguish and confusion merely the result. Thus, we desperately require meaning in our lives, which obviously conventional politics cannot satisfy, even as technology and primitivism—witness the Islamic State—can flow together in new belief systems that assign themselves to traditional religions.

Then there is loneliness. Toward the end of *The Origins of Totalitarianism,* the philosopher Hannah Arendt observes: "What prepares men for totalitarian domination . . . is the fact that loneliness, once a borderline experience usually suffered in certain marginal social conditions like old age, has become an everyday experience of the evergrowing masses of our century." Totalitarianism, she goes on, is the product of the lonely mind that deduces one thing from the other in linear fashion toward the worst possible result, and thus is a "suicidal escape from this reality," since by pressing men and women so close together in howling, marching formations individuality and thus loneliness are obliterated. But even with all of our electronic diversions, is loneliness any less prevalent now than it was when Arendt published her magnum opus in 1951? People are currently more isolated than ever, more prone to the symptoms of the lonely, totalitarian mind, or what psychiatrists call "racing thoughts."

People everywhere—in the West, in the Middle East, in Russia, in China—desperately need something to believe in, if only to alleviate their mental condition. They are dangerously ready for a new catechism given the right circumstances, for what passes as a new fad or cult in the West can migrate toward extremism in less stable or chaotic societies.

The jet-age elites are of little help in translating or alleviating any of this. Cosmopolitan, increasingly denationalized, less and less bound to territory, the elites revel in the overflow of information which they process through 24/7 multitasking. Every one of them is just so brilliant! They can analyze everything while they believe in nothing, and have increasingly less loyalty to the passports they own. This makes them wholly disconnected from the so-called unwashed masses, whose upheavals and yearnings for a new totality, a new catechism, in order to fill the emptiness and loneliness in their souls, regularly surprise and shock these same elites.

The rise of the Islamic State may be only a portent, and its leader Abu Bakr al-Baghdadi but an early example of the disease-variants that follow in the footsteps of twentieth-century totalitarians. Al-Baghdadi arose out of the chaos of the Arab Spring and the American invasion of Iraq. The Arab Spring was not about the rise of democracy, as Western elites initially announced—projecting their own values and experiences onto an alien part of the world about which they comprehend little—but about a fundamental crisis in central authority. That central authority was illegitimate because it was seen as both corrupt and secular. While Western journalists at first fixated on cosmopolitan young urbanites in Arab capitals—because each group saw itself reflected in the other—the Arab masses writhing and toiling underneath yearned for a purity of belief and logic, even as their own ethnic and sectarian divisions, magnified rather than reduced by communications technology, undermine the emergence of any civil society that might assuage their individual demand for dignity and justice. Such conditions have led, and can only lead, to new forms of authoritarianism. And the worse and more prolonged the anarchy, the more extreme and brutal it is, the more utopian and millenarian these new forms of authoritarianism will take.

The same liberal-trending elites in Cairo who seduced Western journalists in early 2011 in Tahrir Square would later be accepting of the new Pharaonic strongman, Abdel Fattah el-Sisi, after they themselves experienced just the slightest whiff of chaos wrought by Egyptian democracy in the form of the Muslim Brotherhood. But Egypt is not a serious concern. An age-old geographic cluster of civilization defined precisely by the Nile Valley, the state there has a long and natural tradition of legitimacy, so that suffocating forms of authoritarianism were not required to hold it together. Countries like Libya, Syria, and Iraq are in another category, however, since their borders do not define ancient, geographic states and population nodes nearly to the degree of Egypt. Thus, they required more extreme forms of authoritarianism bordering on totalitarianism merely in order to survive. That is the root cause for the ideological intensity of the Muammar Qaddafi, Hafez and Bashar al-Assad, and Saddam Hussein regimes. The latter two regimes were Baath Socialist, a variant of a European utopian ideology transferred to the Middle East. Because totalitarianism eviscerates all forms of political organization between the regime at the top and the tribe and extended family at the bottom, the upshot of its demise in Libya, Syria, and Iraq has been anarchy, which, in turn, will not, as I've indicated, lead to liberal democracy but to new forms of tyranny. And because the depth and extent of the chaos in those places has been many times that which Egypt experienced, the form of any new tyranny in those places threatens to border on something utopian in nature.

In Iraq, since 2003, because of an American invasion (which I mistakenly supported) and an arguably precipitous American withdrawal later on, people have experienced a level of Hobbesian bar-

barism and loss of dignity and safety far more profound than what Germans experienced prior to Hitler, and greater than what individual Russians experienced in the course of the collapse of the Romanov dynasty and ensuing civil war, which preceded Lenin and Stalin. Since 2011, Libya and Syria have replicated Iraq. This is to say nothing of the sense of personal alienation and loneliness that even people in these underdeveloped societies have experienced, thanks to the postmodern, technological condition which we all labor under. Add to the mix the alienation of being a young, unemployed Muslim male in Europe, unable to marry, and it becomes actually easy to fathom the psychology of recruits to the Islamic State, for sexual frustration can be appeased much more easily by a totalizing ideology than by being able to vote once every few years in an election.

But doesn't technology empower—by putting people in touch with each other so that they can speak with one voice? Precisely: It is speaking with one voice that is the danger. The freedom of the Internet is a conceit. Most people think that they generate their own ideas; in fact, their ideas are prepared by others who think for them. The very idea that some sermon or blog or tweet has gone *viral* is a sad reflection on the state of individualism in the twenty-first century. The electronic swarm is a negation of loneliness that prepares the way for new ideologies of totalitarianism. Imagine the swarm of electronic followers in countries where all personal dignity has been erased because of war and crime and chaos, where a postmodern form of extreme religiosity is clearly the only panacea.

The ascent of the Islamic State and other jihadist movements, both Sunni and Shiite, is actually not altogether new in imperial and post-imperial history. The seasoned, Paris-based commentator William Pfaff, who covered international politics for decades before he died, observes that the rise of radical populist movements, demanding in many cases the restoration of a lost golden age, occurred twice in mid- and late-nineteenth-century Qing China (the

Taiping and Boxer rebellions), once in mid-nineteenth-century British India (the Sepoy Mutiny), and once in late-nineteenth-century British Sudan (the Mahdist revolt). In that vein, as Pfaff explains, groups such as the Ugandan-based Lord's Resistance Army and the Nigerian-based Boko Haram, which we in the West label, in almost infantile fashion, as merely "terrorist," are, in fact, redemptive millennial movements that are a response to the twin threats of modernism and globalization.

Globalization, as it intensifies, carries the potential to unleash utopian ideologies by diluting concrete, traditional bonds to territory and ethnicity, for in the partial void will come a heightened appeal to more abstract ideals, the very weapons of Utopia. It is not only the Middle East that should concern us. China is in the process of transformation from a developing country to a national security state that in future years and decades could adopt new and dangerous hybrid forms of nationalism and central control as a response to its economic troubles. Russia's Vladimir Putin may yet be the forerunner of even greater xenophobia and nationalism under leaders further to the right than himself, as a response to Russia's weakening social and economic condition. Not only religion, but nationalism, too, in an age of globalization can become yet more ideological and abstract.

We must be both humble and vigilant, therefore. Humble, in the sense that we don't assume Progress. That is, we shouldn't feel safe in smug assumptions about the direction of history. Vigilant, in that we always stand firm in the defense of an individual such as Aleksander Wat, who, however doubt-ridden and self-questioning, refuses to submit to pulverizing forces.

MARCO POLO
REDUX

17.

Traveling China's New Silk Road

THE NATIONAL INTEREST, SEPTEMBER/OCTOBER 2015

The thousands of terra-cotta warriors from the third-century-B.C. Qin Dynasty, first unearthed in the mid-1970s, constitute one of the wonders of the world. I stared down into the vast clay pit where these life-sized soldiers, no two of them exactly alike, stand in a state of freeze-frame marching. They are all headed east. For Qin, though in the heart of today's China, had been the westernmost of the Warring States. Thus, to the east lay all of Qin's enemies. Beyond Qin, in the opposite direction westward, the agricultural cradle that has always defined Chinese civilization begins to give way to the emptier deserts of Central Asia.

A short drive from the site of the terra-cotta warriors in Shaanxi Province brought me to the Great Mosque of Xian, an eclectic confection of Arabic script underneath a traditional, upturned Chinese roof decorated with peacock-blue Persian tiles. The minaret here is easily mistaken for a pagoda. The result makes for an exquisite aesthetic, mixing the Middle East and the Far East, made even more precious by the dust. The Han-related Hui people, who maintain this mosque, account for the easternmost tentacle of Islam on the main body of the Asian mainland: The medieval Silk Road begins and ends right here—in what is, to repeat, the heart of the current Chinese state. For China's political borders now encompass much more than the agricultural core of historic Han China.

Next up was Dunhuang, almost nine hundred miles to the northwest of Xian. Twenty minutes after takeoff, the intricate checkerwork of cereal cultivation began to thin out—a rumor of what would soon become a bleached and bony wasteland, the mountaintops like protruding vertebrae. Politically I was still deep inside China; demographically and ethnically less so, though geographically I had already crossed into Central Asia—into the southwest corner of the Gobi Desert, to be precise. By the time the plane landed the terrain had been reduced to a sheet of sandpaper, almost absent of topographical features.

Dunhuang was founded in middle antiquity as a military outpost of Han China, in the drive to establish and maintain protectorates in the desert and steppe lands to the west of the agricultural cradle. Buddhism, which took root during this period in what is now Pakistan's northwest frontier, would become central to the Silk Road as the belief system of merchants and traders. There are hundreds of caves, their walls covered in medieval Buddhist frescoes, in the friable cliffsides around Dunhuang. In their lace-like delicacy, the tea-rose and mint-green colors of these frescoes seemed washed by milk. The paintings bear the artistic influences of not only Tang China but also Tibet, India, and Sassanian Iran. For Dunhuang was a Silk Road nexus.

Just an hour beyond Dunhuang, hard lava-red hills suddenly give way to a horrifying ashy emptiness. This is the Yangguan Pass, where the protection of imperial China officially came to a halt. I thought of what the eighth-century Tang poet Wang Wei wrote of this very place:

Let us empty another cup of wine.
For, once West of Yangguan Pass, there will be no more friends.

But now I do continue west, yet once again, still well within the borders of the twenty-first-century Chinese state.

In Urumqi, beyond stacks of half-finished apartment blocks, I saw the towering, snow-mantled curtain of the Tien Shan ("Mountains of Heaven") emanating terror and death. I shivered just looking at these gelid mountains. Twenty-one years before, on a previous visit, I found Urumqi a somnolent city of under a million when I arrived on a ramshackle train from Kazakhstan and left on a ramshackle bus for the Chinese border with Kyrgyzstan. No longer. Today Urumqi, the capital of China's westernmost Xinjiang Province, has a population of 3.8 million. It is bursting with traffic jams on webworks of new highways and overpasses, with gleaming skyscrapers all around. The city is a testimony to Beijing's attempt to dominate its Central Asian minority areas by smothering them with development, even as the Chinese build urban nodes for a postmodern Silk Road of long-distance highways, railways, and energy pipelines linking China with the former Soviet republics nearby. For it isn't only the Tien Shan that manifests the reality of Central Asia deep inside China: It is also the signs in Arabic script, evidence of the Turkic Uighur language spoken by more than a third of Urumqi's inhabitants, a language strikingly similar to Turkish proper. (There are, too, signs in the Russian alphabet, indicating the presence of Kazakh, Uzbek, and other Muslim minorities.) When one adds these ethnic Turkic areas to Tibet, you have a third of China's land area. China is a prison house of nations, albeit to a lesser extent than the former Soviet Union.

And yet, whether it is the new highways, the high-speed rail trains that swept by my bus here in Chinese Central Asia, the unending new wind farms on the steppe, or the ceaseless new apartment blocks—or even the very number of terra-cotta warriors themselves—China has always manifested an ambition of jaw-dropping, epic proportions. The sheer scale of it is impressive and frightening, both in antiquity and now. The fissiparous possibilities of China's geography and ethnic makeup appear more than matched by the unifying force of this ambition.

My journey ends in Kashgar, adjacent to the borders of Kyrgyzstan, Afghanistan, Tajikistan, and Pakistan. Eighty percent of the Kashgar region's population of 4.5 million are Muslim Uighur Turks. The signature event here is the Sunday livestock market, where throngs of Uighur men in wispy beards and flat brocaded caps furiously bargain amid packed masses of sheep, lambs, horses, donkeys, cattle, and furry Bactrian camels. The entire scene is veiled by a greasy film of dust, so that your memory of it is in black-and-white rather than color. But as authentic as it might appear to a first-time visitor, the livestock market in 2015 actually represents a more regulated, sanitized version of what I had experienced in 1994. Then, instead of Chinese-built trucks bringing the animals to market, there had been a chaos of donkey carts, and instead of a vast, rectangular space outside town set aside for the weekly event as exists now, the livestock market in the 1990s had been integrated into the bustling, equally chaotic traditional bazaar of Kashgar, with animals jostling against muddy stalls of brass and copper ware, all making for a deafening panorama of visual splendor reminiscent of earlier centuries.

But over twenty-one years, the ability of the Chinese state to extend its reach into the minority desert hinterlands has advanced so much that Kashgar today is a place of new, regimented apartment blocks, with paved streets and a grid pattern, while the animals are kept far from town. It is modernism, deliberately imposed by the Chinese authorities, that is diluting Turkic Uighur culture here. Kashgar is becoming a city of light industry—plastics and electronics—with the workers often imported from the Han core far to the east and housed in these new apartment blocks. The Uighur population fights back by copying mass culture imported from Turkey—the music and dances in the upscale Uighur restaurants are sometimes right out of Turkish television.

Whereas the medieval Great Mosque of Xian exudes an elegant confluence of civilizations—Chinese, Arab, and Persian—here, deeper along the Silk Road in the twenty-first century, there is evidence of a crude clash. One day I witnessed hundreds of Uighur men with their beards and embroidered hats emerge from the fifteenth-century Id Kah Mosque in the center of Kashgar, only to face a well-organized group of Chinese who were engaged in loud line dancing to music from the movie *Rush Hour*. Their festivities were timed to coincide with afternoon Muslim prayers. Thus was mass global culture employed as an affront to a very traditional one.

My entire trip constituted evidence of a postmodern geopolitical drama. The late Harvard China scholar John King Fairbank once said that China's sense of itself is based on the cultural difference that exists between this surrounding belt of desert and the sown of China proper—in other words, between the pastoral and the arable. China's ethnic geography reflects, in the words of Fairbanks and his Boston University colleague Merle Goldman, this "core-periphery" dynamic, with the core being the arable central plain of inner Han China, and the periphery being these pastoral frontier uplands heavily populated by minorities. To the early Chinese, agriculture meant civilization itself: that is, the Middle Kingdom, *Zhongguo*, which owed nothing to these surrounding peoples of the desert and steppe. From this worldview followed the kind of cultural certainty that China shared with Western Christendom.

The fact that the Chinese state today includes both desert and sown reflects the culmination of a long and thus far triumphant historical process, which, in turn, provides the geographical basis for Chinese power. Indeed, the reason why China is now developing a great naval presence in the South and East China seas is that China, finally, in modern times, has the ability to do so, a luxury afforded by its erstwhile conquest of the desert and steppeland periphery going counterclockwise from Manchuria to Inner Mongolia to Xinjiang to Tibet, thus protecting the arable cradle of Han culture from hostile incursions. Secure and dominant on land, Beijing can now go to sea.

The domination of a large part of Islamic Central Asia has a basis in Chinese history—medieval Tang armies threaded their way between Mongolia and Tibet to establish protectorates as far away as Khorasan in northeastern Iran, thus further enabling the Silk Road. At the same time, though, we should remember that East Turkestan—the area of Xinjiang—was taken back by the Manchu Qing Dynasty only in the seventeenth and eighteenth centuries. It is not truly part of historical China to the same degree as the arable cradle.

So the question becomes whether the dominant Han people, who comprise more than 90 percent of China's population and live mainly in the arable cradle, will be able to keep the Uighur Turks, Tibetans, and Inner Mongolians who live on the periphery permanently under control, with a minimum degree of unrest. The fate of the Chinese state will hinge on this geographical issue, especially in the face of economic and political disruptions that loom large.

The next thirty years in Chinese history are not going to be as smooth as the last thirty years. While analysts in the United States might ferociously complain about China's lack of transparency, about its autocratic system, and about its naval aggression in the South and East China seas, China, especially since the end of Deng Xiaoping's rule, has been governed by a collegial group of enlightened autocrats and technocrats, conservative in nature and averse to risk taking, so that China has generated relatively few surprises. This has helped encourage a bipartisan consensus on China policy in Washington, with the differences between Democrats and Republicans muted compared to the disputes that envenom Middle East policy. But more than three decades of double-digit growth, in addition to generating vast and profound contradictions and inefficiencies in the Chinese economy, have also created a more sophisticated, restive, and socially complex society—one that is harder to satisfy. China is now a crucible. The leadership has become ever more centralized and autocratic, with a personality cult beginning to form around President Xi Jinping, even as the economy requires a never-ending stimulus merely to run in place. The dramatic decline of economic growth in recent years is only the beginning of a tumultuous transformation that will test the rulers of the Chinese Communist Party (CCP) as never before.

The decline and fall of dynasties and empires has always been a messy business. And one should never forget that the CCP is another Chinese dynasty that runs an empire of desert and sown, with non-Han peoples on the periphery dominating much of the land area: an area containing the water, copper, iron ore, and other resources upon which inner China relies. Xinjiang, twice the size of Texas, is now becoming a transport corridor for roads, rail, and energy pipelines—part of the new Silk Road connecting China with Central Asia and eventually the Middle East and Europe. Not only is the bazaar in Kashgar full of Chinese-made consumer goods, but so, too, are the bazaars in the nearby former Soviet republics, demonstrating the stubborn dynamism of the Chinese economy at the most basic level. China's economic and strategic reach, moreover, may eventually extend south from Kashgar to the Indian Ocean, as Xi announced in April the building of a major transport system from Xinjiang to the Pakistani port of Gwadar. As a result, Beijing can tolerate no substantial unrest in Xinjiang, even as the security atmosphere features ethnic tension and increasing violent attacks by Uighurs against Han Chinese. Here in East Turkestan is where China's attempt at empire building is most pronounced and also where the Chinese state is most brittle.

Of course, experts have been discussing the possibility of the collapse of the CCP for years. But what would that collapse actually look like? Would it be merely the conversion of a collegial one-party system into a highly centralized and efficient authoritarianism; or a military coup from within that keeps the party nominally in control; or a slow rot that takes years and decades to play out? Remember, while the fall of the Soviet Union happened within a few short years, the Ottoman Empire, the "sick man of Europe," took more than a century to expire. In any event, whether the center transforms into something entirely new or crumbles slowly from within, the relationship between inner China and outer China could somehow change. The places that I visited may increasingly comprise a police state controlled from Beijing—or they could be at the forefront of China's subtle fragmentation, in which China reverts back by degrees to its arable cradle. I believe the former possibility is much greater than the latter one, but the latter one cannot be ruled out.

We have already seen chaos in quite a few Middle Eastern and African states. But China could yet evince unrest of a kind that could engulf not only itself but also other states in Central Asia, which are linguistically and culturally part of historic Turkestan. The adjacent Central Asian republics of the former Soviet Union have yet to experience a post-Soviet upheaval, even as their aged leaders will soon pass from the scene, exposing regimes that lack fundamental legitimacy at the same time that the United States continues its withdrawal from neighboring Afghanistan. In none of these places do ethnic borders coincide with official ones. A place like Kashgar might normally be associated with back-of-beyond travel writing. But, in fact, it could be at the center of the geopolitical world.

Index

"creedal passion periods," 182–84
crime:
  Pakistani networks of, 29
  Russian organized, 24, 37
  at sea, 61, 65–67, 72
  by veterans, 128
Cuba, communist, 148, 156, 180, 207
culture-consciousness, 163, 225
Cunliffe, Barry, 32
Cyprus, invasion of, 18

Dalai Lama, 26
Dan, Uri, 121
Darius, king of Persia, 46–49
Day, George Everette "Bud," 97–101,
  103, 104, 105, 109, 117
Dayan, Moshe, 120
de Gaulle, Charles, 149, 151–52
demilitarized zone (DMZ), 75–77
democracy:
  elements of, 3, 121, 162, 172, 177,
  185
  global promotion of, 233
  as military threat, 197
Democratic Party, 100, 148–49, 153,
  158, 205, 258
  Huntington's affiliation with, 165–66
  1968 Chicago convention of, 112
Deng Xiaoping, 54, 158, 234, 258
Dergue, Ethiopian, 155–56
Desert Storm, 135–36
determinism, in foreign policy, 232–35
DeVoto, Bernard, 238–39
dictatorships:
  benign, 91
  collapse of, 17
  democracy vs., 162, 177, 185
  enlightened, 38, 229, 233
  problem of losing face in, 44
  threat from demise of, 74–93
Dien Bien Phu, 115
diplomacy, 42
  of Kissinger, 143–59, 197–98
  nineteenth-century British, 144–46,
  157
  as paradoxical and flexible, 145–46
  philosophical bases of, 143–211

Diplomacy (Kissinger), 198
domino theory, 155
Donnelly, Thomas, 203
Donovan, David, 113–14
doxa (honor), 215
drug use, by veterans, 127, 128
Dubai, 29, 33
Duke, David, 193
Duty Honor Country (Day), 99–100,
  103, 109

Eastern Europe, 77
Eastern Question, 45
Ecevit, Bulent, 18
Echenberg, Dean, 105–6
ecology, crisis of, 8, 219
economic warfare, 86
economy:
  of city-states, 33–34
  global crises in, 8
  global wealth creation in, 35–36, 39
  in political enlightenment, 179
Egypt, 17, 49, 154, 180, 197, 209,
  247
  ancient, 68
Egyptian-Israeli peace treaty (1979),
  154
Eisenhower, Dwight D., 56, 209
elections, U.S.:
  of 1968, 112
  of 1972, 153
  of 1992, 102
  of 2000, 207
  of 2016, 223
elites:
  masses vs., 246–47
  warriors, 115, 120, 121
Elliott, William Yandell, 167–69
el-Sisi, Abdel Fattah, 247
empire:
  breakdown of, 218–23, 241
  stability preserved by, 218–19
Ending the Vietnam War (Kissinger),
  148, 149, 153–54
End of History and the Last Man, The
  (Fukuyama), 165, 194, 196
England, Lynndie, 140

About the Author

ROBERT D. KAPLAN is the bestselling author of eighteen books on foreign affairs and travel translated into many languages, including *The Return of Marco Polo's World, Earning the Rockies, In Europe's Shadow, Asia's Cauldron, The Revenge of Geography, Monsoon, The Coming Anarchy,* and *Balkan Ghosts.* He is a senior fellow at the Center for a New American Security and a senior advisor at Eurasia Group. For three decades he reported on foreign affairs for *The Atlantic.* He held the national security chair at the United States Naval Academy and was a member of the Pentagon's Defense Policy Board. He is currently a member of the U.S. Navy's Executive Panel. *Foreign Policy* magazine twice named him one of the world's Top 100 Global Thinkers.

robertdkaplan.com
cnas.org

About the Type

This book was set in Sabon, a typeface designed by the well-known German typographer Jan Tschichold (1902–74). Sabon's design is based upon the original letter forms of sixteenth-century French type designer Claude Garamond and was created specifically to be used for three sources: foundry type for hand composition, Linotype, and Monotype. Tschichold named his typeface for the famous Frankfurt typefounder Jacques Sabon (c. 1520–80).